Waiting in Line at the Drugstore
and Other Writings of James Thomas Jackson

Waiting in Line at the Drugstore
and Other Writings of James Thomas Jackson

Collected by June Acosta
Introduction by Charles Champlin
Foreword by David Westheimer

University of North Texas Press

10 9 8 7 6 5 4 3 2 1

Requests for permission to reproduce material from this work should b
sent to:
Permissions
University of North Texas Press
P. O. Box 13856
Denton, TX 76203

The paper used in this book meets the minimum requirements of the
American National Standard for Permanence of Paper for Printed Library
Materials, Z39.48.1984.

Library of Congress Cataloging-in-Publication Data

Jackson, James Thomas, 1925–1985.
    Waiting in line at the drugstore : and other writings of James Thomas
Jackson / collected by June Acosta ; introduction by Charles Champlin ;
foreword by David Westheimer.
        p.   cm.
    ISBN 0–929398–50–5 (pbk.) : $16.95. — ISBN 0–929398–62–9 : $29.95
    1. Afro-Americans--Literary collections.   2. Afro-Americans--Social
conditions.   I. Acosta, June.   II. Title.
    PS3560.A21574W3   1993
305,896'073--dc20   93-32763
                                                                        CIP

iv

So I am
Home.
As the naked failure.
With rhetorical dreams of Emerson,
Whitman and Mr. Sandburg.
Home, partner, with a head full of
Blithe, embroidered hopes and fountain
Springs of books to be.
Home, man, still, to a religious faith . . .
In shoes with well-worn soles . . .

—James Thomas Jackson
From an unpublished poem "Earthville"

Contents

Part I
Essays and Articles

Part II
Fiction and Poetry

Part III

Preface

James Thomas Jackson was born in 1925, in Temple, Texas, the youngest of three children. The family later moved to Houston, where James was educated.

Drafted into the U.S. Army Air Corps in 1943, he served honorably both Stateside and in Europe until 1948. The following two years he spent traveling and working around the country, after which he rejoined the military (Regular Army) in 1950, serving in Germany and Austria with the Army of Occupation until discharged in 1953.

He returned to the Houston area, where he lived and worked until the summer of 1965, when he went to Los Angeles at the invitation of a cousin. The Watts riots had just exploded. When the violence and the fires had cooled, James joined novelist Budd Schulberg's newly formed Watts Writers' Workshop.

From this creative ferment, James emerged to a degree of literary success. Some of his work appeared in the Workshop anthology *From the Ashes —Voices of Watts* and his commentaries and personal experience pieces began to appear in the Los Angeles Times. Two more lengthy works achieved national exposure.

After a long illness, James died in Wadsworth V.A. Hospital in Los Angeles, in early 1985. He left his older siblings, both residing in Texas; and countless friends of many stripes and colors.

He was a man of gentle nobility and kindly wit, of prodigious literary talent, incomplete in its flowering.

James was my dear friend throughout his final years and this book is the fulfillment of a promise made shortly before his death.

—June Acosta

Foreword

Late in January, 1985, novelist and screenwriter Budd Schulberg wrote James Thomas Jackson, a former Houstonian writer and poet and an original member of Schulberg's Watts Writers Workshop, about plans for a 20th anniversary celebration for the Workshop on August 19 of that year.

"You could do a terrific job on the publicity," he wrote, "and if I could only obtain the funds, I would like to see that you were compensated for it."

In February, I wrote about a novel Jackson was close to finishing, "Shade of Darkness," and about a book I hoped he would write next, one dealing with growing up black in Houston, as he did.

James Thomas Jackson did not attend that 20th anniversary celebration or do publicity for it. He did not finish "Shade of Darkness" or write a book about growing up black in Houston. James Thomas Jackson died of cancer on March 25, 1985, at the Los Angeles VA Hospital. He was 59.

The last time I visited him was four days before the end, though of course we did not know that at the time. Between the time I wrote the column about him and its publication in *The Post*, he had learned his illness was terminal. He never got to read *The Post* column about him, but he did hear it. I read the carbons to him in his room at the VA.

Had he finished "Shade of Darkness" and had it been published, it might well have brought him national recognition. Autobiographical, it was a personal and unique view of how integration of the U.S. military affected in an ironic way a sensitive GI doggedly determined to be a writer. But James Thomas Jackson's voice has not been and will not be completely silenced. Though the bulk of his work, much of it various drafts of "Shade of Darkness," languishes now in cardboard cartons, he has been published in a book (*From the Ashes*, a collection of works by Watts Writers Workshop members), in newspapers and in magazines, and he is remembered in many places through his poetry readings with other workshop members.

And the essential James Thomas Jackson is preserved in Houston at Rice's Woodson Research Center. Jackson liked writing letters, even to friends in the same city, when he wasn't writing stories and articles or working at odd jobs to support his writing habit. For the past 20 years, I've been among the recipients of those letters. I never threw one away. Periodically they have gone to the Woodson for safekeeping. They are all there except for those since 1983, which will join his earlier correspondence shortly.

Here are some random selections from letters he wrote in the last years of his life:

"... *getting a grip here and a grip there with a small garden job to do this morning. Sold my recycling cans and newspapers yesterday ... I've been doing this for seven years.*"

"*During the recession of '58 to '60, I labored over twelve months digging an atomic bomb shelter for an ex-Marine bigot keeping his wealth a secret. .... At $1 an hour I was paid in the lower money denominations except pennies.*"

He did construction work, too, and housepainting and odd jobs and for a time swept out a neighborhood bar. He had to work hard to support the habit that consumed him—Writing.

"*Going to the john now. I'll take James Baldwin's* Notes of a Native Son *with me. I was often afraid to read too much of his stuff before. But now . . . trying to get a foothold inside publishers' doors, I need his stuff on Blackness to bolster my sagging one-man literary crusade, with aging pinching the back of my heels.*"

"*It's been a long time since I sold to the* Los Angeles Times *Op-Ed. I wanted an <u>audience</u>. After a nightmarish sleep, I called them before they called me. Weird: all four readers there loved it, voted on it, and it was set into proofreading type.*"

Always writing, the last years of his life in a small, cramped back room writing and rewriting the one work that consumed him more than any other. His autobiographical novel, "Shade of Darkness."

Am enjoying the hell out of myself continuing on the <u>Book</u>. I am there, like yesterday, today, every day. And overlooking nothing. It's absolutely fantastic! What a trip!"

"*. . . deep into Book Two of "Shade of Darkness." Having fun like a dog.*"

Death caught up with James Thomas Jackson before he completed the final chapters. He had hoped the novel would crown his long and often painful journey from high school drop-out to Black artist. Though the novel is yet to be published, this collection of many of his other works, so lovingly assembled and tirelessly submitted by June Acosta, should accomplish for him what fate denied him with "Shade of Darkness."

"*I'll go down fighting <u>not</u> to be a loser.*"

He did and he's not.

—David Westheimer
former *Houston Post* columnist and author of *Von Ryan's Express* and *My Sweet Charlie*, and other novels.

Introduction

"I have to write to be happy, whether I get paid for it or not," Ernest Hemingway wrote to Charles Scribner in 1940. "But it's a hell of a disease to be born with."

When I hear that note, with its mixed overtones of pleasure and frustration, I think also these days of my friend James Thomas Jackson, a writer who shared the pain and the passion and who died of cancer in 1985.

James Thomas was not an unpublished writer. Over the years we ran several of his pieces in Sunday *Calendar* and he had also appeared on the Op Ed page, as well as in other publications. The voice, and occasionally the punctuation (he was fond of dashes), were unmistakable.

He wrote about black artists—poets, playwrights, actors, actresses—he admired, and whose struggles he could identify with because his own struggles had begun early and never really stopped. What those of us who knew him will remember most, I suspect, is that with all the grounds he had for bitterness, James Thomas rarely surrendered to it.

He never denied the realities of his life, and they lent flashes of anger and a kind of wry understatement to his work. ("Writers are forged in injustice as a sword is forged"—Hemingway, "The Green Hills of Africa.")

But he lived for the possibilities of his life as a writer, and if he looked back, it was to see that he had come further, perhaps, than he might have hoped in his early years, even if it was not far enough.

He was born in Temple, Texas, and grew up in Houston, where education was separate and unequal, and he got his high school diploma as a GI drafted into the Air Force. In uniform he read with the thirst of a man emerging from the Sahara, and felt the first stirrings to write.

James Thomas served in Europe, was discharged in 1948, spent two years traveling this country, then re-enlisted, went back to Germany and served in the Army of Occupation until 1953. He had been working ever since, right up to the week he went into the hospital for the last time, on a novel called "Shades of Darkness," based largely on his Army experiences in Germany.

He let me read a large chunk of it, and it was personal, powerful and ironic. The irony, the terrible irony, is that when the Army is at last integrated, the truck company of his story, a proud, well-disciplined outfit, is broken up and his protagonist, a non-com in the former outfit, is put to washing trucks—back to menial status under white control, in the name of progress.

But the novel seemed to me to be about the stirring of change, the teasing but indelible intimation that things could be different. If Germany was not free of anti-black prejudice, it wasn't hard-line Texas, either. It is a look at war and postwar Europe I don't believe we've had from anyone else.

James Thomas went back to Houston after his hitch, tried to write, found a helpful and encouraging friend in the novelist and *Houston Post* columnist David Westheimer (*Von Ryan's Express*). Westheimer remembers that once, when James Thomas was denied admission to a Houston theater, he went home and burned books by white authors. It was one of his rare surrenders.

In 1965, he decided to move to Los Angeles. With magnificent timing, as Westheimer recalled in a column, James Thomas arrived in Watts on the first night of the riots, turned around and drove into the desert and slept in his car until things calmed down.

Not long after, he became a charter member of Budd Schulberg's Watts Writers Workshop and was published in its 1967 anthology, *From the Ashes*. The friendship with Schulberg never stopped, and they had corresponded earlier this year about the 20th anniversary of the workshop coming in August.

At Schulberg's suggestion James Thomas—as he identified himself on the phone; never James, certainly never Jim—came to me, proposing to write for our Sunday arts magazine, called *Calendar*.

And so he did. Irregularly, idiosyncratically, entertainingly, personally and, above all, passionately. He wrote profiles of black performers, which were as valuable for his own appreciative insights as for the interviews as such. He wrote essays on films and television events touching the black experience. His opinions, forceful but fair, were measured against a life that had never been easy but that had seemed to leave him, despite all, with a profound philosophical optimism that better days were coming.

His style was all his own, and he occasionally upset the inhibited traditionalists of our copy desk with his delight in dashes, not just quick dashes but dashes that went on hyphen after hyphen (almost lacerating the paper thanks to the force with which he hit the typewriter keys). His dashes were true punctuation—pauses for dramatic effect, for letting a point sink in, for allowing an insight to be savored.

He was a voice, and in memory I have trouble sorting out the voice I read on paper from the actual voice, low and mellifluous, occasionally roughened a bit by cigarettes and a taste of wine, that I had heard so often on the telephone or across my desk. James Thomas Jackson was in fact all one voice; read his prose and you heard him, urgently singing.

If they are smart (so I think), newspapers are collections of voices, varied and distinct, speaking of news events near and far, talking of sports and other pleasures, appreciating the arts, communicating the writer's sense of how we live and feel in our moment of time. But newspapers also have duties and parameters and, more often than they should be, they are tethered by duty, defined into a collection of airtight compartments. It was and is a source of great regret to me that we were unable to print some of the strongest and most poignant of James Thomas Jackson's writing—his voice at its most eloquent. But against the pressure of timeliness, we simply could not accommodate this most personal of his work. Books were its proper home. I read some of these writings in James Thomas's lifetime, including long excerpts from his major work-in-progress, the novel/memoir of his experiences in World War II. I have read more of the work since he left us, as it has been lovingly assembled and edited by his friend June Acosta. It is all strongly affecting, and it is, I believe, a body of work that forms a particular and important testimony, both positive and negative, about life in the United States in the middle of the twentieth century.

James Thomas Jackson answered to no stereotype. He thought of himself as a man and a writer. Those were his primary givens, not his race or his economic circumstances (which were mostly vile). And it was as a man of letters that he hoped to be judged.

I'm afraid that he delivered more to the promise of Los Angeles than Los Angeles delivered to him. He painted houses and did caretaking and janitorial work and lawn-tending to keep the typewriter clacking. It galled him not to be able to write full time; the miracle was that he had energy left over to write at all. But the passion that kept the words coming also gave his words their special and original force. It is no idle compliment to say that James Thomas Jackson was an inspiration (and a chiding challenge) to those of us who write with no obstacles but our own inertia.

He was a brave man and a vivid voice, and he is long overdue to find at last the wider audiences he deserves.

—Charles Champlin
Arts Editor Emeritus of the *Los Angeles Times.*

PART I

Essays and Articles

Waiting in Line
at the Drugstore

I am black. I am a writer and I want to place full credit where it belongs for the direction my life has taken: on a photography studio and a drugstore on Main Street in Houston, Texas.

When I was thirteen, I dropped out of school, bought a bike for $13 (secondhand and innately durable) and went to work as a messenger for the Owl Foto Studio. Each day we processed film which I picked up as raw rolls on my three routes. That was great: a bike and job are supreme joys to a thirteen-year-old.

The Owl Studio, on a nondescript street named Brazos (very Texan), was located in a white stucco building that blended unobtrusively into the rest of the neighborhood, which was mostly residential. The area was predominantly white, and though it did not smack of affluence, it was not altogether poverty stricken either. Six blocks away was the drugstore, where I had to go first thing each morning for coffee, cakes, doughnuts, jelly rolls, milk, cigarettes, whatever—anything the folks at the Owl wanted. My trip amounted to picking up "breakfast" for a crew of six: three printer-developers, one wash-dry man, the roll-film man and the foreman. The drugstore was the biggest challenge of my young life. Being thirteen is doubtless bad enough for white male youths, but for blacks—me in particular—it was pure dee hell. Going to this drugstore each morning was part of my job; it was required of me. With my dropping out of school and all, my parents would have whipped my behind till it roped like okra if I had tried to supply them with reasons for not wanting to go. So, I gritted my teeth and, buoyed by the power of my Western Flyer, rode on down there.

The place had your typical drugstore look: sundries, greeting cards, cosmetics, women's "things," pharmaceuticals—but most instantly fetching was the large, U-shaped lunch counter. White-uniformed waitresses dispensed eats and sweet drinks of varying kinds: from cakes, donuts and pies to cups of the freshest smelling, strongest tasting coffee one could ask for. In the morning, there were countless servings of ham, bacon, sausages and eggs and mounds of hash-brown potatoes. At lunch there was a "Blue Plate Special"—three vegetables and a meat dish. Oh, they were together, no doubt about that.

My beef was that I was forbidden to sit at that counter. If any black wanted service whether for himself or, like me, for those he worked for—he simply had to stand and wait until all the white folks were served. Those blacks who went contrary to this were worked over something fierce, often by those mild-mannered Milquetoasts who looked as if they wouldn't hurt a fly. A fly, no; but an uppity nigger, in a minute.

I had once witnessed the beating of a black brother at the drugstore and heard tales of other beatings elsewhere. Clean and sanitary as the drugstore was, I preferred the ghetto (though we didn't call it that then). There, at least, we had the freedom to roam all over our stretch of black territory and could shuck our feelings of enforced inferiority as soon as we were on common ground.

Yet I went to the drugstore each morning with my order of coffee, cakes and whatever, written out and clutched firmly in my hand. And each time I was confronted with rows of white folks, seated at the counter and clamoring for attention. I did what I was expected to do: I waited, all the while hating it.

Especially that kind of waiting. As those white faces stared at my black face, I stood conspicuously in a spot near the counter, wanting not to be there, to be somewhere else.

My film pickups were not like this at all. I simply went in a store, picked up a small sack of roll film and split. After all, we provided twenty-four-hour service, and every son-of-a-buck and his brother wanted to see how his pictures came out. It was only the drugstore bit that bugged me.

While waiting near the counter one morning, I realized that I was leaning on a bookcase. I had seen it before but had ignored it because I was in a hurry to get served and get the hell out of there. The case was about four feet high and held perhaps six rows of hardcover books. The sign said "Lending Library." I began looking idly at the books, studying the titles and names of authors, so many unfamiliar to me. But the jackets were impressive, alluring, eye-catching.

One book caught my fancy: *Out of the Night*, the bestseller by Jan Valtin. I opened it, glanced at the fly pages and came across a poem by William Ernest Henley:

> Out of the night that covers me
> Black as the pit from pole to pole
> I thank whatever gods may be
> For my unconquerable soul.

Then I turned to the beginning of Valtin's narrative, read that first page, and then the second. Eleven pages later, going on twelve, hoping to get to thirteen, I heard the white waitress call my name. My order was ready. I folded a corner of the page and tried to hide the book so no one would take it before I could get back the next day.

I picked up the food and wheeled back to the studio—slowly. My mind was a fog—I had never begun a real book before. All the way back, I felt different from before. Something was happening to me, and I didn't quite know what to make of it. Somehow I didn't feel the "badness" that I usually felt when I returned from the drugstore.

The next day, my usual waiting was not the same. I went from page thirteen to page twenty-seven . . . twenty-eight, pinned a corner down, returned to the studio, delivered my routes, went home, thought and wondered. God, I wondered, when would

5

tomorrow come? The promise of tomorrow, of course, was the difference.

Many mornings later I finished reading Valtin's book. But there was another that looked interesting: *The Grapes of Wrath* by John Steinbeck. (We weren't as poor, I discovered, as those people.) Then *Tobacco Road* by Erskine Caldwell.

A year passed, and I discovered a black library branch at Booker T. Washington High. An elderly friend of mine in the ghetto who had noticed the change in me made a list of things to ask for: Countee Cullen's poem "Heritage," Charles W. Chestnutt's "The Wife of His Youth," Walter White's "Fire in the Flint"; also Frederick Douglass, Paul Lawrence Dunbar, Jean Toomer—how was I to read them all?

Find a way, my friend said.

All the while I kept going to the drugstore each morning. I must have read every worthwhile book on that "Lending Library" shelf. But during this period, something strange happened: my waiting time got shorter and shorter each morning. I could hardly get five pages read before my order was handed to me with—of all things—a sense of graciousness from the waitresses. I didn't understand it.

Later on I went off to World War II. My mind and attitudes were primed for the books yet to come and for the words that were to come out of me. I was eighteen then and a drop-out, but I was deep into the wonderful world of literature and life. I found myself, and my niche, in the word. Who would have thought that a drugstore could provide such a vista for anyone? And my waits at the counter? I keep wondering: which way would I have gone had I not waited?

Good question.

Once Upon a Time
in Houston

In Houston's predominantly black Fourth Ward, I grew up in a cul-de-sac.

My street, Crosby, dead-ended with our house. Unasphalted, it stayed that way until well after my eighteenth birthday when I entered the armed services during World War II. Our tiniest black ghetto—five wards in all and listed numerically—was Watts, California-sized, perhaps: 2 x 2 x 2 miles, and downtown Houston's eyesore of a backyard. It was still pretty much that way when I left it for Los Angeles, California, in August, 1965.

Our ghetto, because of Houston's downtown nearness, was ever a mass of contradictions in social, commercial and even cultural mores. We could "trip" from the sublime to the ridiculous in an instant, depending on how one kept score. A black customer could be refused use of a restroom, while a black employee—male or female—not only cleaned them but used them at will; even though double bathrooms were installed within the major premises. On our jobs, both domestic and residential, we entered by rear doors and had possession of the places all day during our chores. At evening tide we departed through the same rear doors. These double-standard confusions were many, varied, and blew our black minds for as long as it took to "adapt"—if we wanted to survive race prejudices—without going plumb nuts in the process. Our ghetto was our saving grace: in our combined blackness, faith in our churches and trust in eventual justice overall made manifest our striving for entity—through the front door.

I have fond boyhood memories though. Horses from Phoenix Phil's Dairy were kept in a large corrugated tin barn just around the corner from our house. Their clip-clopping and clanking bottle milk clatter, both empty and full, mornings and afternoons, sufficed as timepieces to in- and out-of-house patrons more than any Woolworth, Schultz-United or J. C. Penney alarm clock. One morning a horse driver's car engine caught fire, parked right in front of our house. The white owner (blacks cleaned the stables, tended the horses) tried using my father's water hose but to no avail. Another white, a passing derelict a short block away on our Cleveland cross street, rushed back to assist. Snatching the hose out of the frustrated driver's hand, he was yelling "Sand! Sand! Sand!" Grabbing handfuls of it he splayed it all over the car fire. In an instant the fire was extinguished. He, alone, of all of us was blest with knowledge of so handy an expedient; and we had a whole city block of the stuff.

Conversely, Phoenix Phil's Dairy was located at the last edge of the street ending a Fourth Ward boundary, becoming the foot of this part of Houston's downtown commerce. It faced a portion of poor white and struggling metropoles taking up where we left off. On the roof and high above the dairy's white brick edifice, where our milk was daily bottled and loaded into an early dawn's horse-drawn truck, was a huge Phoenix Phil sign. A colorful commercial sign of a white, pink-cheeked boy-child of three, wearing an outsized, deliveryman's cap of white crown, black-bibbed and dressed in striped blue overalls. The right strap of them hung down unfastened. In one hand he was carrying a giant quart of white bottled milk. The tot's commercial name was "Phoenix Phil." This logo told us Fourth Warders in particular, and all persons entering and departing this area in general, that this milk was baby-pure good. I went away to serve my country remembering that particular sign as did, I'm sure, many of my black and white playmates (who lived on our fringes), and always expected it to be there when we returned. Sometime in the late fifties, the sign and the old ownership went. "Phoenix was sold to Foremost," was the word we all received.

Back to Crosby Street. Over the wooden and very tall fence of Crosby Street lived some white folks—as they did, always near the edge of Fourth Ward's perimeter. This house, a two-story, painted white, had a large tree which offered much shade deeply planted near its back stairs. I remember the middle-aged couple's name as the Benfords. They appeared to live coolly and quietly. Sheriff Benford was a no-nonsense man in his job. (To this day I see him only a decade removed from a Texas Ranger.) He was reputed to "kick asses and take names," indiscriminately. Our high fence limited association, except for my occasional day's work inside their light, bright and airy home doing some cleaning chores, in which case one or the other was nice as pie to me. A-okay. Sheriff Benford's presence "over the fence" just might have dispelled many burglary attempts from our humble abode, and nothing but respect passed back and forth from our good neighbor fence.

The Benfords' house also greeted the end of Calhoun where it curved out, became Baldwin and headed south past well-tended shrubbery, umbrella trees and white, early plantation houses well to the rear. Presenting a moody but wealth-accrued quietness, Baldwin seemed the most sedate street of my childhood. And at Christmas time, peeking through a key-holed fence, it looked forebodingly fetching with bright lights streaming through moss and shrubbery alike. It gave my young mind all sorts of wistful thoughts of a quiet, comfortable culture that never seemed to come our way.

One summer when I was ten or eleven, my new next door black neighbor, D. J. (Dan Johnny) Houghton and I started out walking from Calhoun's end. Adventurous in every way, we hopped and crawled over the eight-foot-high fence and started hiking up Calhoun's then unpaved street, taking turns carrying an empty five-gallon bucket, going "crawdad" hunting. ("Crayfish," the shrimp's bastard kin, living in bottoms of shallow creek water.) It would be a five-mile walk each way, a hot Texas summer with bristling heat, and the distance to Bray's Bayou and our foraging end mattered not one whit. The area was white folks' suburbs (then) whose occupants showed no inclination to bother us and certainly we had no intention of bothering them. Houston then had places in white areas we blacks weren't about to go, especially those inhabited by poor whites who were mean as hell to "niggers." Those we encountered that day were simply indifferent. Plus, luck being with us, we hand-caught a whole bucket full of this muddy, creek fish delicacy.

D. J. and I struggled the whole way back with our "catch," using a broken broom handle to equalize the bucket's water-added weight. (D. J.'s cleverness: not wanting to ruin our bounty by stupidity.) I credit myself for being eager and adventurous, but D. J. was my own black Davy Crockett. We rested quite a lot and changed arm grips; we even used people's hydrants for fresher water in our return odyssey, and our catch was unspoiled when we reached home base.

Once back home we were instant heroes. Black folks' love for "exotic" foods combined with a "mean" Depression made the crawdads a godsend, and from kids our age! Our neighbors said we had "pluck."

Both our parents had us distribute our goodies to as many in our block as possible. Fried crawdad odors permeated our area that night. Both D. J.'s and my plates were huge from our parents' frying: heaps of home-fried potatoes accompanied the now golden devils, along with our staple, "Happy Jack" cornbread, skillet fried, and all the ketchup we wanted. I asked my mother if we should offer the Benfords' some, but a wagging maternal finger warned me against it. (It seemed white folks had a thing against black folks giving them things.) "Not to white folks," the wagging finger said. It was also the first time I heard the old saw, "like bringing coals to Newcastle," and later, one I was ever trying to comprehend, that black people were "inferior to white." No matter, D. J. and I would eat now and think later, having lots of growing up to do. So we ate our "exotic," muddy creek crawdads with ravenous relish and laughed like two fools at absolutely nothing at all.

Of Roses and a Black Family's Unusual Visitor

My mother was a God-fearing woman who loved roses.

Her husband and children (myself included) also loved roses and feared God. In our family, the two went together, ever so nicely, at most times. But it was left to my father to teach me something about compassion.

Both Mother and Father had, it seemed, an almost innate understanding of the fact that people often failed as well as succeeded through no action of their own. My mother, in particular, thought of human lives as she thought of the roses that grew in the front yard: sometimes they wilted, sometimes they almost died; yet with a "little loving care," a "little gentleness," a "little concern," those roses always bloomed again.

When I was growing up during the depression years, we lived in the southern latitude of a pronouncedly black ghetto in Houston—a fact that never distracted us for long. Life was sometimes a hell or, at best, a restricted pleasure. There was often much hunger among our neighbors and those whom my mother called "the less fortunate."

That expression of hers drove me to a multitude of soul searchings—who, I wanted to know, could be "less fortunate?"

11

After all, we were already black, already deprived of innumerable economic advantages. Even then, at my tender age, I knew that we were scorned, derided, hated for our immutable blackness.

For a long time, though, I was proud of our black "freedom." We had, at least, blackness in common. And it was so beautifully black! For instance—

The blind man next door to us who delighted me with stories even more engrossing than those I read to him from the Holy Bible.

The elderly spinster three houses down, whose lawn I cut once a month for a few quarters. (I always used a hoe and botched it each time—but she forgave me.)

The Pullman porter, next door to her, who on departing for work carried that distinctive-looking, black "doctor's" bag, with the bold watch chain slung across his stomach; who worked on the Santa Fe and had a pretty wife.

The woman fortune teller down the street, with her many mysteries that held all of us children in an ever-circumspective awe.

The gospel singer with the peg leg who lived around the corner, who got outrageously drunk every Saturday night and gave a one-man soul-show in his backyard.

Such was the beauty of our isolated black land. It was our domain and only rarely was it broached by the appearance of either youthful white faces who wanted to play with us, or the curious sight of a white journeying mendicant, invading our black ghetto with flimflam wares.

Why, I thought, if we were so inferior, so unequal, so unfit to mingle with whites—why should they come to our part of town to peddle? They had removed us from their dominant scenes and restricted us from associations within our mutual city, leaving us with only wistful looks at an expanding and growing place which, even then, my own hod-carrying father was sweating to help build.

They made us ride buses in the one small section allotted us—packed black sardines, well to the rear, like slaves on some ship from African shores, bound for shores like these.

The word was that we were smelly, wore the same clothes all the time, had no culture, no intellect, couldn't think. That our cooking pots reeked with the pungent odors of chit'lin's, red beans and neck bones. That our bodies—when we bathed—smelled of Octagon, Ivory or the even more disinfecting odor of Lifebuoy. That our streets and gutters ran rife with the litter of empty whiskey bottles. That our houses bled and flaked with a blatant cry for paint.

Then the picture changed. This man came. This white man in tatterdemallion clothes came to our black ghetto. His last recourse. He was raggedy as a twenty-nine-cent mop in a Baptist church in '32. He looked real bummy, and my mother fed him. That day she was cooking red beans and rice, collard greens and neck bones. The collard greens came from our own back yard.

My father arrived home early that day, smelling of mortar—a "perfume" I had learned to love the smell of. It meant prosperity, really. Mother fixed a big plate. (The white man's was big but no bigger than Father's—never bigger than the breadwinner's.) We all ate as though nothing unusual was happening. Washing all the food down with Poly-Pop, a watery strawberry flavoring with lots of sugar.

At the dinner table I studied the mighty symbol of authority. White face, blue eyes, blond hair, badly in need of a shave and hungry like a dog. He was too hungry to smile.

After the meal Father gave the man a pair of pants, a shirt, one of his hats and two cigars. My mother filched about $1.90 from our "don't go" money bank. He looked like a new man when he left: shaved, cleaned up some with pomade perking up his hair. I almost hated to see him go. There was so much I wanted to know. So much I wanted him to tell me.

Father understood that I was curious, and talked with me later. I can remember his words today.

"James," he said, "he is a white man with problems. He is not wanted. He is hated and despised among his own people. He is what is known as po' white trash. That sounds bad and, for him, it is bad. But that's the way things go.

"He is a white man with nothing. But in this house he is treated with kindness and understanding . . .

13

"Now," he added, done with his seriousness, "Don't you think your mother's rose bushes could use a little water? It seems to me they haven't had a drop to drink all day."

It was time to lay a "little loving care" elsewhere.

Terry and Me

His given name was Terrence.

He hated it with a passion, and would fight like a wildcat if any other boy called him that to his face. He was TERRY, damn it! Terrence was a name for sissies!

Many's the time I saw a swollen eye or a cut lip on him, because he demanded and fought for that sovereignty. In truth, at eleven going on twelve (the same as me), he was the out-fightingest white boy I was to meet in my young life.

Terry lived in the Calhoun-Bagby section of Houston, a minuscule pocket of white-painted homes, many with garage apartments well to the rear used as servants' quarters—black servants (colored or negro, we were called then). I never saw any others, although I had heard that some poor whites played that role too.

Whenever I went to Terry's house, it was because I was recommended to his mother by some other white woman in the area as a "good worker" and "dependable," meaning I didn't steal or loaf.

That was just fine with me. Extra work meant extra pay. In my family during the Great Depression, every little bit helped. I was tough and eager, and there were many things that black maids doing "day work" just didn't have the time or strength to do; and Terry, being white, and in keeping with the "status quo," was not prevailed upon by his parents to do such menial chores as chimeyflue cleaning, lugging trash to the alley, digging up flower beds and the like.

It was an unwritten code of the South that the white youth of my time and in my city were still to be pampered. Let the strong black youth and the black adult males do the work! It was one of the last holdovers from slavery days that a compromising white society clung to with all the power it had left.

In the 1930's, those servants' quarters were another holdover, a slowly vanishing pseudo-integration, curious and inexplicable to my young mind. Black servants were ever at the beck and call of their white "masters," long after the Emancipation Proclamation was signed. (I'd been told repeatedly that even *that* glorious news got to Texas late, to be forever etched into our young minds as the Nineteenth of June, 1863. The edict culminated in a "gentleman's agreement," a kind of black freedmen's holiday thereafter known as "Juneteenth." Over the years, this all-black Fourth of July was observed by most Houston blacks as a legal holiday, with lots of red soda pop and pink barbecue as the prime criteria for festivities.)

In the meantime, we all—black and white alike—would live the dichotomy or double standard of "For Whites Only" and "for blacks only" for the greater part of our days. It was our social and cultural milieu, familiar albeit unfair. That's the way it was. The Big Change would come, but slowly.

The area in which Terry lived was a giant stone's throw over the fence from my house on our cul-de-sac ghetto street.

For the young, what was the distance? We were fleet of foot; and for Houston itself, which took roots from everywhere, the mores that governed the young were less rigid. Two boys from two houses, two ways—ways that converged for a time. Our lives intermingled so much, we could very well have lived next door to each other.

Terry's folks were in the conglomerate economically, only a generation or two removed from being sharecroppers, small farmers. His mother and father were practical planners: not hurting severely for material wants, yet not well-to-do either.

The white-painted houses of that enclave were unostentatious: an image distinction. Our own grimy-looking house could have used a paint job something fierce. Ah, but to do it! To change that grimy image would wreak social havoc, in those two close neighborhoods! A black family painting its house, and maybe even white!

In those days, all of our family worked. My father was a hod carrier mostly, doing construction work. My stepmother was a domestic, working in several white women's homes until she got a steady job in one. We three Jackson kids did after-school and weekend work. My brother hustled jobs of all kinds; my sister sweated in her school cafeteria; and I, the youngest, shined shoes, threw handbills for the local small grocery markets, besides the aforementioned household odd jobs. Everybody roved about to earn money, to stave off starvation and our "Blue Norther" winters. We simply dug in there; grubbed and scratched and lugged, for our creature comforts. It was our birthright, familiar though fearsome.

One of my tasks on alternate Saturdays was at Terry's house. Terry suffered from acute attacks of asthma. Excessive dust and grime were an anathema to him, and he hated his affliction ferociously. Mother Nature played no favorites, and I was grateful I'd been spared.

I, healthy as the young weeds I chopped, cleaned their sooty chimney, swept, dusted, raked, did anything manful, to make those extra coins. (Most of my earnings went into the Jackson "family pot," though I always managed to filter me a bit of change for "sneakin' in" Saturday movies and other indulgences. Saturdays were fine and had to last me, for on Sundays my time was "uselessly" restricted to religious activities.)

Terry always tried to help me work, and his mother gave him the very devil for it. For two reasons: the one on account of his health; the other, unspoken but understood by all, the perpetuity of the white superiority bit. Terry pooh-poohed the maternal restrictions, and got slapped in the face for his disobedience. I tried my damnedest any number of times to get him to back off,

17

mostly because I didn't want him to jeopardize my job. He seemed to understand this, and did back off—grudgingly—and always with a slow wink when he thought his mother wasn't looking, and he felt like he was scoring triumphs. Then we'd conspire—or at least he would—to compensate for his not being permitted to help me with my work. Such loyalty!

He was the first white friend I'd ever had, however inadvertently, and I didn't know how to tell him to let things ride as they were. So damned much explaining! God, I wasn't a sage! I was only part of the damned system! Learning to survive the best way I could.

Separateness was the order of the day. In my young mind, I knew that code. Terry ignored it; but hell, it wasn't his black experience to live out, it was mine. I had a family to answer to, and a whole ghetto of blacks, ordinary folks plus the privileged and influential, like preachers and teachers, not to mention the NAACP!

I was getting used to my blackness, feeling pride in my black youth, enjoying the sanctuary of being among my own people. If I responded to Terry's friendly, well-intentioned impulses, I'd have trouble functioning. What was he after, anyway? He had it good in his own white world, and I didn't envy him for it. I couldn't take him with me where I went. Our physical identities were too pronouncedly different. The double standard of the white system wouldn't stand for it, nor would the black system, which was not as harsh, perhaps, but certainly none the less solidly in place. Now, if he'd just let me do my work and earn my pay, everything would be copacetic.

But neither the system nor the double standard knew Terry. The hell of it was: neither did I.

On this Saturday, by the time I had finished his house and was ready to go, Terry already had his plans laid. Unbeknownst to me, he had cleverly rifled his parents' icebox and food cupboards, cutting off big chunks of roast beef and ham, copping a few eggs and a shaft of butter; filching some white potatoes, yams, onions, turnips, tomatoes—whatever an eleven-year-old boy figured a family might like to eat. He'd even poured some flour into a brown paper bag. (Everybody saved brown paper bags in those days.) All were rammed into a sturdy shopping bag with cardboard handles and stashed surreptitiously near the alley through which I'd leave.

Then I was finished, got paid, and was off through the alley toward my home shores. There at the mouth of the alley was none other than my conspiratorial friend, Terry, beckoning me frantically to "Come on, come on, hurry!" holding his big shopping bag with both hands, while I, halted dead in my escape, was suddenly, unwillingly caught up in the vortex of that idiot's shenanigans, thieving from his own folks, clearly expecting to follow along home with me.

In desperation, I tried to reason with him to return all that food, to stay and allow me to go, to use some sense. To no avail. With all that wheezing and snorting of his stifled asthma, coupled with his apparent earnestness to prove himself a friend, I was rendered as senseless as he.

So, two culprits—one black, one white—we moved on fleeted feet toward Darktown, both of us as conspicuous as bugs in a bowl of rice.

It was only the protection of the gods who watch over fools and idiots that allowed us to arrive in the safety of the ghetto, without mishap.

Once home, I laid down the law to my well-intentioned friend. It took some doing, but at last I got his promise of no more such larcenous tomfoolery in the future. Luckily, my folks were all off attending to their own particular business. I stowed the groceries, and we went out into the streets again.

Then things got worse, or so it seemed. Since he was there, in Blacktown, what the hell was I gonna do with him? I couldn't just tell him to go, with being indebted to him and all, for the food; and he didn't want to leave. He acted like he had all the reason in the world to be there, like he was one of us.

We stood out like two bandaged sore thumbs. Stares and gapes abounded. All the black brothers and sisters, especially the older ones, gawked at us like we were two freaks from a circus. We traversed through areas where I, alone, moved so ordinarily and without amazement; trying to seem like two normal boys, going about boys' affairs.

It wasn't easy for a loner like me; besides, I was feeling a nudging of the race thing, the differentiation, boiling in my innards.

But Terry was so damned ingratiating, he put at ease every black we met, with his natural gregariousness, greeting everybody with a "Hi! I'm Terry!" followed by "What's your name?" Then the whopper-stopper: "me and James are friends." (Now why didn't I think of that?) Right off the bat, he had that Terry business straightened out.

Finally we went to where I always went on Saturdays, to the picture show. Saturday offered a double feature, a cartoon and a serial.

Terry seemed to have a pocket full of money, but I insisted on paying for my ownself's ticket. We had the same battle at the concession stand, with the popcorn, candy and cold drinks. He was easily hurt, I noticed, so I yielded and let him treat: "Go 'head an' pay fer it, fer goshsakes!"

In the gloom of the movie house, we lapped up all the cinematic adventures. There were some moments when we were confronted with stares, curious rather than threatening; but the movie was engrossing, and our presence together went unchallenged. A white boy in a black theater wasn't too uncommon, really. Black people had been babysitting, movie-sitting, white kids even younger than Terry for as long as I could remember. Strange as it seemed, many whites in those days couldn't see themselves trusting any other race as servants.

By the time we exited the movie, it was late and very dark outside. Terry was apprehensive, but since it was my turf, I consoled him, then decided to walk him "piece-way" home— close enough to see that he would get there safely, yet with enough latitude to shoot me an azimuth to mine.

The dark was bad enough, what with remembering stories of young boys being carted off to God-knows-where; but my own apprehension covered more grisly misfortunes suffered by too many of my race: lynchings, burnings, other savageries.

Their street lights were nearly as sparse as ours (and ours were very few and far between), but finally we arrived in seeing distance of his house (it had a short campanile tower, the only one on the block like it) and we prepared our departures.

I asked him if he was ready, told him to check the air for dust, and take a deep breath for his asthma. Then: "O.K. . . . . . on your Mark . . . .Get Set . . . . .Ready? . . . . . .GO!!"

He was off and running. Like a turkey through the corn. Lickety-split, his white, short-sleeved shirt bobbing eerily in the darkness, then disappearing. At last, I heard a familiarly yelled "O-Ka-a-a-a-a-y!" in the distance, signifying he had made it home.

Then I was off, getting the hell out of there, that white area, outrunning all those imagined white goblins set to pounce on a young black intruder in their midst.

I barely slowed when I reached Darktown, fearing some of our own goblins too, when sudden shadows appeared in my flight path. I remembered parental admonishments: "At night, always walk the middle of the streets, if possible." A fellow could see more, have more room to maneuver. Getting a second wind, I hauled ass to the safety of our house. A lamp was burning, as always, until everybody in the Jackson household was in for the night.

Finally, with the day's excursions behind me, I settled onto my floor pallet, and my drowsy thoughts turned to dreams of my new-found white friend, benevolent thief Terry.

Strange, I never saw him again.

His parents must have learned about our newly-budded comradeship, and determined to put an end to it. Although I was never called back to Terry's house, I got other weekend jobs, met other people, found books and libraries full of principles and enduring philosophies to sustain me when human relationships faltered.

I did learn, eventually, that Terry and his folks moved to Arizona, then to someplace else, thence to oblivion, leaving me with only the memory of his being.

For a long time, I kept remembering the sight of him standing at the mouth of that alley, with a shopping bag full of his parents' groceries, waving frantically for me to: "Come on, come on, hurry up!" Then later, that same night, my own whispered urgency. "On your mark .... get set .... ready.... GO!!" and him, running like a bat out of hell, going zigzag to the safety of his house; and me, doing the same thing, running like a molly trooper in the opposite direction, with the bond that joined us stretching, strong—the two of us warmed by the knowledge that we had found something precious: true friendship, and that intangible could never be taken from us by anyone of any race.

On Learning Values, and People

My first full-time, everyday job, working "with" white folks, and not just "for" them, was in 1938, at Greene's Pharmacy in Houston. There, even though blacks did not sit at the counter to eat like white customers did, the "color line" was a little thinner than lots of other places in Houston.

I'd put in plenty of after-school and weekend hours "odd-jobbing"—everything from cleanup and yard work (mostly by recommendation of one white family to another that I was strong and honest), to delivering handbills for local stores.

Out of money I made, I was finally able to buy a second-hand bike. Like it did to all kids in the late 1930s, the bike meant freedom and mobility to me, like a horse meant to one of my Western movie heroes.

I'd just turned thirteen. Being in love with a deliciously cute brownskin that I wouldn't make any kind of waves with, I upped and quit school. I applied for and got a Social Security card (the thing to do at that time), and was hired on at Greene's as a delivery boy.

The pay was eight dollars a week; the work lasted every day from 3:00 to 11:00, a shift I hated. Sometimes I switched around and worked the 7:30 to 3:00 shift, but that was rare. The last hired

23

(meaning me) had the late swing, and was obliged to help clean up behind the food counter after returning from deliveries. I earned that eight dollars!

But I did get tips: a dime here, a quarter there, all from delivering prescriptions, sandwiches, malts, soft drinks and the like. We delivered prescriptions by the boxcar load, it seemed—there were a lot of sick folks!—also sundries, "personal" things, and food, of course.

The most popular sandwich was a "Western." That was a triple decker of roast beef, tomatoes, lettuce, and pickles, with mustard or mayonnaise. Only ham and cheese—grilled or plain—ran a close second. In all, it was a compatibly homogenous pharmacy. Mr. Greene had something for everybody, every ailment. He was a long, lanky drink of water with glassy blue eyes—the most perfectionist pharmacist I've ever known. The august diplomas in back of his checkout counter fully attested to his academic training. In black folks' jargon, he "took care of business."

The other two delivery boys were Johnny and Mack. Other aspirants came and went. We remained. We learned our streets, alleys, areas—those "hunky" and "po' cracker" neighborhoods where they hated blacks with a passion; those that were moderate and more liberal; those that were affluent—or well off. Sometimes it wasn't easy for us to tell the difference between the last two.

With our tips, we sometimes realized twenty to twenty-five dollars a week in our six-day work stint. We were rarely off on a Saturday or Sunday, which was good, in a way, because tips were more numerous then.

We weren't Uncle Toms, either—which may have cost us some tips. We fought against any "hunky" or "po' cracker" allowing himself to "rub a nigger's head for luck," and got a few bruises for our pains. We didn't kiss asses, and heaven help the black slob who did. He was sent to a Coventry from which there was no returning.

Johnnny was a favorite with the customers—especially the females. Mack and I were black in color, but Johnny was tan—more vulgarly referred to by blacks as "shit-colored"—and heavily muscular with handsome features. There was an unwritten code predominant in the South I grew up in that a black of Johnny's color naturally had "some white in him," and therefore was superior to a pronouncedly *black* black. A damn lie to be sure, since most of our greatest black leaders were *black* blacks. To accentuate the stigma, the anonymous poem was on nearly every black man's lips:

> If you're white, you're right
> If you're yellow, you're mellow
> If you're brown, stick around
> But if you're black—git back!

Because of Johnny's handsomeness and tawny skin, Mack and I often had great apprehension for his safety, to say nothing of our own as potential co-conspirators in some verboten liaison. There were too many overly aggressive white women filtering in and out of our pharmacy, getting close and far too chummy with him. Some were so damn bold—and stupid—that they asked for no one but him to deliver their orders, causing more than one raised eyebrow from Mr. Greene, who took almost all the orders.

Worse, if the jealous homely waitress behind the counter took the order when some dizzy dame cooingly specified that no one but Johnny deliver it, the jeopardy was even worse. The only thing that saved Johnny from a lynching or castration resulting from her acid tongue was the fact that she bad-mouthed everybody who worked at the pharmacy, including Mr. Greene's sweetie, Margaret, another waitress. This was her undoing, because Mr. Greene wasn't about to have his love life "bizness" put in the streets by some foul-mouthed "bitch" as he was heard to say. So the homely waitress finally got fired. Somehow nothing untoward ever happened to Johnny while he worked at Greene's, although the white-girl customers kept getting bolder and bolder. When he left on his own, however, we got it through the black grapevine that one very affluent white girl who always asked for him was pregnant.

After Johnny left, my biggest concern was my association with "Mr. Lloyd," who cooked lunch and did short orders.

According to Johnny and Mack, who wouldn't work with him, he was "one real prejudiced white man." He kept a fifth of Old Crow in the wooden, pull-out rice bin at his right knee each and every day. He was the most efficient cook I ever knew. He opened shop every day at seven, making breakfast for the many clerical minions who worked near and about our pharmacy area. I had always worked in his kitchen during my dallying time: peeling potatoes, cutting celery, cleaning spinach, unstringing green beans, skimming carrots or beets. On his good days, he called me Jimmy and taught me many things about running the kitchen. I didn't have much love for him, but I was curious to find out how one white man could justify blaming all America's woes and troubles on the black race. He wasn't violent—except in his talk—and that was water off a duck's back so long as he didn't raise his hand to strike us. And his words were usually under his breath—sotto voce—as though he was thinking twice about saying them. Many times I heard him call us "jigs," "pickaninnies" or "scobies." We called him "Mr. Lloyd" as part of the Southern code. That didn't mean we had to love him.

Oftentimes, I think Lloyd hated the world in general. What made all of his anger finally come to a head was Margaret being taken off her duties as waitress and assigned to the kitchen. She may have been a young, vivacious redhead, pretty as a speckled pup under a calico quilt, but she couldn't cook for beans!

That was when the sawdust hit the fan—and literally. Lloyd kicked over the revolving fan which rested on one end of his order table, and it fell into the sawdust which we—mostly I—sprinkled on the floor each day. He wanted no part of a "she-male"—his words—in his kitchen. Always quick-tempered, and even more so now, he left fuming, slamming his apron down here, his chef's hat there, even starting to remove his white trousers out on the sidewalk. He decided against the idea, then vanished.

Our customers came as usual, but there was no Lloyd. Margaret didn't know rye bread from white bread, and there were customers on every one of our twenty-two seats around the L-shaped counter *and* our two tables-for-four. All were impatient to eat before their allotted lunch times were gone.

Mr. Greene had to leave his pharmacy cubicle to pinch hit for his angry and departed cook. First rattle out of the box, he cussed out Margaret for being such a "dumb bitch." Siding with Lloyd, he berated himself for thinking she would be a great helpmate for him. They lashed out at each other in that tiny kitchen, each hurling invectives at the other with growing compounded angers that carried the length and breadth of the entire pharmacy. Finally Margaret stormed out of the kitchen, issuing all kinds of parting shots at Mr. Greene's age and sexual impotence and some other private secrets that surely Mr. Greene would have preferred to remain private. The hush in her wake was enough to speak reams of gossip for days.

In the meantime, the show had to go on. While he was deciphering the waitresses' order scrawls, I was standing silent to his rear, watching his movements. I was surprised to hear him call my name, especially in a solicitous tone: "James, how in hell does Lloyd get these things together? I mean, I can't even get 'em to *look* like Lloyd does." Mr. Greene wanted to get out of this dilemma. ("And a little child shall lead them," was the cynical thought that popped into my head.) I found myself directing him, with just the faintest hint of condescension:

"No, Mr. Greene, this is what Mr. Lloyd does for a 'Western' sandwich, see: a thick slice of roast beef, a lot of mayonnaise—if they want it, otherwise use mustard—a steak tomato slice, a wide hunk of lettuce; okay, put some hootenany there; sauce—hot sauce, out of this little bowl, that's it, spice it up a bit; there, that's fine, there you go. Now this order is egg salad—make it on toast, it'll weigh heavier, make the guy think he's getting more for his money; give him a li'l extra mayonnaise, too; sprinkle a little relish on it, perk it up some. Mr. Lloyd always says, 'the guy's probably on a tight budget.' This one's for four ham salads. Mr. Lloyd always lays these on kinda thick. The waitresses says they tip good when he does that. And it's better to use it than to let it spoil. I'm putting a rasher of bacon on now for the bacon and tomato sands. She should have six or seven of them. Put a lot of lettuce and a big tomato slice on each one. You know how bacon shrinks. It's a good seller. You should have some grilled ham and cheese there. They're both there, already sliced. On a couple of 'em, put the sliced onions separate. If they don't eat 'em the waitresses will bring 'em back—on the Q.T. If they eat 'em they'll be buying gum and mints on the way out. That's the way Mr. Lloyd does it. It's simple."

Of course nothing is all that simple. But I was putting my new-found knowledge to use and that made me feel good. Mr. Greene had come out of his great shell of respectability to learn something from someone he considered inferior. At the time, I didn't have the sense to hold grudges. Putting what I had learned to worthwhile use didn't seem like too much condescending to me. Acting on the old black axiom "if a man don't know, he must don't know," I figured I did what I should have done. It would have been easy to just hate white folks and leave it at that, but we Jacksons weren't quite made that way.

Believe it or not, Mr. Lloyd came back the next day, early in the morning, full of profuse apologies. Just like old time, he sent me to get his first fifth of Old Crow for the day. Mr. Greene was happily back in his pharmaceutical cubicle. I never saw Margaret again.

I went on to other jobs and other situations. I would remember Mr. Lloyd, though, his "jug" in the rice bin, and helping Mr. Greene prepare those luncheons that day. And remembering too that I had not lost one ounce of respect, either for myself or my fellow man. You can't beat that.

Juneteenth Was Freedom Day—A Long Time Ago

In the long receded used-to-be, Father's Day was marked on our calendars as today. June 19. That was before it was changed to fall on Sunday to accomodate the widely commercial shenanigans of merchants the country over.

But to my own humbly parented black family in Texas, now far into its third generation in this land, the 19th of June has a much deeper meaning. That meaning applies not only to me as a black southerner but also to other blacks, North or South, who may sit in silence about it, who may still seem to feel a shame in observing this particular day. Supposedly we black Texans—and the white folks, too, I imagine—got the word late about the Emancipation Proclamation. News that it had been signed, they say, arrived in Texas about June 19, 1863. At any rate, from my cradle up, "Juneteenth" was black folks' day. Freedom. No blacks worked. Most had that day off as an official holiday from their white employers—as opposed to their former masters and mistresses.

We'd have picnics galore, riding in mule-drawn wagons, bedded down in fresh-cut hay, heading out to some isolated pasture or undulating meadow in the Texas plains outside Houston where birds sang and crows cawed. Red soda pop bubbled, and pink barbecue assailed our nostrils from the crack of dawn till way past twilight's last gleaming. We children romped and ate and sprinted and yelled with abandon, until our throats were hoarse and our bellies distended. But it didn't just involve gorging ourselves on barbecue and soda pop, or the black male adults over imbibing the "hard stuff." We had solemn ceremonies, too, with prayers and speeches by some of the most eloquent black speakers of Texas. Their thunderous rhetoric rained like block-buster bombs on our attentive ears. We were somebody then. We had come from a mighty, mighty long way; we were the chosen few, and we were proud to beat the band. It was one wonderful black world on that day, the one day in the year that was entirely ours. Hundreds of blacks scattered over so wide an area, having programs just like ours—it was magnificent. Unbelievable. Most of all, we didn't feel alone. We were not only family, we also knew that we were many *in* the family. A nation within a nation, whose great and only pride came from our hands, our sweat, our minds and our sacred black honor.

On those grassy Texas plains in the 1930s, it was, to borrow from Charles Dickens, the worst of times, and the very best of times. Because we brought back to our shacks and shanties a new Jerusalem that was to outdo that of antiquity. And for that vision we rejoiced. Oh, how we rejoiced!

As the years passed and we grew older, many of us still could not completely embrace America's Fourth of July—Independence Day—because it had no direct connection to us. We saw it mostly as a big day for white folks. Oh, some blacks had to figure in what it was all about, since we figured in so much else. So that gave us sort of a right to whoop it up right along with the whites. At most, the white folks' Independence Day gave us an extra holiday.

We were Americans and no longer slaves, it's true, but our special segregated day, June 19, said that America was as much our country as it was theirs. A source of pride. A weird paradox at best. The most outrageous sort of social separateness within our still-floundering country was forcing, inexorably, the nation's growth toward humaneness.

Perhaps it was uneasiness over this blacks-only holiday—our own "Fourth of July," you might say—that eventually caused our southern black society to shy away from the Juneteenth celebrations that we kids had once so revered.

By the time I entered the Army Air Corps soon after my eighteenth birthday, I couldn't remember "Juneteenth" having been celebrated for several years. By the time I had finished my hitch in the service, there was barely a whisper of "Juneteenth" in Houston, the city where I grew up. It was only when I visited the small town of my birth—Temple, Texas—that I found some vestige of it yet observed on that date—half-hearted, and lacking any real fervor, or even remembrance of its significance.

The Fourth of July now was the big event, even in Temple. And blacks—like whites—took it as their very own. Right along with Father's Day, they made much ado about whatever. The times had gone a-changing.

But in the long memory I have cultivated over my lifetime, the "Juneteenth" of my pre-adolescent years will always linger. For it meant much more than Negro Freedom Day; it was Negro *History* Day. Even in our youth, we were not only learning our roots, we were also planting seeds: in our own inherited land, and in our own time. That was all we had, then.

Looking back on those "Juneteenths," I find no shame, nothing to forgive. But I am sure not about to forget, either. None of us should ever forget what slavery was really like—not when our foreparents were part of it. Because freedom is that part of a person's life that is ever sacred. Once it is trodden on, that's where, and when, the fight for emancipation begins. And the fight continues forever—through life everlasting.

So what June 19 commemorated was the indomitable spirit in every man. As we celebrated that day, we blacks knew only this: that freedom can *always* be taken away. And that wouldn't do. No. That wouldn't do at all.

Hopeth All Things

Part I—At the end of World War II, as a draftee into Sam's Army Air Corps and part of the Occupation Forces in Italy, I found myself signing up for three more years.

Much as I loved my home city of Houston, and certain as I was that I'd inevitably return to that Mecca of Meccas, my urge for adventure was foremost. The United States Armed Forces offered me that, I believed, plus the security of room and board, and a monthly stipend to boot! I was not yet twenty-one, and heady with youth and the prestige of being a soldier of a conquering army.

By spring 1946, my all black battalion was stationed outside of Naples.

On a certain fateful Sunday, I was in Naples, alone, sightseeing. As the day unfolded, I was the typical American tourist: taking pictures of Mount Vesuvius; walking the length and breadth of Via Roma; stopping on Garibaldi Square; throwing peanuts to the pigeons; ogling the hippy, leggy Neapolitan beauties; and generally sopping up the atmosphere before attending "The Barber of Seville" at the San Carlos Opera House.

I was far removed from the tumult that was in eruption, beginning in another part of the city and spreading to our base, eighteen kilometers away. A full-blown race riot, sparked by a minor incident between black and white servicemen, exploded into a violent conflagration of emotions, unmatched even in the recent war against a foreign enemy! Some of my comrades were beaten senseless. A white soldier was killed in retaliation. Savagery on both sides escalated quickly.

All of this I did not learn until I arrived back at my barracks at day's end. By then, the fighting was over, and calm restored.

Following a cursory investigation, many blacks were general courts-martialed and sentenced to long prison terms. The rest of us, the innocent with the guilty, were herded off like cattle, in our convoy trucks, to a valley of desolation that should have been called Limbo. Here we waited. And waited. And still waited, believing we were on permanent exile, an anathema to the U. S. Army.

Northeast across the lower calf of the Italian boot, wedged deeply within the sandy core of a gargantuan bowl of tufa dust, between Foggia and Manfredonia, the military deposited us— until they got around to sending us home to the States. Here is where our unofficial Peace Corps began, back there in that early June of 1946.

Everybody in the area seemed to know our background. White soldiers had already dominated Foggia, and yes indeedy, the word had preceded us six leagues to the fore, in story and song:

> From the placid Highlands of Scotland,
> To the shores of Tripoli,
> From the peak of Mount Vesuvius,
> To the Plains of Normandie,
> From merry old, old England,
> With its vast Trafalgar Square,
> Wherever these n——rs appear,
> Don't welcome them anywhere!

Then more, pitched somewhere between bawdiness and obscenity, rendered by a chorus of white American servicemen, wherever they gathered.

We endured the insults in stoic silence, harkening back to remembered admonitions, learned at mothers' knees, on how to get along in the white world. We bided our time. Meanwhile, we had already come from one clashing holocaust with other white soldiers of that apparent ilk, and were still waiting for the ultimate penalties from it. Another confrontation was certainly the last thing we would provoke.

When any of us approached the town of Foggia, the women, children and even the raunchy-looking dogs fled at the sight of our dark faces. Their men stared daggers at us, and our "brother" GI's either turned their backs, or fell into the rhythms of that aforementioned derogatory ditty.

We weren't welcome and we knew it; but we were too proud to force ourselves into their social setup.

So we tried another tack: Manfredonia, overland a few kilometers, beside the Adriatic Sea. The white servicemen wanted nothing to do with the town because they thought it too filthy, which it was; and its people too excruciatingly poor, which was also true. Yet they, as we, were too proud to beg the "Amici" for anything.

After surveying the entire village by jeep, our white C.O. made his decision: Clean it up! (We had learned, bit by bit, day by day, that this white man was made out of some good stuff.) He was in a bind, either way—with his superiors, for obvious reasons, and with us, his charges. We were already war-weary, riot-weary, and homesick-weary—emotions not conducive to high morale or good soldiering.

We filled up our D.D.T. tanks, and moved in to "de-filthy" the area. We sprayed every person, every animal, every hut and hovel, every nook and cranny, with acres of the stuff. We attacked the plumbing systems—repaired them, laid new pipe—replacing what had been devastated by the war's bomb. We made the water potable, and hung Lister bags all over the place. The clean-up over, we were chesty with justifiable pride. After all, we were Air Corps Engineers, and had the expertise. What next?

In the kitchens of our battalion there was far more food stocked than we needed. So a plan was born for one huge, open-house "blowout." With the sanction of our C.O., we formed a committee to consider a time and place for our celebration, then negotiated with a village scribe to hand-print bills and posters announcing it to the citizens.

Weeks of intense preparation followed. The spirit of our mission enveloped us with an almost religious fervor, casting out shame and despair—though routine service assignments suffered.

I was in Special Services then and was ordered to assemble an entertainment group. I attacked my assignment with glee. We already had a standard spiritual quartet which had carried the rousing religious songs of our people into some strange parts of the world previously unexposed to it.

I gathered six musicians from three companies to form a combo. These fellows had accumulated a choice collection of secondhand instruments from shops on Naples' side streets. A talented jazz vocalist from Milwaukee, and a couple of natural born clowns for comic balance completed our bill. We were on our way.

Our mess sergeant, a man of great wit, forbearance and wisdom, not to mention culinary prowess (we dubbed him Sir Food), got his crews to rattling pots and pans; and, as expected, created a menu fit for the princely palates of any realm in the world. On a Sunday, we set up shop for our "peace and friendship" breakthrough in a grassy area at the outskirts of the village. Two mobile kitchens fairly rocked with the alchemy going on inside their ovens and cauldrons. Outside, long wooden serving tables groaned and creaked with the weight of bowls and platters and tureens, all filled to the brims. GI blankets, laid randomly, finalized the Sunday picnic motif.

At first, only a few children, old men and some emaciated mongrel dogs sidled up, undoubtedly lured by the mess sergeant's pungently pleasant cooking aromas. Soon, the trickle of guests swelled to a flood, and it seemed that the entire population of Manfredonia and for miles around, had gathered to sample our hospitality.

Immaculate, spit-and-polished black soldiers on K.P. duty, eyes beaming, smiles broad, ladled food onto GI stainless steel dinnerware, with grace and flourish, as though they were serving royalty; poured gallons of fruit punch and coffee into GI cups; urged second and even third helpings. Our guests ate and drank as though they hadn't enjoyed a good meal in months—this, we learned later, was true for many.

The entertainers moved through the crowd, regaling all with "down home" rhythms, songs, antics brought from the states. Language barriers fell, and other contrived and artificial social barriers that separate humans from their human kin; all fell, stamped into the ground by dancing feet. The day ended on a soaring high. We had established a "friendship" beachhead. Gradually, from that day onward, we entered into a normal social stratum that put our erstwhile moroseness to flight.

A pretty little brown-skinned Red Cross worker was transferred to our Manfredonia area. A "sister"! We welcomed her and gave her the same affectionate respect accorded our own blood sisters, stateside. She, along with soldier volunteers and many of the locals—men, women and even children—helped prepare a partly gutted but still habitable building for our own service club. After all, it was summertime. A couple of skylights—compliments of American bombardiers—let the sunshine and fresh air in! They removed debris, swept up the dust, and strung varicolored bunting throughout the rooms, combining the American spirit with the Italian. The work became a joyous festivity, resulting in a feeling of union we never lost.

We soldiers felt fully blessed then, living and working among good friends, with the Adriatic Sea in our backyard. We splish-splashed in ebullient blue waters like little slum kids on a first outing in the country, purified and cleansed of all past indiscretions.

After a time, even the merchants of Foggia and its city fathers solicited our trade and invited us to enjoy apertifs with them at their sidewalk cafes; some even welcomed us into their homes. But we remained cautious and wary about responding to the overtures, remembering the insult and rejection that had gone before.

In the main, Manfredonia was ours. Most of us did all our socializing there, even enlarging and rehabilitating our service club for the village citizens to use after we'd gone, as soon we must.

Summer was over. There was a finality in the season's change that signalled moving on. The Army was ready to move us, so we got ready to leave Manfredonia.

It was a teary leave-taking for all, yet not as much sad as triumphant. We had emerged from disgrace into the warmth and comradeship freely given us by these simple people. We would never forget them.

On a windy November day in 1946, we left for home.

Part II—By year's end 1946, I was stateside again. The euphoria of victory on two European fronts lingered—over Germany, of course, and my all-black battalion's personal public relations triumph in Manfredonia.

That inevitably yielded to the hard reality of segregation in the South; Tampa, Florida, to be exact, where I was stationed at an Army Air Base. Yet I was young and full of hope: for myself, for my country, and for change within the despicable system that had spawned me. The war had disrupted established lives, ways, behaviors, habits, mores, customs. Surely all that disruption would spill over and hasten the coming of real change. Full integration of the services was around the corner, we black veterans rumored among ourselves.

Meantime, I was "in" for another three years, and determined to be the best damned soldier in the United States Military; and to take every advantage of the opportunities offered.

This post-war Army, like a good parent, encouraged continuing education, and I grabbed for a bootstrap: a high school diploma. I'd dropped out at thirteen to go to work, though I'd been "favored" academically and considered "apt" (to succeed or fail—take your pick). Here was a golden chance to remedy that, via a plethora of correspondence courses.

In short order, I breezed through the Army's GED tests— General Educational Development—and received my Certificate of Completion. If and when I returned to civilian life, I figured I was ready for Howard or Fish—or Harvard, Columbia, and Stanford, for that matter.

Our base boasted an on-the-job training School of Information that provided me my first clerical MOS (Military Occupational Specialty). I became a Public Relations, non-commissioned officer. In conjunction with my public relations role, I was also a certified Special Services NCO and Information Specialist. This last I liked most of all. Now they had the real me! Within the Army's vast table of organizations, that was one hell of an august title, particularly for a black dropout. I was a qualified, self-propelled individual, willing and eager to share all that enthusiasm. When my orders came, I could hardly believe my luck. I was to be a teacher, an English teacher.

With the war over, many in my battalion were re-enlistees, out to make a career of this thing; battle-scarred black warriors, heroes from the fighting fields of Europe—Casino, the Po Valley, the Bulge, the French liberation, the Austrian and German campaigns—were willing to make any sacrifice to learn the 3 Rs, to boost IQ scores up to some standard "stay-in" Army level. A paradox. Veteraned soldiers, trained, disciplined, physically taut machines, were now told they must become academicians of some sort, certified on paper, in order to remain in this grand alliance of comrades. Forthwith. Most who wanted to stay in lacked the proper qualifications.

That the same Uncle Sam now offering to educate them had given short shrift to their intellectual development throughout their boyhoods (years of poverty, deprivation and mental starvation), was another paradox, but one for head-shaking and amazement rather than bitterness. The Army's educational institutes did not lack for students in 1947.

Many of these men were already non-coms of the first three or four grades; some had gained their beloved stripes from service tours that began and advanced upwards from the old Civilian Conservation Corps of the pre-war depression years. Some were born leaders, and others merely law-abiders. Many came from camps and fields and stations where they served stateside duties during the war. Many more, of course, came from battles "over there"—but they all had one inexorable thing in common: they were "in" and wanted to stay there. They had come too far from the desolate battlegrounds of their youth—where the enemies were bigotry, social revilement, hunger, insecurity—to turn back now. The Army offered a way out, even with its disturbingly routine ramifications.

The lure presented was a re-enlistment plan that paid huge bonuses and promised others after re-enlistment terminated. This vast, expensive, financial *quid pro quo* of the military, had begun in the early summer of 1945.

All those glittering dollars, those steady three meals a day, plus the rarest and most abiding kind of camaraderie with their fellows, gave weight to the decisions to re-enlist, out-classing passioned vows never to raise their right hands again for any more of the Army's whims, regulations, discriminations, early risings, parades, chastisements, inspections, and restrictions.

Commitments already made, any lingering doubts were banished by a last long look into the futures that might have been, had civilian life been re-embraced: a continuation of ignorance, poverty, and social insignificance. Those from the South, especially, saw an endless row of white teeth, gleaming brightly in dark faces, yassuh-ing and nawsuh-ing every day of their lives, for the maintenance of pittance-pay jobs. They saw themselves as continually tragic clowns, shuffling and stumbling from derision to scorn, while quelling the anguish inside. Then they rejected it.

In the North and West, true, the wartime need for skilled men and women of any color had resulted in partial integration in the plants and factories. Unfortunately, most of the potential re-enlistees were as yet unskilled and could not qualify for those jobs. These men too rejected civilian life.

My little Information and Education office swelled with the stampeding presence of these knowledge-hungry men. We had classes day and night, with four black instructors (including myself) running the show. Our white I&E officer—a fine fellow—was there in title only, and didn't interfere with our methods.

This was all pure fun for us. Our typewriters sang off key and on, as a phalanx of fingers huntpecked out queries to applicants' grammar schools in search of grades and curriculums. In time, the replies followed, many with personal comments that bespoke the perspicacity and powers of observation possessed by small town and country schoolteachers. It was no surprise to learn that some of our recruits for re-enlistment had shown a certain determination and stick-to-it-iveness as very young boys.

Meantime, our own program was well underway, commencing with the same basic tenets and principles those long-ago school ma'ams had sought to instill.

"In the beginning was the word." Never more true than now! My God-fearing Baptist family in Houston might frown on my sacrilege; yet I was witnessing a divine creation of a kind: the exploding enlightenment of human minds, virgin intellects embracing knowledge—and I, a witness to the drama!

They struggled, and with such passion: grown men in their twenties and thirties, stammering as they read aloud passages from the simplest primary readers; inarticulate as infants yet absurdly beautiful, grasping at the broadly variable syntaxes of English, grasping with serious intent for the meanings of these words and their purposes. Voices of the canebrake, the mills, the farms of America's rural South—soft, serene, or guttural, echoing through our classrooms.

Most of them fared better, faster in basic arithmetic—numbers and the rhythms of numbers being a part of their/our earliest childhood days and the counting of fingers, toes, and heartbeats.

They made passing grades in history and geography, studying with a soldier's dogged perseverance, a do-or-die attitude that far transcended any college student's aspiration toward a degree. They were pushing toward victory, toward a real and visible citadel!

English remained their biggest stumbling block. They dreaded coming to me for their weekly bouts, less because of my youth than my attitude. Language and words were my passions; they had no such love. They were struggling to master the practical side of English; I was trying to instill beauty. We were both learning.

I learned that they had to discover a connection between English and their own lives, so I tried to communicate that this study of words was the fountain spring from which all the other knowledge would come. They would be facing other instructors every week, with more detailed and involved subjects; therefore, the English literature I tried to make familiar to them embraced a principle that underlay all else.

I used simple readings whenever possible. I tried to share with them the dignity which could be found in the literary things that I loved. I had them read "When Malindy Sings," "Notes to a Brown Girl," "We Who Wear the Mask," and many of Paul Lawrence Dunbar's epic dialects. I watched them wade through Countee Cullen's "Color" and "Copper Sun." These were my own books, given to me by a woman I worked for as a teenager in Houston. I cherished them as creations of pure artistry from the rich, tormented experience of our own people. I also owned, and shared, "Montage of a Dream Deferred," "Not Without Laughter," and many of Langston Hughes' earlier works. Walt Whitman's *Leaves of Grass* I loved because it spoke to all mankind, of whatever creed or race.

Oscar Micheaux's *The Wind from Nowhere* and *The Case of Mrs. Wingate*—both adventurous social confrontation novels with black heroes—were not only standard fare in my classroom, but in the barracks as well. My students devoured them greedily, passing them from man to man, apparently finding a new world in reading alone.

Afterwards, books abounded everywhere. The post library was full of browsers, kibitzers, seekers after wisdom and truth. Impromptu literary discussions erupted in the mess hall (especially during breakfast chow, when minds are at their sharpest), the Recreation Hall, the PX, the Service Club, any place where soldiers had some time to themselves.

A few native New Yorkers, comfortably familiar with the world's largest library of books by, about, and for blacks—the Schoenbrun Institute—enlightened their incredulous comrades concerning that grand cornerstone of black learning and black pride. It became a Mecca for many, who were determined to see it for themselves someday.

The entire course was an accelerated one—Army's standards—and for some, too soon over. The higher brass began its

41

weeding out, and military life fell back into its former day-to-day routine. Yet even the rejects had been awakened to something new and precious that would stay with them forever.

I, too, fell back into a former routine: an interior, highly personal push for literary/journalistic exposure, and surely, I thought, inevitable success. My love of writing had begun during my years as a draftee; the obligatory letters home had flowed smoothly from my pen, arousing envy and awe in my comrades, who would sit for hours in agonizing silence, in the throes of a genuine writer's block, struggling to transfer thoughts and feelings to blank pages. I functioned as a kind of khaki-clad Cyrano, creating newsy or romantic missives for them—at first gratis, later for a small fee. Never had cigarette and beer money been earned more easily! Thus was born my writing career.

Now, wanting to practice my chosen craft for real, I persuaded the editors of the two Negro newspapers in Tampa, the *Florida Sentinel* and the *Tampa Bulletin*, to run my weekly columns about the battalion and its individual members. Gratis, again. No matter. I was in print, in an authentic commercial publication.

As a fledgling journalist, following my own innate curiosities, I roamed about in my free time, exploring the territory, always looking for new opportunities, new experiences, gaining entry into places and situations by virtue of my Army status: P.R. man for the battalion. The dual role felt comfortable.

The P.R. man was as important to the battalion's health, happiness and morale as the C.O.—more so, maybe—the catalyst from which all good and pleasant things evolved. The P.R. man was a scout and peacemaker, leading the way, unanimously selected—aye, even scapegoated—to find something new, exciting, different; some way, somehow, when old interests waned.

Webster defines public relations thus: "The art or science of developing reciprocal understanding and good will between a person, firm or institution and the public." Webster didn't know about segregation in the South, or what a monumental challenge this P.R. man had taken on! But in spite of segregation, there existed a black elite in every city, and I sought out Tampa's. Downtown or its environs, my instincts were as sharp and true as a hound dog's nose! I ferreted out cocktail gatherings, garden parties, black show productions, tours, excursions; all the nice, polite, civilized affairs that a soldier by himself couldn't get a toehold on, but which his P.R. man was required or invited to attend.

By stumbling around, I discovered a school—just starting—in downtown Tampa, run by a white woman, who rebelliously wanted to buck the southern system by teaching blacks to fly Piper Cub planes. She was kind and businesslike, a nonconforming maverick in the long tradition of her sisters. There have always been southern white women who defied their own lords and masters and ofttimes the law, to ease life for blacks doubtless identifying their own enslavement in the cloistered South with ours. For whatever reasons, our patroness was a rebel.

I made the announcement at my weekly I&E class; and forthwith, seven adventurous young bucks joined me in enrolling in the school.

Our C.O. gave us ample time off in the afternoons to attend our classes; and we headed enthusiastically for the wild, blue yonder—carrying, like a banner, the memory of the heroic Tuskegee airmen, who had to battle the U. S. Government for permission to learn to fly, before ever having a go at the enemy.

The school—short-staffed, run on the proverbial shoestring—occupied a little building in downtown Tampa. One memorable instructor, an aging avant-gardist, expounded in resonant rolling tones, with a huge cigar pleasurably clenched between two fingers, waving, stabbing the air for emphasis: meteorology, navigation, gliding, banking, turning, landing. Here was the ideal teacher, mature and experienced, standing in front of his students dispensing knowledge as though we were all simply in the throes of a good conversation.

I could understand the book and classroom lessons pretty well, but once I was airborne with the instructor, I was more interested in the infinite than the finite: in cloud formations, in vivid Van Gogh-ish patterns of the land below, in compelling beckonings of horizons beyond.

The Muses were with me then, set by my side in an extra cockpit. The drone of our single engine was like the overture to *Finlandia*, Siegfried's *March on the Rhine*, the climax of *Tristan and*

Isolde. Everything in the world and of the world encompassed me fully except a nagging motivation to fly this airplane. Flying was definitely not my thing. Disinclined mechanically anyway, I was simply along for the ride.

I bowed out gracefully after three weeks, having foolishly spent good GI school money on something that didn't even interest me, other than for ego satisfaction; and of course, for sparking interest in my buddies. Some of our original eight completed the course without me, really learned to fly. Others enrolled thereafter.

It was a first for blacks in that segregated part of the U.S. Morale had been low for some time, since the end of the Army's whirlwind academic program for re-enlistees. That battalion needed a good joke to unwind tense and beaten spirits. We first eight were their prime comedians; and me? Hell, I was top banana!

Being an integral part of that grand union of black service-men provided me with a bank of solid gold memories to draw from for a lifetime—memories as sharp-edged and immaculate as their long ago realities: all the seas crossed; the distant shores seen and loved; the harbors, the great cities, the mountain fast-nesses; the inland sunlit hills and medieval villages. Dover's White Cliffs, Newcastle-on-Tyne, the beaches at Normandie, Amsterdam, Vienna, the Black Forest, Innsbruck, Linz, the Isle of Capri, Casserta, the Leaning Tower of Pisa—and a vast throng of lovely people.

Then home to the United States of America, and its memo-ries no less vivid. My first entry into Boston and the smell of Freedom in the September air. A tangy mingling of autumn, the sea, and my own recollections of schoolboy readings. Smaller, more intimate memories, reaching ever backward. My father's rarely bestowed embrace, moments before I boarded the railway car in Houston to carry me (eighteen and just drafted) to camp. His quickly blinked-back tear glitter.

The list is endless, the thoughts are ever recurring, making necessary the craft of writing, the lifelong task of gleaning from the memories these stories which will speak to others. I spend my

life watching, listening, striving to understand each day's experiences; ever hoping for more wisdom, more fluency, in my quest
to translate my people's triumphs and travails into literature! For
when the world will want to understand.

A yardstick I've always carried with me since the days of my
first communion is the thirteenth chapter of First Corinthians: "
. . . beareth all things, hopeth all things, believeth all things,
endureth all things . . . love never faileth. . . ." That must surely be
true somewhere out there in the Universe.

In Search of Country

In the early spring of 1948 I decided to make a vagabond tour of the United States.

I had already served five years in the Army Air Corps during World War II. Back then I had hopscotched from one post, camp or station to another via whatever Army plane was available. I was afraid of flying, but that mattered not one whit to Uncle Sam: he said go and I went. Traveling was not that new to me, anyway; our parents often scattered us Jackson kids—of which we were three—to not too distant relatives in summer after school was out.

Back home in Houston after my honorable discharge, I was free, footloose and utterably *miserable*. I wanted something better, but didn't have the foggiest notion as to what. One thing was for sure: it wasn't to be found in the big "H."

I needed *goals*, some *distant* ones to wipe away my confused state; but I lacked the know-what. I needed something to replace the callousness that the segregated Army had engendered in me, not to mention southern mores that had dimmed my black being for—God knows—so many years. I didn't have the patience— and certainly not the opportunity—to search for it on my home grounds. Well as I loved it, Houston wasn't ready for my soul-searching. Only one thing to do, then: hit the road. So, with money from a pawned Benrus watch and a day's pay from a cleaned-up construction site, I left the Houston scene.

By bus, though, always by bus. No riding "rattlers" for me: the fear of being maimed—like so many of the racial kinsmen I had met in childhood-adolescence—too grim in my mind; to say nothing of severe head whippings—and behind kickings—by malicious white brakemen. I went first to Dallas—to get the feel of traveling—then Wichita Falls, where I had spent eight weeks in Air Corps Basic Training. On to Indianapolis, Indiana—simply because I liked the sound of the name. An altercation with a small group of black-hating white bigots during some job-hunting soon put that fantasy to flight. I savored a little taste of St. Louis, Missouri, luckily finding a fine brownskin that with her charms, almost drew an ending to my wanderlust. Her name was 'Delia and it was yet ringing in my ears when I reached the Big Apple of New York City. While there I tried the Harlem, Brooklyn, and Fulton areas. I couldn't cut it. Not my kind of city at all: too damn big, too friendless, just an asphalted, concreted jungle where making any kind of friend was damn near impossible for a hick from the "sticks" like me. Not like Houston: a "hello, stranger" at 6:00 A.M., a "welcome, friend" by 6:00 P.M. type of town. New York, so crowded with folks, seemed to breed a lot of loneliness. And mine was no exception.

Every time my bus hit a new town, the first thing I did was get a job. Most and *preferably* in a cafe or restaurant: bus boy, dishwasher, janitor, it didn't matter. My stomach did. (Back in those days my appetites doted heavily on food. That's changed considerably now. Many—ever so many—missed-meal-cramps have eternally routed those "three squares a day" rituals to flight.) Learning about people was also a main criteria then. I've never knocked colleges and universities, but nothing—nothing—ever taught me more about life than people themselves, especially those from the common clay like me. That had been my growing-up way in Houston: as a youth reading to the blind and bedridden, and to the grossly illiterate blacks who compounded our ghetto. Even though I could have enrolled in a college or university under the Educational GI Bill—GED graduate, USAFI Correspondence Courses fueled and blessed—I didn't have it in me to do so.

So I drifted from one city to another, fascinated by their names and distance and, after departing, realizing that there was really no Utopia for a black man anywhere in the United States, North or South. And if there was one, it was more likely to be found in the person himself.

I stayed in Boston, Massachusetts, for a spell, which is where I was when the papers heralded the news that the North Koreans had crossed the 38th Parallel. Still eligible for re-induction, I at first shuddered at the thought of going back in. Especially to some outlandish place called "Korea," whose politics were beyond me anyway. I had paid my dues. Now I wanted something for me in return. I didn't know what, but I knew it wasn't that!

I was in Italy on the ass-end of World War II and I didn't want anymore of it. Memories of the 1946 race riot there and its aftermath were still with me. There had been little justice for our black men involved in that upheaval, holocaust and subsequent courts-martial. So many of our black "boys" had received long prison sentences.

But then I thought of my piddling job at Boston's General Hospital, about my restlessness, about grubbing out a day-to-day existence and hustling jobs and finding places to sleep. I quit my job and re-enlisted; it was damn near a relief to be back in "Sam's" care.

The day of departure dawned thirty days later at the Worcester enlistment station. I met—nay, was given—five peach-fuzzed, milk-faced white youths by the Recruiting Sergeant. I was to become their boss afficionado, their guardian all the way from Worcester, Massachusetts to Bremerhaven, Germany. And even beyond to their post, camp or station. Just great. The last thing in the world I wanted—or needed—was to be responsible for somebody else, and some brats to boot! (Leadership? My rear end! Them kind of cats are born, not picked in an instant like me. And white boys too? Oh man!)

But there I was—and there they were. They called me "Sarge" and I was barely a Pfc. Their parents had come to see us off to Fort Dix, New Jersey. Cousins by the dozens, it seemed; friends, gushing, over-acting, inanely emotional female sweethearts—good grief!—grandfathers, grandmothers—some with canes. Such slobberings you never did see. And the fathers—the biggest asses of them all. Bribing me with fives and tens, ramming those beautiful green bills into my pockets with the admonitions. "Look after my boy, Sarge—he's all I got," and so on and so on and so on. Whew! Those baby-faced warriors—(warriors? Hell, we were going the other way, thank God!)—had fifty and one-hundred dollar bills stitched in their drawers! Fat cats in every sense of the word. They had come from places smaller than Worcester and were now "off to see the world," through the chaperoneship of—Guess Who's Taking Whom To Dinner?

I didn't even know my own feelings in this matter then. I was almost as bedazzled as they were. But I was committed to the task by UNCLE SAMUEL; I was signed up for three years—just like they were. All of us were on our way, and that was that. I couldn't even get away from the boys to enjoy a few stiff shots of some strong bourbon. No sir. This was one time I had a responsibility whether I liked it or not. And I damn sure didn't like it, in spite of all the money in my pocket.

We started doing our soldierly things at Fort Dix. (They were in a hurry to process us and get us the hell out of there, which was really jake with me.) Unfortunately, we went everywhere together, on duty and off: mess hall, service club, movie house, Army lectures, indoctrinations, physical education field. I played gin rummy with them, a game I despise, until it poured out of my ears. I tried to teach them whist—black folks style: "cut-throating"—but they invariably got back to gin rummy. They drank malted milks and milk shakes by the boxcar load, ate candy, cookies and cheeseburgers you wouldn't believe! Neither one could drink more than two bottles of Dix's bland three-point-two beer without getting sick. What I'd heard as a boy, that white kids got a charge out of vomiting at night and then bragging about it the next day, seemed to be true. Where I came from, that was a quick way to the pokey and a fixed label as untrustworthy. My "boys," however, apparently thought their behavior was "manly."

49

We could have gone downtown on pass and we did—once. We were stared at like freaks. Full integration in the Armed Forces had not yet been achieved in 1950. Our enforced comradely "togetherness" made me feel as unwelcome as a fly in a pot of rice. But they lapped up their experiences, doing what white people normally do, without hesitation or ponderous thought of acceptance or rejection.

Yet they revered me as 'Ol Sarge—a nearly twenty-five years-old Ol' Sarge. And therefore a man of the world. The hell I was. If they only knew how much of life I had yet to learn! And how I longed to mingle with some black brothers, to gawk at some cute and gloriously-behinded black sisters, and indulge in some good ol' black bullshit one more time before I left the good ol' U.S. of A. Just once more, to get a little bourbon drunk and rap like an idiot about beautifully mundane things! God, that was living! And I missed it with these young (terribly so!) white charges.

Thank God we weren't at Dix any longer than necessary. At last we were on our way. My white charges tickled me at one point when we were on our way to the Staten Island Ferry. We had come out of Grand Central Station, going through Harlem for our transit. All those black faces like Wham! hit them at once and, obviously—from the boys' fear-stricken faces, they must have remembered all the disparaging stories their folks told them in their Yankee boondocks about blacks who suddenly got mad and fought back. Scared the living snot out of them. They stayed so close to me there was barely room for people approaching us to pass: what with our bulky duffel and "AWOL" bags lumbering down New York's busy sidewalks. I couldn't help but gloat a bit, remembering how many times I had been pushed off a Houston sidewalk so a white man could pass, when I was a pre-teener growing up. Or, how futile I felt when I couldn't, on a physical par, in justice, fight back without losing some part of my anatomy— or even my life.

At last we were on the ship. Well underway now, passing the Statue of Liberty, I remembered Emma Lazarus' poem, "The New Colossus," inscribed on the pedestal: "Give me your tired, your poor, Your huddled masses yearning to breathe free . . ." Saying it quietly to myself; my "boys" listening to me in awe and one saying: "Gollee! You know that? We had that in school!" And me thinking about Freedom, the quintessence of it, and of what it must have meant to Emma Lazarus who, like Phyllis Wheatly, was knocked down by an untreated virus that would not let her live out her day. Now here I was, fleeing, fleeing the land where true Freedom was supposed to exist, but was in reality so limited. Now, paradoxically, I was leading five white examples of the American heritage to a place they would defend the soil of another country that was neither theirs nor mine. The first three days of seasickness finally overcome, all of us were riding the crest of our new adventure. Five young white boys from the New England "sticks," barely seventeen-years-old apiece, hardly ever further than Worcester in their lifetimes—clinging to me like I was their mother hen and Father Goose combined. Yet still black: nothing was going to change that. The sum total of what I was they still considered bullshit.

Our sailing days were sweet. No details to attend to. No K.P. or guard duty. One would think these guys were all Senators' sons, and me their traveling major-domo. We weren't called on to do anything. This was really some new Army. I wondered and probed and searched and finally decided to hell with it. Enjoy it for what it's worth. I knew I'd get back to the bone of my blackness sooner or later. The system always had a way of sidetracking things for awhile by issuing a little false glitter. Believe me, I'd get back into my "place" before too long. I'd bet a fat man on it. Blacks had said it for ages: "What goes around, comes around." They were always right. I'm just glad I've had the sense to remember the axiom. It's kept me from going off the deep end ignorantly.

Soon we were walking down the gangplank at Bremerhaven, Germany, me and my charges. Complete with an Army band playing some of the hits of the day. A huge banner above our heads proclaimed blatantly: "YOU'VE HAD IT!" It was to speak for us both ways: entering and departing. How very damn clever!

I checked our train and departure times to a military installation some one-hundred-fifty kilometres distant. We lolled around the German Bahnhof eating those delicious hard salami sandwiches and drinking lukewarm *limonade*. My "boys" were full of awe at the quaint countryside just beyond the station. We scrambled through our guide books after each German sentence we heard, and never understood a damn thing.

The day was summer-beautiful and bright, the temperature moderate, the cobwebs clearing from my head, hopes surging, adrenalin bubbling in my loins because I was at the beginning of Anywhere. "Try adventure" my being seemed to say. Good enough. Ironically, by this time, I was thoroughly enjoying my company. They were so young, so totally inexperienced, so damned ignorant; and I was so damned "hipped" it was pitiful. I couldn't blame them for their apprehensive attitudes of the raunchy and funky ghettos they probably (rightly) assumed I had come from. My charges had their "whiteness" going for them. Who knows what I—Ol' Sarge—could do about the races if my cards were played right? At this moment, aye, at this juncture, even, they were mine to do something with. The prospect suddenly had merit. I could teach. Maybe I was even heading for an integrated outfit. If these five whites of mine were an indication of the changing times, I could reshuffle my thinking, put some old angers aside, find some other positive thoughts, and, hell, just get down to it. Why not? A new land, another country, damn near another identity. Heck, yes. Why not?

Our train came and we went. On arrival a white Pfc helped us load our gear from the depot on a six-by-six truck. I rode up front with him. He had been informed of our coming and let me know, during that eight-kilometre ride, that the army's policy of "separateness" was still in effect. My brief elation at the thought of an integrated life in a "new" Army went flying out the truck window. And I was back to a black soberness real quick.

I handed the white Sergeant-Major in the Orderly Room my "boys'" manilla Orders Jackets. (They had waited outside.) The Sergeant-Major thanked me with an authoritative unctuousness that would have done his race proud. Outside his door, I merely gave my "boys" what seemed to all eyes like a perfunctory wave. Inside me, though, was an anger and a bitterness that had no resolve at all, not ever.

Wordlessly, I walked out to the street. My five charges—to a MAN—sprang up to an almost attention. And followed me.

Another white soldier, a Corporal, checked to be sure my bag was still in back of the truck, then raced around the front of the cab to sit with the driver. My "boys" still followed, wonderingly. I climbed aboard the back of the truck. It started, smoke coughed from the exhaust pipe, and the truck eased out into the street. One or two of my "men" began confusedly perfunctory waves. Then all of them, looking more curious, slowly began to follow in the truck's wake. More black smoke from the truck's rear reached me where I stood, holding the overhead struts, looking back at them. Their waves became more frantic, as if something wasn't yet clear to them, and they all wanted to ask what it was.

The truck moved on. The white men kept waving, more profusely now, and I waved too, wanting to shout something— even some inane parting comment. The truck turned a corner, the driver hitting his higher, faster gear. The waving arms, mine and theirs, becoming more and more magnanimous. I was leaving something behind, something I didn't know much about—or maybe I did know, but I didn't dare let myself think it, or realize it, as part of my being.

The driver reached his last gear. He was speeding me back to the station where the train would take me to *my* destination, to *my* place. Even as I realized what was going down in my initiation to another country, I knew I had added an inner strength: baffling, fine, noble, a part of Americana that gave my life—even as a life-searching black—immediate value. What I did with it from this day on would surely revert back to this day: this day in particular.

While I was absorbing this new idea, my charges were in the streets, running far behind the truck, waving like crazy. I saw them running, running like idiots and waving, while the truck went faster and faster, and there was nothing at all between me and those waving white arms but the natural-designed distance between earth and space and sky.

Wheel in the Midst
of a Wheel

Ezekiel saw the wheel,
Way up, in the middle of the air
Ezekiel saw the wheel . . .
Way in the middle of the air. . . .
—Old black spiritual

The route the tornado took seemed of special significance. It entered adversely from the North, sweeping tall corn stalks flat. It then conjured bare sections of wasteland in a solo choreographed dance that unleashed cone-shaped dust whirlpools, with changes so sudden and explicit it almost dared a darkening sky to interfere. Frame shacks, mundane (yet treasured) objects within its fore, collapsed and splintered into hundreds of over-sized toothpicks. They flew helter-skelter in ways resembling a fusillade of bow-gunned arrows. Were its force and reach less than destructive, it could have been any child's captivating Saturday afternoon cinema cartoon.

Meteorology was in its infancy. The small western city's townspeople were grossly unaware of the black funnel's approach like an undiapered infant, especially in the so-called boondocks, gleefully playing with nature's own dirt and dust, totally uninhibited. Warnings of unnatural impending elements invading this partly impoverished township were reckoned by individual human discomforts: itching or spasmodic paining (from once broken limbs), arthritic swellings of gnarled fingers; shoulder discomforts; a generally vacant feeling in the back of the head. This especially among elders—with hot blood vessels shooting up unaccountably in various parts of the body. The right hand itched and burned concurrently: always a *sign* of incoming "bad news."

The first building to fall was the bank. It crumpled like a busted, waterfilled paper bag. Vocal alarms now became cries, only partly getting panic-issued messages to panic-ridden people. This bulwark of wealth fell into ruins, its sides and facade bursting, scattering money in four angular directions. Where was the accountant who could make a tally of windblown ledgers?

Other storefronts along the funnel's wake shook, swayed, groaned, trembled, buckled and slithered themselves down to the ground, its absolute nudity now covered with debris of crinkled architecture. The violent force of the tornado's magnitude moved on.

Once there had been a lynching.

The wind, too, lynched in its sweep. Like a great, spiraling broom swishing ever back and forth, ever forward, its powerful black straws rooting out concrete-anchored stanchions right along with fragile wood studs. Steel rods, naked, begged heaven for a clothing mercy.

The wind swept past a county seat of registry, a school of learning, a court of justice. It invaded a den of commerce, a lair of incumbent white idlers. The giant broom scattered debris; millinery and men's suits flew like custom fashion showings in a charlatan's contrived seance across stark streets. Coveted china cups, saucers, pewter bowls and wash basins danced rondelets in the air, like stringless puppets without their masters.

The number of dead, dying and injured mounted. Panicked

small children wandered the streets, faces bleeding from the blows of whimsically flying particles. Old men, young men, women of any age, luckless to be caught in open terrain, were swept away like Peter Pans. Some rose and were swept down again; some clawed the ground with fingernails cut to the quick, not wanting to be captured in that ride again. The broom confirmed their fears: it appeared to backtrack for "missed" objects, as if wanting to do no less than a perfect job.

Numerous live electric wires lashed about. Snapped free from their tall, telephone pole moorings, they danced snake-crazily, coiled themselves about any object—animate or inanimate—that strayed into its path, its sparkles erratically splaying. It decreed death to all that ventured near.

The tree died.
The tree.
The branches.
The rope marks showed.

The footpaths were remembered. Their impressions stood up starkly amidst the gleam of day. The tree bent and bent and bent and finally it broke. It rolled thunderously into the gutter and stayed there; long branches of its citizen-proud horticultural genus withered and snapped off one by one; a far cry from the township's "grand ol' tree" that had shaded lemonade drinkers of a would-be-superior race.

Rains whipped spray in the broom's wake. Each of the large, hail-like drops seemed a full cup. However panic-stricken at the funnel's onslaught, the sufferers shared a memory now goading them to reflect: the route of the funnel was the same one the lynchers had taken!

Abruptly the winds changed. Atop the domed pedestal of the courthouse, the blindfolded alabaster woman fainted. She toppled over backwards, the scales still in her hands, her feet severed neatly from their ivory base. Her once lovely Grecian body floated in tiny particles, swept along by a maddening water's flow. The steel thongs that once girdled her massive white thighs stood obscenely upright above the domed court-house, vacant of their abused and left-for-shame virgin.

The Negro youth's body had jerked convulsively as the hanging rope tightened. His flailing legs and arms danced a macabre rondo in the baseless air. A few in the crowd argued with nausea, lost the battle, vomited in spite of themselves, upon themselves and others in their once crowded, gleeful midst; yet even these were not wholly willing to avert their eyes from the grim scene of race-proclaimed "justice" before them."

When it was over and done with, they filed silently away: to their long homes and their short homes; to their rich homes and their poor homes; to their uncertained and repressing frightened boasts over kindling kitchen stove fires; to their cabbage cooking boils and armadillo stews; to their gin tonics and Jim Beam bourbons and paté de foie gras servings from trembling black hands. Into those hands a largesse of "Li'l Abner" pork chops would be regally placed for later eating in on-the-lot shanties with black garden-grown potatoes and turnips. This "overly generous" white gesture of wayward guilt feelings fused with the times' unbreakable axiom of "keeping them in their place." Serving as a token toward treating their black servants "fairly," the lie fooled no one. It merely served as a mollifying alternative to sudden, random beatings— both designed to keep descendents of freed slaves in tow.

All would be well again at hearth and home. The rulers could walk home to brief, front spring porches (perfect for "courting"), or to wide verandahs. Or they could stand, coupled, under ivy-strewn, lattice-laid porte-cochere's. The town would be home, still, to the conspicuously absent servile black "neighbors," today too frightened (or, would they be vengeful?) to speak out about this hideous deed. They would still walk streets which had held rope-dragged, live bodies from end to end of its growing, amidst whoops and howls.

Was this justice?

Wasn't there a hidden, untold truth somewhere? Wasn't one of their fair, flaxen-haired white goddesses caught in the sexual act in a woodshed with a black youth of her own age, without coercion and blown out of proportion by blatant cries of black rape? And didn't she keep a peculiar silence as he was dragged away beseeching her to speak? Didn't that one-eyed, blindfolded bitch die in the storm?

Where reasoning was absent, strife prevailed. The white goddesses' honor prevailed. Another fly whisk at imagined dust, another gin tonic, another Jim Beam double shot (without ice). Justice was served. The race kept pure.

Then as suddenly as it had begun, it ended. The dark funnel disappeared. The sky lightened. The blue emerged. The winds following the funnel abated, but flood waters set in. Streets, many of them without macadam asphalt smoothness, became soaring rivers. Alleys, in their usual overflow of uncanned garbage, spewed their disseminate litter along impromptu waterways.

The sun, however, slipped (earlier than usual, some thought) below the horizon. An aurora of many colors, producing brilliant lights, gleamed its many-colored rainbow for the longest time— long enough for all to see then, just as suddenly, vanished.

Which was the sign, the storm or the rainbow?

Was the funnel a sign of wrath and vengeance for an evil deed done by a seemingly friendly township in the twenty-five-year-old past?

The wise ones were silent. They had watched the movements and faces of the known guilty going their ways in the aftermath of that holocaust day. One of the watchers began to quote the prophet Ezekiel, who saw a wheel in the midst of a wheel, way up, in the middle of the air, raining down vengeance.

It was then that the wise one saw the guilty weep. He knew the reasons for their weeping, but he "shuffled" on, keeping his thoughts to himself, believing the wheel would always turn.

Once I Crossed the Rubicon

The three years I spent as a soldier in Austria—from July 1950 to August 1953—were pure storybook enchantment. It was the most idyllic place in the world for a veteran soldier who wanted to get away from America and away from war—both civilian and military.

But the Army still held a few surprises. I was sure, when I re-enlisted, that the old segregated Army was dead. I found out how wrong I was when I was once again assigned to an all Negro company. The sting of that was lessened when I found out I was to serve as an Information Officer. To me, this was duck soup.

The Information Refresher School they sent me to—outside Frankfort, Germany, a city called Buëdingen—was rich in metaphors and how-to-do-its. All of it was a fledgling writer's dream. Our teachers were the most: half were Americans—both soldier and civilian—half were Germans. Not a black in the bunch! All had august degrees in journalism, sociology, psychiatry, political and military science, history, or public relations. Their props were perfect: maps, color slides, films, all sorts of visual aids. The teachers themselves were enthusiastic, voluble, highly informative.

For eight one-hour classes per day it was go, go, go. It was no place for dunderheads. Those of us who remained *learned*. Learned to quickly digest public information; to disseminate it and project it to any size class from ten to twelve hundred. I made it somehow, graduating one month after starting, with a class considerably smaller than I'd started with.

When I returned to my Company and started teaching, we really had some lively discussion periods. And, alas, some poor ones. There were times when I couldn't reach my charges at all, even with all the material at my command. Too much of what I was expected to teach was considered irrelevant by my students. They preferred watching the Army Signal Corps films, "The Negro Soldier" and "The Negro Sailor."

My articles—feature stories and the like—about individuals in my Company served me in good stead, as they were printed in our weekly Command newspaper, *The Argus*. Another part of my duties as Information Instructor was sending my students to various Army schools when the quarterly quotas opened. Meanwhile, through constantly drilling them in remedial reading skills, I was able to help them boost their IQs. Together with my I&E sergeant we gave them tests, and helped get diplomas from their different schools back home.

We were a segregated from the rest of the Army, sure. But we knew there was a new world a'comin'. And we were fighting against the odds. Then, in the Spring of 1951, our proud Company was integrated. I was in limbo as to how I felt about that hard-won battle, especially since, in this case, down came my little house of cards.

Black men from my Company were grouped into eights, tens and twelves and inculcated into heretofore all-white companies in the Transportation Battalion proper. I went with seven more Negroes—("Black" was not a term we used then—we didn't like it!) to an all-white Headquarters and Service Company. The leitmotif of our movement into this, the "brainy" Company—this sprinkling of pepper into the salt shaker—was to get the "best of the blacks" first: those with school diplomas, the best conduct records, and so on. But the work they gave us never came close to matching my Information Officer job; we were to be *Railway Transportation Clerks*!

A Railway Transportation School was hastily set up in a seldom used storage room, especially for our benefit. We eight were taught the basic rudiments of shipping men, baggage and freight, as well as making out monolithic Way Bills, written in English, German and French.

Two white officers patiently—and I daresay, tolerantly, because this was damned sure unbelievable Greek to us—taught us all these things as well as ticket selling and correspondence protocol. For one week we crammed stuff into our craniums that should have taken a month, at least. Every man passed. Then we were sent to railway stations throughout Austria, wherever American soldiers were stationed and military trains ran. We were given new military occupational specialty numbers—MOS— and new identities. Of sorts. I was mourning over the loss of my previous position as Information Specialist, so I decided the best thing for me was to go as far as possible. I requested *distance*. Turned out not to be the best idea.

The six months I spent as a baggage clerk in Munich's *hauptbahnhof*—main train station—in a section reserved for the United States Forces, were the most boring and humdrum of any job I have ever held. There were only two military trains running—morning and night. This was the famous Mozart, originating in Vienna.

During their tenure, American troops, Department of the Army civilians and the like entered and departed Austria through Munich. Ergo, the Munich station. The train's entire idea was as romantic, really—and intriguing, too—as the country it rolled through. Traveling eastward across the center of Europe on its run to Vienna—"Veen"—crossing the iron curtained bridge at Linz (a sort of "abandon all hope, ye who enter here"), it ran forebodingly near iron curtain countries like Czechoslovakia and Hungary, zipping and wailing through more than two hundred miles of Russian zone. No one, but *no one*, could go through that zone without having that famous—or infamous—Grey Pass. Returning westward to Munich the train went through pleasant and peasanted communities in Austria, up towards Lower Bavaria, entering and halting at that peacefully placid no man's check-point land of Freilassing, the border checkpoint that separates Austria from Germany. I traveled the entire length of it more than once and each time the mystery and intrigue of the journey fascinated me as no other European journey did. Back in those days one simply hadn't lived if one had not ridden the Mozart to "Veen" to see the Changing of the Guard. The pomp, spectacle and pageantry of that military show was worth the ofttimes tedious ride back, with the perpetual harassment by certain Russian officials at various checkpoints along the way.

I missed my old job, and yet I was impressed with this idea of clerical advancement. If only I could work up to a job where I could do some good! My tasks here were so menial it hurt. There were three white soldiers over me, one corporal, two pfc's. Four with the lieutenant. Two were from the Midwest, one from the East (the lieutenant), one from the South. I never once doubted that there were latent prejudices within our group. A black man knows these things inherently, is ever embroiled in them. If any of them knew I had been an Information Instructor they never mentioned it.

Actually, work-wise, there was not much to do except check the baggage of soldiers entering and deporting twice a day for the two train trips; between those times, just be available. According to the unwritten soldier's code, "I had it knocked!" Yet here I was, squawking. I couldn't help it though; I hated being idle. In my bones, I felt like a glorified Red Cap—especially with the red arm bands we wore—carrying bags for people of both colors. I knew, too, that the soldiers traveling through envied us, seeing us doing practically nothing, living in Munich's downtown hotel—the Columbia—and wearing Class A uniforms each day rather than work fatigues, meeting civilians, especially all those fantastic "foxes"—of a universal blend—that they themselves would hardly be at liberty to meet. Our comrades' comments were many and almost entirely unanimous: "Bird Nest on the ground!" "Riding a gravy train/using biscuits for wheels./Every time the train stops/He just hops off and sops!" It bugged me, but there I was and had to stay until something else happened.

So there I remained. The gregariousness of Munich over-whelmed me. It was like a little New York. I have always felt like some strange non-entity in big cities anyway; like a hick from the sticks, which, in essence I really was. But I needed some outer escape, some new, transitive learnings to fill this empty void. I decided to make the best of this lingering frustration. So I went forth.

Munich had abundant interests. There was Dachau, the infamous concentration camp—just a few miles out from town. There were old castles, forts, moats, to explore. I learned how to bargain with black marketeers for cigarettes and Nescafe, like a housewife arguing with a butcher over a questionable piece of meat. I met the Hall Johnson Choir—again—and we rehashed old memories of Camp Ellington Field back there in 1944. At one of the most popular German music halls—the Deustches Museum—I saw an adult musical group of that age known as the JATP: Jazz At the Philharmonic, conducted by Norman Granz. All my jazz idols were there: Ella Fitzgerald, "Flip" Phillips, Lester "Prez" Young, Hank Jones—everybody. Later on I saw Les Brown. I saw my first American film in a foreign country—*Samson and Delilah*—and had tons of difficulty understanding language dubbings. I walked through Munich's parks and forests, rode her shimmer-ing, sausage-tailed streetcars—*die strassenbohn*—and ate beef-steak I never knew existed before. Not even in Texas, my home state, which, as everyone knows, is "heifer heaven." I made friends with people of many races, from many worlds. Watched sculptors doing their massive works out in the open. My note-books filled to overflowing. I read more library books from the American Way Service Club than I had in months. I even person-ally knew a woman spy. That is, I knew it after she was caught—by our roving Counter Intelligence Corps agents, dressed in G.I. garb and acting the part—and I saw her picture printed in the *Stars & Stripes*. She was a fox, too!

Suddenly the line ended. Troops and other Department of Army personnel entering into Austria were to come and go through Leghorn—Livorno—Italy, via Innsbruck and the Brenner Pass. The Munich station folded. We packed our bags, our four-hundred-day cuckoo clocks, took our last Mozart ride from

Munich back to our Austrian base area of Linz-Salzburg. In a short course of time—from sugar to shit—I went from one apathetically dismal job assignment in our Transportation Motor Pool to an even worse one. Ever hoping that of all our far-flung railway locations I would ultimately get the kind of assignment that would do me and Uncle Sam the most good. It did not look forthcoming. So I sulked, brooded. Gave up completely. Finally, I did what I thought any other self-respecting, one-hundred percent, red-blooded American boy would do: I said to hell with it all and went AWOLoose!

I went to a place in Austria called Ebensee because an Austrian fraulein of whom I was fond often talked to me about it. To get there I rode a hinterland bus—located from a country road about a mile or so from our camp—to a town called Lambach. Then another country-type bus to Gmunden. From there by an excursion ship down a placid river—nameless, because I've forgotten—to the base of the city itself. Mountains flank either side of this river-hillside town. The time was summer and the brilliant blue skies with floating white clouds intensified the aura of wide-eyed tourists vacationing in a strange land. A cable car running upwards at a forty-five degree angle carries about twenty-five passengers to the mountain summit. Another one runs downward. Width-wise, they pass one another, mid-way, at a distance of about thirty feet. At that height, passengers stare at one another across the gap, with no distractions in between except a distant, hazy horizon. At that time I didn't believe there was another sight in all of God's world as fine as that brief moment when the cable cars passed, and people looked at one another with their sheepish grins, as though all had defied nature's law of gravity. The only noise was the softly monotonous purring of the cable car's motors and an occasional sea gull flapping its wings in the air above our heads. Great God Almighty! I thought. How close could a mere mortal come to infinity!

The top of this summit was surprisingly like an ordinary little country village, although quaint, like much of Austria with its streets, shops, stores, and byways, and its alleys called *gasses.*

The first three days there I was drunk as a Cooty Brown and couldn't care less. I had rented a nice bungalow where I rewrote some of my story ideas. The fourth, fifth, sixth and seventh days I drank myself sober, picked socialistic and philosophical arguments with *gasthaus* proprietors, visited American schoolteachers—male and female—and an Austrian lay priest. My thinking German was nil. My oral German was street and gutter talk—bedroom terrible—with a few choice expletives thrown in to get my stupid points across. In my mental stupor, I was a prime jackass; the original, white, Ugly American had nothing on me. And I performed magnificently! While I was inebriated I could wail without self-consciousness. But, of all the fine wines in the world—and they had them, including Five Star Cognac and Napoleon Brandy—nothing could give me the kick I needed to sustain my fading bravado. Conscientiousness crept back into my being. Faces and figures of my parents and kin kept flitting across my mind's eye. The figure of my sister especially, ever remembering me in her prayers, returned to sober me. My family didn't have to be here on this mountain top for me to remember how I grew up. The Forces of Right were beginning to win their battles.

So back I came. However resignedly. Back down from this precipice of folly. The ride down the cable car. The meeting of one going up. The sheepish looks of passengers across the way. That warm, personal, powerful feeling of infinity now checked because I was returning to moral retribution, punishment, and a more probable nothingness. I couldn't retreat anymore. I had to face reality.

The Army stockade was miserable. Naturally. The first day I was there—after my sentence—a sergeant, highly reminiscent of "Fatso" in James Jones' *From Here to Eternity*, made me clean out a cesspool. It was the filthiest job I had ever done, and I had had some pips! He stood over me, gloating, as I cleaned out the scum, unclogging the drain with my bare hands. My fatigues were soggy and filthy with muck and stank to high heaven by the time I finally crawled out. Up to this time, it was a known fact to everyone but me that this white man was "hell on AWOL's, hard on Jews, and pur-dee death on niggers." But I thought of Countee Cullen and Richard Wright and Chester Himes and every black writer I had ever read, as well as the Johnson brothers' "Negro National Anthem," and I cleaned out that scum with a morbid passion. (I'll fix him, I thought. I'll satirize his white ass in a short story. He won't even recognize his ownself. The prick!)

But of all the despicable things I did as punishment for my wrongdoing nothing—absolutely *nothing*—made me feel as low as I did at Retreat. This is held at five o'clock P.M. every day of a soldier's life. The flag comes down. Either a bugler blows this immortal curtain call through a megaphone near the flag pole, or a high-volumed phonograph recording is played, so that it can be heard over the whole area. This somber music alerts everyone on the post grounds to stop what they're doing, face the music, and salute until the last note is played. But in the stockade, with our endless courtyard lineups or formations, surrounded by four ever-present manned gun turrets in either direction, we would first be called to attention and then, instead of facing the music, we were ordered to turn our backs to it, snatch off our fatigue caps, and stand in frozen immobility until the last note was played. (Shades of Franz Kafka!) This order grabbed me. Its message was that we weren't fit to embrace the flag. Sure, I engaged in rhetoric about its treatment of Afro-Americans, but America was still the only country I knew. And I didn't like being deprived of what blacks had gained in building it, fighting for it, dying for it, and caring for it, not even for three minutes. It was a blow I never did get used to.

Fortunately, I didn't have to stay long in that place. When my case was reviewed it was deemed that my sentence did not match my "crime," and I was released and sent back to my Company.

News of my incarceration had spread far and wide among white members of my unit. Many were young recruits just in from the states who had never seen a real "eight ball" before. I didn't want that "eight ball" bit. I had more to do with my life than tote that stereotype around. When I was a boy growing up in Texas, those words were used referring to all Negroes, and I didn't like it then.

The other seven blacks from my service company were at outlying railway stations in Austria, more distant than Salzburg. I hoped that I would get lucky too; the white soldiers had Salzburg sewed up too well. I discovered that other railway transportation offices were set up in distinct parts of Austria: Zell am See, Solbad Hall, Innsbruck, Kufstein, Passau—they even had some of our guys in Livorno—Leghorn. They were cropping up all over the place! Transportation personnel of my outfit were assigned to ship and receive soldiers and supplies. The home base was in Salzburg now—it had been moved from Linz—and my unit was billeted just a few miles from that quaintly marvelous city in Klessheim, along with other detached service units plus a divisional headquarters. The small railway task force that was left here as a remnant of our Company was automatically assigned to the motor pool. The menial work was simple: servicing jeeps and trucks and doing routine military jobs such as walking guard, an occasional hour or two of unenthusiastic dismounted drill, and alternate K.P. duty. Guard walking was a lonely endeavor at best, but K.P. was maddening.

Here military life was quiet and routine. Too quiet and routine to suit me. We were compelled to spend one hour each week in Troop Discussion Period. (My old stomping ground, although watered down with apathy, glossed over in tedium. In a word: a drag.) The instructors, each week a new one and always a non-commissioned officer of the first three grades, exhibited no joy in their work at all. All that good material, I thought, held in a vacuum, its import bouncing off walls, seeming to penetrate no minds at all. Soldiers are hard to teach anyway—especially subjects not directly related to basically fighting men. One either had to be a zealous simpleton—like me, I suppose, naturally and unequivocally in love with knowledge and the desire to impart it—or, an officious ass: a role these instructors preferred to assume, to command their charges' respect. I never did find a third way that was binding. Soldiers are different from other people anyway. I endured this routine apathy plus my new distinction of being "eight ballish" because I now realized I could not go back to my first love. This army world was integrated in its own way and I was inherently compelled to go along with their changes. I couldn't turn back the clock. And I wasn't sure I wanted to.

The transportation office was huge and busied. Many desks and typewriters. IN, OUT and HOLD baskets were filled to overflowing with transportation data of all kinds. I liked seeing the activity such busyness generated. I only hated that I was not an integral part. I knew that I could fit in, but with my black skin, plus the bad record I had recently acquired, I knew I wouldn't be trusted or tried. I was still the only Negro in the home base. Quite suddenly I graduated from the status of "grease monkey helper" to that of jeep driver. My task now was to carry two sergeants to the downtown Salzburg railway station office in the mornings. After that I parked my jeep in front of the home transportation office and made myself "available," acting as courier to anyone who needed me.

Some Negroes—like some whites—are made for this sort of thing. I wasn't. I wanted a post at one of our outlying places, way down the line. Where the office was just big enough for two and an interpreter. Where one had to forage for coal. To go out in the snow drifts and check box cars at distant sidings; converse challengingly with Austrian freightmen and brakemen; to learn something tangible of their rustic ruggedness; to have a hot coffee with them or a cold beer; to put my imperfect German to a test and, in the doing learn more; to reach out my Southern hand and upbringing across this sea of color, custom and color distinction, send it all to flight with the handshake of fellowship that had guided me from one nebulous situation to the other, ever filling my cup, both ways; to find the humane side of people in another land. Because I believed my father, who had been a soldier before me, and succeeded in doing all this; because I believed my brother, who had also been a fighting soldier and continued the chain—the two of us seeing more European countries in war and peace than any one of the previous generations of Jacksons could ever have imagined. I was the younger brother, the question mark, yet, ever the "hopeful" one. I wanted an experience I could take back to America with me when I was a soldier no more.

I knew that such an assignment existed. It was at Innsbruck. A small, dilapidated upstairs transportation office, up above Innsbruck's main station depot. It was run by a Negro sergeant friend of mine. He was a musician—and a damned good one. I had helped him get his high school diploma from Robbins, Illinois, and we had attended the same music school for army bandsmen at Dachau before I flunked out. I knew this man's assistant, a white soldier, was being returned to the states for discharge, leaving a vacancy. The sergeant had already put in a request for me on two occasions that I knew of, even going to the trouble of coming all the way up to Salzburg to speak to my commanding officer. His efforts on my behalf had been futile.

I was frustrated, and kept walking "the straight and narrow path" to prove I was worthy of the assignment. Meanwhile, something happened that gave me even more motivation. The State Department sponsored a *Porgy and Bess* tour at the state opera house in Vienna. Although I was still on Restriction, I badgered my former Information & Education officer to help me get a pass to "Veen" to see this great operatic folk work. He spoke to my C.O., who gave me all sorts of dire threats and admonishments if I messed up again but, joyously, he let me go.

When I arrived in Vienna, the tickets were already sold out. But I hadn't come two hundred miles to miss this great work. I button-holed one of the managers and told her my plight. When the opera doors opened I walked in and got me a seat in the fourteenth row. Close enough. William Warfield, Leontyne Price, Cab Calloway—as "Sportin' Life"—burst forth like four o'clocks in triumph, singing the magnificent stagings of George and Ira Gershwin's greatest lyrical musical. At the finale everybody stood and clapped and stomped as all the actors came on stage for a final bow. I counted fourteen curtain calls, and still a lot of exuberant applauding and stomping. The people standing behind me turned out to be the state department aide and his wife. After watching my hands get sore from pounding, they asked me if I wanted to attend an after-theater party and meet the cast. Does a hog love slop, I thought. This was the first—and only—time I have ridden in a Mercedes-Benz limousine!

The party was a natural ball. Ol' Cab turned them out with his standards: "Minnie the Moocher," "St. James Infirmary," his irrepressible "Hi De Hi De Hi De Ho," and all that splendid jazz from an era long gone. William Warfield sang songs in German, French and English. Here, I thought, is the only baritone who can top my former baritone idol, Paul Robeson. Leontyne Price was incomparable. I felt a great hope, that this lovely, soul-girl-woman from the Mississippi Delta, could be lauded and applauded and taken to the bosoms of these people in one of the greatest musical capitols of the world. The two were newlyweds, and their performances were all the more poignant in the love they openly expressed for each other.

That was a party that *was* a party! It lasted all night long. There were sixty-six members of the cast and crew and, on my program I collected sixty-five autographs. The only one I didn't get was that of "Porgy's" goat. He couldn't make the party. In quarantine. More's the pity.

The party got me stirred up for excitement, so once I got back to home base I traveled whenever I could. I went to Salzburg again, and this time I really saw it. The Mirabell Gardens, the Hohenzollern Castle, *Getreidegasse* (the little alley and the house where Mozart was born which is now a shrine). The Mozarteum, where his music played all day on magnificently constructed, high-placed pipe organs. What I failed to catch in the army band school I grasped in Mozart's lively spirit. The pipe organs played "Ein Kleine nacht Muzik," "Coci Fan Tutti," "The Marriage of Figaro," or Don Giovanni; many arias, fugues. I followed the River Salzach for a long distance; I sat alone in *gasthauses*, *Wein Stuberls* and argued—politely—the merits of Wagner, Strauss, Stravinsky, Nietsche, Schopenhauer, Beethoven, Liszt and Dean Dixon, with an occasional Salzburger. I drank a sweet and strong wine called Refosco and many bottles of Lowenbrau beer. I felt less "eight-ballish" now, as though I had discovered a new set of values that had lain dormant within me all the while.

It made me want even more to do something noteworthy with my life—in this clime—before my enlistment was up. So far, none of my friend's requests for me to join him in Innsbruck had come through. I was still a courier, seated in a corner of the transportation office, listening to the steady click-clacking of busy typewriters and the rustling of papers. Waiting—always, that ever-hating, cotton-picking, waiting—to rise up at some officer's beckoning, and drive him to some place and return to do the same thing again. Day after miserable day.

The first snows had already fallen. And beneath this brooding I still had hopes.

As Afro-American blacks have said for generations, God was in the plan. He came to me this time in the guise of a small-statured, grey-haired white lady from some obscure city in Georgia, who happened to hold an important post in the railway transportation office. I think she was a G.S. six or seven—a reasonably high enough rating. Occasionally I would drive her to her hotel in downtown Salzburg at the end of a work day. I have always dug people that are a little different from those made of such repetitiously similar common clay. This woman, in the first place, never wanted me to take the main, well-trodden road back to Salzburg. She preferred the country lanes—and so did I: past the many-stiled cedar posts, the earthy farm houses in the distance with their thatched roofs; the quaint hominess of rural Salzburg. By her very demeanor, this woman made me like her instantly, color aside. She talked only when she had something to say. Otherwise she was regally silent.

On one particular Friday, I was at my lowest depths of depression and I wanted to say *something*. I didn't know what she could possibly do about my little ol' problems, but by God, I wanted *somebody* to know how I felt about *something*! I was hoping that by some quirk of fate, she would open a door and I could spill out my message quite naturally. But when she didn't, my impulsive self didn't give my shy self a chance to change my mind. I was blurting out my problems before I knew it. She listened impassively as I talked.

"I admit that I've messed up and made mistakes—and what soldier worth his salt hasn't. So, okay. But before I messed up I was a hot shot Information and Education Specialist—even if I have to say it myself—and a feature writer for the Command newspaper. I've studied for everything I've learned. None of it has come to me in a silver spoon. I still have my MOS's. But that don't matter now: the writing or the Information-Instructor role. I believe in time I'll be a writer—and a damned good one—because I believe in people and their problems, aims and achievements. As for reading I've always done that and will always. Maybe I'll have a chance to combine the two at some other place in time, provided I don't flip my lid here and now in wanting something that I believe will be forever unavailable to me. The only thing that does matter *now* is that the other colored soldiers who came into this Company with me—and the new ones that came after too—are stationed in RTO's as clerks and what-nots all up and down the line. And I want to be stationed in one, too."

I can imagine how intense my face looked to her. It is so constructed that it is damn nigh impossible to conceal my emotions. And when I get angry or thoroughly disgusted I get carried away. I've often wondered, since then, why that woman didn't jump out of that jeep and go running down the snow-packed road yelling, "Madman! Madman!" But she never once changed her own look of intense concentration. I told her the whole story, finding other farm roads to drive down as I did so. We must have traversed the whole of Salzburg, going over those untouristed tracks, the Hohenzollern Castle looking like an unassailable citadel in the distance.

"Right now I'm flunking around the motor pool—when I'm not driving—and it looks like I'll never get out." Just talking about the business made me feel deflated. In the beginning, blowing off this steam had warmed me up, but the more I talked the more I felt the wintry air bristling through the jeep's seams.

She surprised me when she spoke: "Have you spoken with your Commanding Officer about another assignment?"

"Yes, I have." And then I explained about my sergeant-friend and the open job in Innsbruck. "My C.O. has promised me that *sometime* he would get me an assignment. But I think he's just pulling my leg." I took my eyes off the road long enough to look into her eyes, knowing full well that what I was about to say was not the most discreet thing in the world to say, armywise. Many GI's—figuratively speaking—have been hanged for saying a lot less. Well, I am often a blunderbug in the fickle world of social graces; and it's hard for me to hold my tongue.

"This man, my C.O., is *not* sympathetic to my abilities. He's the type of Southerner that doesn't care about giving a Negro a *second* chance. Whenever I ask him about the Innsbruck job, he gives me a stock answer that is usually negative. Just between you and me and the lamppost, I know I'll never get *anything* from him. I'm not entirely a fool. I know what I can do for the Army, and it certainly is not here in the motor pool where I am no more than just some black non-entity."

She looked at me for a pretty good while. I kept my eyes on the road ahead but I could feel her stare. What I had said now all seemed useless. Only the view in front of me soothed my drooping spirits. This was certainly not a Texan's kind of winter, but it was sure peaceful country. The wooden fences were winding turn-stiles along our way. Snow covered every meadow. Wayside crucifixes passed us with their dim, religiously symbolic luster. The sky was perennially overcast with the gossamer haze of winter. I filled the silence by thinking about my long-term goal to go back to Texas and tell my two nephews about this wide world I had seen. Brighter vistas would open up in the world for Negroes—for blacks. I could see them shaping up here and now. And, God bless, I sure wanted to get my licks in on the changes. I damned sure didn't want to come back a nobody, as an Army fuck-up. I wanted to take part in something!

I don't know how I must have looked to her at that time. But as we rolled across the Salzach River Bridge enroute to her hotel, her defiant voice said just one thing: "Well, one thing's for certain: They're not going to pull *my* leg!"

And they didn't either. The following Tuesday morning my duffel bag was packed and I was standing on the train station platform in the Salzburg station, waiting for my train to Innsbruck. It was bitterly cold but I didn't care. Inside my soul I was an oven of flame. I had finally gotten another chance.

On Faith and Being "Born Again"

When I was baptized at age eight, the whole religious front in the South was segregated. My memory of baptism—being "born again" has remained sacred—fearful and joyful together—through some tough times.

Total immersion, at the strong hands of the Reverend, into a small tub, located a few feet behind his pulpit. It was swift and short, and mercifully the tears starting in my eyes didn't show because I was wet all over! Joyful then, with the same strong hands raising me up, thrusting me toward waiting arms, warm towels, proud embraces, smiles and shouts.

All of us who experienced—endured—such a ritual, took its symbolism, its tenets, with us wherever we went. We would never be completely alone, so long as we believed.

* * * * *

During a two-year vagabond tour of America from 1948 to 1950, I entered upon some hard times in Philadelphia, the city of brotherly love. Jobs for strangers were nonexistent, and I had been sleeping on a cot in a Salvation Army house for seven days.

It was a refuge, sure, but the food was terrible: donuts and coffee three times a day. A fantastic insult to the stomach of a twenty-four-year-old man who couldn't steal a job as a pot washer. A fellow traveler who occupied a cot next to mine boasted he had not gone to bed hungry since he'd been there. He tried to turn me on to his methods: "Get yourself a coat and tie and dust off your shoes—I'm sure they've got some cast-offs here somewhere. Don't be ashamed to wear them if they don't fit too good, or they look too funny. Go to this place"—he gave me an address—"look humble and say: 'Peace, Father, it is wonderful.'"

This was the first I had heard of the Father Divine sect. Calling any man Father—other than my dad or that other, invincible One I had been taught to fear and love, was more than I could fathom. I told my friend as much. Expletives deleted, he answered: "You wanna eat, dontcha? You're tired of donuts, aintcha?"

I said yes, but argued some more about going against my principles.

"Well, starve, then!," he said. More expletives deleted.

Then came the real battle. Conscience vs. stomach. Stomach vs. conscience. God, I was hungry! My mouth drooled at the thought of those feasts Father Divine hosted for his followers: neck bones, ham, collard greens, corn bread, potato salad, red beans, rice, yams, ham hocks. Hell. I was going crazy! And for the first time in my life I left the faith, the faith that had carried me this far but was now vying against the lusts of my stomach. I had to find a way around my principles. Finally, it came to me: "him that asketh, gitteth; him that seeketh, findeth; to him that knocketh, a voice says 'come in, Brother, Peace is wonderful.'"

Lightning didn't strike me down. I entered into the temple of a man—a black man—who proclaimed himself "God." And I did eat—as the Scriptures said—again and again I *did eat*. And my luck changed, and I found work, and I went on.

* * * * *

Another time, I was in Columbus, Ohio, jobless, alone, sad and defeated. It was a weekday. This huge cathedral stood open; someone was playing the pipe organ: perhaps Schubert, Wagner, Mozart, no matter. Sanctuary beckoned me in my hour of crisis. I went in through the open doors, knelt in a lonely pew, talked to that Man, bared my soul, asked for guidance, cried a bit, felt better, and walked out feeling I had a new lease on life, and bless God, I did, too. I started working the next morning and earned enough money to go home and see my folks.

* * * * *

Back home in Houston one day during the Recession, I was out walking on a Sunday. I was trying to find some odd jobs. But I had no luck in finding anything. Matter of fact, the local constabulary asked me to leave a white area because I "looked like a suspicious character." (That meant black in my language.) Deflated, I walked on back toward my ghetto. There on the fringe of it was another cathedral: huge, high and imposing. More Wagner, Brahms, Beethoven maybe, pealed out from its pipe organs. Litanies without number. Caressing the soul, making promises. My landlady's fears assuaged. Debts that could—and would—be paid. When one believes, and follows that belief, faith will banish all tears, make all things right. People would study war no more; life would be gentle and sweet; prosperity would come once again in the land God gave to Cain. These promises were for me. The South had changed, I thought. I was somebody once more. I could sense it. A church door was open and I could feel the entreaties of its sanctuary beckoning me. Tomorrow was another day. Lord, today, my life could change.

I mounted the steep stairs. The huge and high oaken doors were suddenly thrust open by a white hand. A matching white face quickly turned to anger at seeing my black one. "What do you want, boy?" and me, a thirty-some-year-old "boy" answering: "nothing . . . nothing at all . . . not a goddamn thing. . . ."

Descending the steps I remembered the cathedral at Columbus, and Father Divine's temple in Philadelphia, and my full belly, both times finding comfort, and having to answer only to that great, invisible, invincible, omnipotent One. But I was born black, so today worship would be denied me. There would be no Beethoven, no Wagner, no Lizst, not even a Gian Carlo-Menotti. For that matter, they would deny me Aaron Copeland, Dean Dixon, or Duke Ellington if they could, because I was just some poor black bastard who only wanted to spend a few minutes inside what was supposed to be a sanctuary.

"What do you want, boy?"

Not a goddamn thing. There wasn't a goddamn thing in there I wanted anymore.

* * * * *

As soon as I crossed the line back into my ghetto territory, the Spirit hit me. That should have been my aim in the first place. All our Amazing Graces were there for me to embrace. Regardless of my wanderings, and for whatever vagabonded reasons, the ghetto was my beginning place. It would be my sanctuary while life showed me what to do next.

* * * * *

As time passes, the remembered images of those "religious experiences" follow, one after another, like the scenes from a movie, complete with sound. The voices of my family, of Father Divine's welcoming shout to "Come in and eat!" The thundering peal of that Columbus organ, and, almost drowned out and dying away, the whine of the church caretaker who turned me away.

Most vivid is the image of that wet, shivering, shiney-eyed eight-year-old, and the thrill of his new-born faith.

A damned happy image to remember, after all.

The Burning of the Books

After having written damn near everything else without selling anything—poems, essays, short stories, vignettes, many chapters of my intended novel, "Shade of Darkness"—I now wanted to write this play. I was deep into it by now, and at first I had a dead aim for that fine television series, "Naked City." Their theme music fractured me—it was so poignant. And that intense, all-consuming actor, Paul Burke, was damn sure the right guy for one of my principal characters. My black male actor was not too clearly in focus: Sidney Poitier was naturally my first choice; but that super star was real busy then, and might not have the time; but there were some other boss black male actors that could do it, I told myself. But I didn't know about writing for the telly any more than I did writing for the stage.

I kept remembering an expression a USO lady had told me once, after reading some of my book chapters, that I "really wrote from the seat of my pants!" I liked that expression and tried my best to live up to it. Books I had read a jillion of—it seemed—but that alone wouldn't suffice unless the writer *in* me was thoroughly hipped to my craft. All I knew was that I was stone gone behind this story. But I kept working, the story got too long for television and, worse still, it got too *strong!* So, I decided to forget it as a "Naked City" venture and center it for a *live* stage.

The late Sunday night Play of the Week television show my landlord-friend and I viewed at his upstairs apartment in Houston wasn't helping to make my decisions any easier either; they only kept me more engrossed—and more determined to make my story a stage play. But first, I had to see me a real play.

It happened that I had read an article in *Time* magazine about a play on the boards titled *A Man For All Seasons.* I flipped behind the title. It sounded Biblical—and it was. I had read *Time's* synopsis of it and was moved. My mind was instantly made up. I had to see this play, but I had no money.

Then—thank the Jesus!—a little luck came my way. I walked up on a job where a builder was just beginning an eight-unit, one-bedroom apartment complex. Touched by my insistent pleas that I could do any of the laborer's semi-skilled nuances the job called for—from plumber's helper, to pouring concrete to carpenter's helper—he hired me on the spot. I jumped into my work with a passion. (Construction work's my bag anyway. WALLS RISE UP! Head and hands and muscle toning; plus free fresh air and the blue sky above; nothing like it in the whole wide world for me. My father was a hod carrier and he fair ate that mess up, inadvertently passing it on to me!)

Next, I would need something to wear. At this juncture I was three-by-type dude: three pairs of pants, three shirts, three pairs of under-plunders—tops and bottoms—one thin wind breaker jacket, one pair of shoes. No economical Thom McAns for me, not with these Li'l Abner size 13's. My lack of conventional or stylish wardrobes didn't usually bother me in the least. (My parents and snobbish associates maybe, but me—to hell with it.) This Creole landlord-friend of mine—Joe—disagreed. He bought me a double-breasted suit when he learned I was aiming to see this play. (He would not be able to go with me, much as he would've liked to, but he was a gourmet cook at one of Houston's finest French-flavored restaurants.) He paid ten bucks for it at Goodwill. I liked the conservative gray-blue color, but the double-breasted bit had to go. After all, this was Texas, not California. The trousers needed altering also. So I took it to a tailor from the West Indies where he taped me off and assured me he would reduce it to a single-breasted and make it "stylish." Eighteen bucks. A monumental sum back there in the almost mid-sixties, for a laborer making $1.25 an hour. But my black people—like whites—liked to see a man in a suit and white shirt and tie from time to time.

In the meantime I worked on, each week getting out from under my minor debts—which were all major to me. Watching the calendar in the *Houston Post*'s NOW section for the play's arrival. Finally the great day came. I was tubbed and rubbed and thoroughly scrubbed—white folks' theater, you know: down South and all that—and absolutely "togged out." Hair cut, new shoes shined to a high gloss. (I had been a shoe shine boy in my youth, so that was no problem.) I was the picture of sartorial decorum, a gentleman of the "system," a bon vivant of the new world, one in which I had labored like a dog to help make. Not as sharp by price tags as I was *clean*, just *acceptable*. White shirt (Arrow), maroon knit tie, tied with a Windsor knot—man, I was ready!

I arrived at the theater—Houston's newest and finest—with about twenty minutes to spare. Took my place in line, was impressed by the splendor of its artistic, theatrical look. I was deciding on an appropriate seat, say about the fourteenth or sixteenth row, judging from the seating diagram on the wall by me and the amount of money in my pocket. After all, tomorrow was still another day; and one always had to eat.

I told the tall blonde, high-coiffured woman behind the glass cage the ticket price I had decided on. (I even allowed myself a few seconds to admire those huge breasts of hers with a sensual look. Wow, was I ever being reckless!) She then gave me the most innocent look in the world as she said: "I'm sorry, but we don't have any days for Nigras to see this play."

Nigras? What's *them*?

My thinking was out of focus. This was in 1963 or 1964. I had been in two wars for my "country." Everything was "equal in the arts." For patrons and artists alike. Nigras? It must have been a thousand years since I heard that word. That was slavery time days, wasn't it? I was a writer now, wasn't I? I was somebody, a human being, all the time, right? Had I stumbled into a surrealist, four-dimensional world from which there was no returning? All of a sudden this bitch was ugly. Then I quickly recovered my balance: from black poet to black Nigra in jig time.

"You mean I can't get a ticket to see this play?"

"Those are the rules, sir. I don't make the rules. I just work here."

Sir? On top of all them Nigras?

In a daze I walked over to the wall board where the cast members' photos were so prominently displayed: Paul Schofield's the most outstanding. (Of course, he had been my main man!) In costume of Sir Thomas More. All the others juxtaposed around him, as well it should be.

Now my mind was running five-hundred to the minute. I kept staring at Paul's face, not even seeing it, really. Just looking, thinking, unbelieving, fighting within me that old, ancient, Southern-bred feeling of social inferiority that I thought I had whipped by now. I thought I had rid it out of my body, my psyche, my mind, out of my now—I felt—fully grown artistic soul. Now I didn't see Paul's face at all. I saw remembrances of my first opera at the San Carlos Opera House—*Tosca*—and the last one, *Rigoletto*, in Naples, Italy; after the War, as an American soldier, trying to learn what "culture" and "art" was all about, especially since such cultures were verboten to us blacks when I was a youth growing up in Houston. Now this, in my first real initiation of prejudice's extension onto a road I had chosen and nurtured myself on. I still couldn't believe my ears had heard that white woman right. How could one believe what couldn't really be true?

"Something you want, boy?" And I turned to see a white man in a security guard uniform, slightly more than five feet tall, his face red and laced with blue broken veins, his belly large with obesity, his lips moving constantly from chewing tobacco—some of its spittle spilling down his chin. A .38 or .39 revolver—what did it matter—with a wooden butt grip jutted half out of his holster: a fast draw, perhaps? The most amazing thought oc-

81

curred to me: this cat had the bluest eyes I had ever seen!

"No," I heard myself saying. "Not a damn thing." And then I faced those blue eyes again. "Not a goddamn thing." And I started walking away—slowly, but deliberately. I was through with it. So far as I was concerned, the *Man For All Seasons* was a man that never was. I went out into the Infinity from which I came.

Back home I took a good look at where I lived. I surveyed this humble abode. Not much and me. I looked at my handmade—by me—bookshelf, five rows high, nailed to studs on the wall. Some of its treasures I had carried with me through the Italy of World War II's aftermath, some through travels in Austria and Germany, others were from a favorite bookstore in downtown Houston. So many of these were written by white writers. I would begin here.

Outside my pad there was a fifty-five gallon empty oil drum where we—me and my neighbors, me and my end-of-year rejection slips—burned our trash from time to me. It was empty that night. And the night was late. So I started grabbing books. Everything written by a white—now a hunkie, some peckerwood—was being ripped, then ignited. Once the fire was going it was easy. The flames began to roar. And I began to pour. Books I had bought, books I had found, books I had stolen surreptitiously from libraries—books I had needed for CULTURE. I watched them all go up in flames. It was a very dark night and there I was, one lone black nigger was out there in front of that funny-looking house that my landlord owned, burning books. Of all things. In a white neighborhood, maybe, I would have been arrested. But this was the ghetto, Houston's ugly backyard, where niggers often did crazy things.

There went Sinclair Lewis and his *Babbit* and *Main Street* and *Kingsblood Royal*; Erskine Caldwell's *Tobacco Road* and *God's Little Acre*; John Steinbeck's *The Grapes of Wrath, Cannery Row, Tortilla Flat.* (I had read passages of it to black GI's in the tufa dust wastelands of southern Italy, after our race riot, when morale was low and there was no USO or Field Library—except my own.) Burning them now not out of hate, but out of their utter uselessness—to me. New white writers I had recently become acquainted with: Monica Baldwin's *I Leap Over the Wall*; I didn't hate her either but she was white and she flat had to go. Thomas Wolfe went with disgust and revulsion now: *The Web and the Rock*; *Look Homeward, Angel*; and *You Can't Go Home Again*—burn motherfucker, burn! And for a damn good reason too, since it took me a century of being brainwashed to learn that this dude hated niggers and jews with a passion; he was even didactic about it, and his publishers printed his every word. You *know* he had to go! Rip, rip, rip! And here's ol' Cornelius Ryan, author of *The Longest Day*, the story of the D-Day landings, where he didn't even have a nigger shining a white officer's boots—for what *that* was worth. Others—so many others—including the one I despised most of all: Harriet Beecher Stowe and her damned *Uncle Tom's Cabin*. Why had I kept that one? If it hadn't been for a book like this, there *never* would have been an Uncle Tom epithet in our vocabulary. I wished at that moment I could speak for the umpteen jillion times the thought of Tom's supposedly noble actions toward Little Eva swirled through my people's brains. How many of us black males, reading of how niggers were treated back in those days, entertained the thought if we had been Tom, we would have decided "to hell with this shit" and throttled that dangerous little bitch so we could escape! Or planted her little ass up in a tree somewhere away from wolves and possums or something, cause that posse was getting closer and closer to them all the time. And what did Tom's noble act get him? Aside from not a goddamn thing, he helped further perpetuate the feet of white men on black asses for eons to come. Bullshit.

So burn, books, burn. And burn they did. All that night. I kept only four: James Baldwin's *Nobody Knows My Name*, Ralph Ellison's *Invisible Man* and Chester Himes' *If He Hollers Let Him Go*. I also gave Elizabeth Browning a break. She had written so beautifully about us "colored" folk in *Songs of the Portugese* that I hurriedly—before I changed my mind—tucked that book under my mattress. But everything else written by whites that were in that house had to go. And go they went.

That was then, of course: *that* time, *that* era. I've long since gone back to reading everybody. (I've had to, to stay up.)

I don't regret my actions that night one iota. In the more than ten years I've lived in Los Angeles, *A Man For All Seasons* has been in movies and on stages here several times. I refused to see it each time it was advertised. Sometimes I was more than able, financially, to go and see it, but I wouldn't. Twice I was offered free tickets through my involvement with the Watts Writer's Workshop, and twice I refused. Finally, one night when I was fishing for something to watch on the tube, there it was. Half with reluctance I saw it—in its entirety. And loved it, trauma or no. As for the play I was writing—*Bye, Bye, Black Sheep*—it had traveled (in manuscript form) around the world, addressed to Bobby Breen of the *Porgy and Bess* troupe. (Isn't that ironic? A full-length, four-act play, arriving at every place the addressee was, only to miss him by the mere caprice of time and fate.) Three years of writing this one and only "masterpiece," poured out of my black experience, only to have the manuscript arrive at where they had "just left." A Jackson luck. Or a "never-was-meant-to-be." Whichever. No one can't say I didn't have one hell of a go at it though.

Friends and family going to and from Houston these days tell me it has changed considerably since "my time." So be it. I've done so many things writing-wise in and out of the Watts Writer's Workshop that *that* night in Houston has lost a great deal of its sting. I've seen so darn many plays here—good, bad, indifferent, better, best—that my travails of *that* night seem hardly to have occurred—except in that long memory of mine. It isn't too likely that what happened to me will happen to another black—or another minority, even—and that should be good. Hell's bells! That's the way it should have been then.

Written in Los Angeles
July 30, 1978

84

*Looking Back—
and Ahead*

Mayor Tom Bradley of Los Angeles was instrumental in making the whole month of February Black History Month. Before we only celebrated a week. The month idea is far better. God knows, the "half ain't never been told," as the old rhyme runs, what with the media's overwhelming whiteness ofttimes "snowing" our accomplishments by bringing out the same old names time and time again: Booker T. Washington, George Washington Carver, or W.E.B. DuBois. Rightly so. These are names deserving recognition. And yet a great many of us—both black and white—know all that. The historical melody of these names lingers on.

But what we must all do now is to reach back for more of the black achievers our black souls and psyches tell us are there. We can do this without forgetting the well-known achievers—like George Washington Carver who, from the lowly peanut—(the "goober")—invented 125 different products, including a lipstick! Like Dr. Martin Luther King, Jr., whose Montgomery Bus Boycott exposed the hypocrisy of a city's bus franchise so dependent on its black riders—the very ones they forced to ride in the back!

(One anecdote coming from the boycott's travail was that of an elderly black woman with a cane, trying her hardest to keep up with the more strident marchers. Bus doors beside her opened, the white driver whose empty bus seemed to command entry, tried his ingratiating best to entice her: "Come on in, Auntie, they'll understand." "No, they won't," the matriarch replied. "I've got two grandchildren on this march, and though I lag behind, I'll get there, eventually. And I'll be with them. That's what this march is all about.")

We hold memories of our accomplishments as self-evidence: manifold examples of the good, the bad, the ugly. We could pick any time, any clime, any situation, and some representative of our black kin were there, and often being mistreated.

—Hitler's rejection of Jesse Owens, who went on to earn a batch of medals in the 1936 Olympics.

—The unwarranted dishonorable discharge of an entire company of black soldiers in Brownsville, Texas during World War I, sanctioned by then U.S. President Theodore Roosevelt, who could have pardoned them but didn't, causing them to live out the rest of their lives not only in dishonor, but—worst of all—in economic disgrace.

—The U.S. Army's LSD experiments on James R. Thornwell, who was made a mental cripple at a remote farm mill in the south of France. (And at last, after sixteen years of mental anguish, his being "fully exonerated" by the U.S. government, which paid him over $600,000 and admitted that charges against him were fabricated.)

—Althea Gibson, first black woman ever to win a Wimbledon Tennis championship (the first of any, in that field) in competition against a sea of whites.

—Marian Anderson, Mattiwalda Dobbs, Leontyne Price, who broke down the barriers by singing in formerly all-white fabled halls of opera. Right along with their male counterparts, Paul Robeson, William Warfield and Roland Hayes—just to name a few. Even in triumph, with their talents of mastering moods, languages and dramatic content, their success was never entirely easy: their blackness ever preceded them, nine leagues to the fore.

The "Black Experience" covers a vast expanse of time, clime and events. Small issues often loom large overnight, as when a segregated army post evoked the need for a "special" air base: a "Black Air Force" was started in Tuskeegee, Alabama, at the outset of World War II. This Black Armada destroyed 260 German planes, damaged 148, sank a Nazi destroyer and blew apart hundreds of military vehicles when strafing convoys.

Those who came back—sixty-six did not—did so with Distinguished Flying Crosses, legions of Merit, Silver Stars, Purple Hearts, Bronze Stars. They were members of the 99th, 100th, 301st and 302d Pursuit Squadrons; known collectively as the 303d Fighter Group of the 12th and 15th Air Force in Europe. Almost 1000 black cadets were trained as Army Air Corps pilots at the all-black Tuskeegee Army Air Base during World War II.

Not to be forgotten, either, are members of the 24th Infantry Division, the 25th Infantry Regiment, who ran the capricious gambit between North and South Korea, resulting in one of our nation's highest casualty rates for that war.

Neither should we forget Vietnam, and the black soldiers who traversed its death-laden rice paddies, its bomb-ridden, off-trail roads, its sniper-infested trees, dung holes and dried palm-covered pits. Our blackness was there, too, and collectively, both white and black came back home to an almost ignominious future.

Still, in the aftermath of three wars, Hollywood and its first cousin, television, have yet to present our heroic black participation in the above endeavors. They don't care a fig or give a damn. But truth can't stay buried forever. I know it, you know it, Hollywood knows it.

"A mind is a terrible thing to waste," say the United Negro College Fund Television commercials. The logo speaks reams. So does an admonishment issued to a greedy and uncaring woman character in a Rex Stout mystery novel: "Madame, what does your mind do with its time?"

Both are appropos for today as well as yesterday. "Black Is Beautiful" of the 60s and, "I'm Black And I'm Proud" of the 70s have not died, and are yet applicable. Now, in the 80s, the more we apply those logos to our continual struggles, the greater dividends our soul thrusts should reap. For our blackness is targeted, and is ever a target. Our black history reveals a catalyst (of faith, mostly) that has propelled so many of us to rise above non-entity status. We can certainly produce more whether the world thinks of us as the "chosen few" or not. And for what that's worth, who knows? Maybe we are, already.

Awakening to a
Common Suffering—
and Pride

Before you say you've read enough about *Roots*, wait a minute. Let me tell you what I hear being said among black groups.

By that I don't mean the NAACP, the urban league or the like. No, the discussions I mean are among members of the black working class who, whether you notice or not, walk every day in your midst:

Construction workers, not just the ones who dig the hole but the concrete hardnosers and the welders, and after them the carpenters' helpers and the dry-wall hangers and the painters and the moving men;

Postal workers, from the white-collar types to the maintenance people who labor all those abominable hours while the rest of Los Angeles is sleeping;

Clerks and ditch-diggers, barkeeps and day workers, lawyers and garbagemen and secretaries, and all the other beautiful brownskins you see driving to work at 7:00 in the morning in their Datsuns and Pintos and Chevies and Fords and Chryslers and Mercedeses, even.

Roots awakened them all to *themselves* as nothing had before. The real blacks like me, black blacks who have thoroughly African features, suddenly found ourselves viewing something close—so awfully close—to the way we once were all those decades, generations and centuries ago.

Afterward, how pleasant it was to hear black voices expressing opinions about particular episodes—telling how they cried and laughed and how their furies were aroused when they saw black actors and actresses portray the common suffering of our past.

In all my years of movie and TV watching, I've never seen and loved and admired such acting by my black brothers and sisters. Yet I have reservations—and I understand the cast had reservations, too—about the authenticity of the characters as scripted.

When you look behind the scenes, you find something curious: the lengthy screenplay for TV's eight-part *Roots* was written by four men—Bill Blinn, Ernest Kinoy, James Lee and Charles Cohen. All of them are white, which could have something to do with authenticity—or lack of it. Yet the network says all scripts were approved by Alex Haley himself, so I won't fault the screenwriters too much. We blacks have a saying: "They did the best they could."

Though their screenplay is no match for Haley's original, it sure pulled a lot of people off the streets to discover the saga of Kunta Kinte. It even drove some of them—millions, I hope—to seek out the roots of *Roots*, for it is in book form that the story is pure soul.

Yet, for all its shortcomings, the TV version made black history pulsate with power. It said: "Baby doll, we have arrived. We are here."

We blacks have done a lot of hard dying in our time—whether by hanging—lynching or (and this too is a form of death) by castration—but in *Roots* the mostly black cast took the script, and gave us *life*. Through their art, they awakened latent pride in a people who were starving for it.

Nor will that pride go away ever again, for *Roots* and its influence will endure. When, years ago, I took history in high school, our teacher kept admonishing us: "Be proud, be proud—you're from a mighty race." But the textbooks didn't bear her out, and neither did everyday experience, and it is only now that I *believe.*

Black history has been suppressed—especially by Hollywood—for too many years, but after *Roots* that's bound to change. (Hell, we never wanted to be pacified, which seemed to be the intent of movie makers; we wanted to be presented.) No longer will our story be segregated in black theaters, black movies, black television, black whatever. Now our experience interests everyone—and the ratings are there to prove it.

At last we are for real. We didn't invent our history: no one in his right mind wanted (or wants) to be enslaved. But we have a past that can't be ignored, and 1977 turns out to be the year Alex Haley laid it on us.

Now, by continuing to dig for our roots and laying them bare, we can gain the strength to go on and achieve what we merit: the freedom, honor, dignity and respect that should have come naturally all along. Now we can do this without begging and bitching and borrowing, without burnings and lynchings, without all those things done to us which have too long robbed us of our humanity.

As the actors and actresses in *Roots* brought the characters to stirring life, so Haley has renewed the lives of all those blacks who read the book or watched it on TV.

That is no small accomplishment, and all I can say to Alex Haley is, with great honor to him and heightened respect for myself: "Thank you, brother."

My Africa—
It is All This, and More

In the midst of Black History Month I have been thinking about my personal black heroes. Paul Robeson was one, at a time when black people were in sore need of them, and to this day his deep baritone rings still in my ears.

But I have other idols in my private pantheon. Among them are two black brothers, James Weldon Johnson and Paul Rosamond Johnson. I was first introduced to their work by my high school music teacher, who was a beautiful black rebel in her own right.

She had us sing the Johnson brothers' hymn—the Negro national anthem—"Lift Every Voice and Sing" *before* the "Star Spangled Banner." She did, that is, if none of the white faculty members were present. She tried to get us to sing it softly if she thought they were anywhere near, but her efforts always failed terribly.

Francis Scott Key's lyrics were all right with us, but not in the same league with the Johnson Brothers' soul-ensnaring bombast:

> Sing a song full of faith that the dark past has taught us;
> Sing a song full of hope that the present has brought us,
> Facing the rising sun of our new day begun,
> Let us march on till victory—is won.

After we had put our voices into that with fervor, there was never a dry eye in the classroom.

Long before I came along my father sang it—or so he said. My sister sang it. My brother and I sang it in church on Sundays. In 1945, the Wings Over Jordan Choir sang it in the segregated mess hall at Houston's Ellington Air Force Base, and the rafters threatened to collapse. Every black soldier in that tarpapered barrack stood with his hand over his heart as tears rolled down his cheeks, and then stood to join the choir in singing a song of freedom that was yet—and still is—so many years away.

The Johnson brothers asked us to lift our voices in song, but they wound up lifting our hearts. Dr. Martin Luther King, Jr., lifted our hearts in another way—but he, of course, is more than just a personal hero.

I pay no attention to allegations against him that have surfaced lately to besmirch his name. What does matter is that he was a messiah to innumerable blacks and, one must, admit, innumerable whites. (The whites marched along with us in the civil rights movement, were abused and even died for Dr. King's causes and dreams, because they are the universal causes and dreams of mankind.)

As we blacks are fond of saying, "God doesn't love ugly." (To which someone will always answer, "Naw, and He ain't too crazy about pretty, either.") So, no matter what is said about him, we loved Dr. King in the '60s, and our love is only compounded now.

The powers-that-be can proclaim his birthday a national holiday. The most popular pundits in American can write about him in heart-rending essays that have no soul whatsoever. The politicians can stand pompous, officious, stately—shed a crocodile tear or two—and yet not mean a word they say.

We blacks will know when our heroes are respected and when we ourselves are respected. The most amazing thing I remember from my early adult years growing up in the South is that I always understood what was going on. I knew (and I was not alone) when some light-complexioned blacks were "passing." The whites did not catch on.

93

We also knew when whites had it in for members of our race, and how to stay one step ahead of them. Wasn't Harriet Tubman, illiterate that she was, a bona fide example of this? She organized the "underground railway" before the Civil War and helped free slaves, using the simplest of codes—a gospel song, "Steal Away," when it was too dangerous to travel. That was generalship of the first order, it seems to me. And heroic.

We blacks have always studied our adversaries. We have had to, in order to survive. As a result, we have often seemed passive and have suffered because of it. All the same, in our struggle to keep ourselves intact, informed and "cool," we have seen new black hero-leaders spring up from the pits—always bringing light.

Phillip Randolph, Mary McLeod Bethune, Joe Louis, Walter White, Thurgood Marshall, Marian Anderson, Dorie Miller, K. Gavilan, Chester Himes, Richard Wright, Leontyne Price, William Warfield, Count Basie, Duke Ellington, James Baldwin, Sarah Vaughan—all swim in our subconscious.

So does Countee Cullen's "Heritage":

What is Africa to me!
Copper sun or scarlet sea,
Jungle star or jungle track,
Strong bronzed men, or regal black
Women from whose loins I sprang
When the birds of Eden sang?
One three centuries removed
From the scenes his fathers loved,
Spicy grove, cinnamon tree,
What is Africa to me?

It is everything to me, past and present, all one.

It is a quiet night in a Mississippi marshland where I walk with a brown girl whose skin is as smooth as velvet.

It is crickets scratching in a Texas night when there has been no rain, and frogs bellyaching ("blew-it, blew-it") when there has been too much.

It is the trace of a whirlwind—a hurricane—that blew away a tiny Southern hamlet years after a black man had been dragged through its streets to be lynched for a rape he did not commit.

It is the castigation of black brother soldiers who, in time of war, in a foreign land, defended themselves in a race riot.

It is Marian Anderson singing triumphant at the Lincoln Memorial in 1963 after the tumult and shouting of the March on Washington had died away.

It is my father balancing me on his shoulder to see Franklin Delano Roosevelt traveling down a Houston street in an open car.

It is me, years later, as a draftee, parading down that same street as a black soldier—last in line, of course.

It is me glancing surreptitiously from my place in the parade to see my father and his proud visage, and never missing a step.

It is my nineteen-year-old heart, swelling with pride along with his, because I was helping defend America's free shores, yet knowing down deep that this was a lie—that it would take more years than allotted me to gain all-encompassing freedom.

This is what Africa means to me. It is my people and my heroes—all this and more.

Many black struggles and many black heroes have gone before us. But the fight is still with us. Every black person who leaves his home in the morning has *that* fight to face before all others. It matters little that one is an artist, another a businessman, another a laborer—whatever a person does, blackness precedes ten leagues to the fore.

It is our race, our nation within a nation, our category. Out of it have emerged heroes and heroines—but not enough. We've come a long way, and we've still got a long way to go. Tomorrow *has* to be made better. After all, what's one more fight? Or several? We've been in the arena too long to quit now.

Black Friday: The Day Kennedy Was Shot

(All the action and dialogue in it are true. I was a part-time laborer at Masury-Seidlitz Paint Factory and Warehouse at that time, and on that fateful Friday. We black Houstonians had moved about with our fingers crossed, after hearing the rumors from many bigots that Kennedy was going to be <u>had</u> in Houston. And when he left the big "H" that Thursday we breathed a giant sigh of relief. When the bullet pierced his skull that next day, that Friday, this white knight fighting our black cause, being wasted in Dallas—of all places—that weekend was too great to be borne. Consequently, I chronicled our feelings and regrets the way I <u>knew</u> we felt.)

It was such a beautiful day.

Like the others that had preceded it in the past three weeks of a Houston, Texas, Indian summer, it made one feel good just to be alive and enjoying it. Texas blue skies, white cumulus clouds, seem to the natives—like me—like no other skies anywhere on God's green earth. I should know: I had seen a bunch of 'em in my time. And in a bunch of places.

This Friday, November 22, 1963, it was going on three o'clock P.M. on the culminating day of my employment. I had

96

been here at this Paint Warehouse-Factory for three continuous weeks as a part-time worker. My friends had gotten me the job. (I had worked here part-time before, but never more than a week at most.) This was the time when the recession was dwindling after more than four years of unemployment hell. It had been a fair bitch: socking it to business, businessmen, and the poor, hard-working blacks and whites alike. The average semiskilled laborer couldn't *steal* a job. Crimes of many dimensions were on the rampage during that time. Politics—in the main—were to blame for damned near everything. But now things were shaping up, they were visibly shaping up, and even I could breathe a little sigh of relief.

I was glad to have this job for several reasons. First and most of all: the money. (Really, everything else followed its lead.) A dollar fifty an hour (*good* pay by comparison: I had worked for one dollar an hour up to 1960 after I had come home from the wars in 1956; then President John F. Kennedy had upped it a quarter, and now this Paint Company had a set minimum of a dollar fifty, with time and a half for overtime; so I could swim along real well with continuous employment at this rate, even being single); I could groove real good.

I had my own pad now. My landlord's wife had died, his grown daughter had her own house nearby, and his grown son occupied the upstairs part of this one. It had a phone, still connected, which both—or all three—of us used; the son had an extension. (The daughter bugged me some, coming over at oddball hours of the day and night to use the phone—that's the truth! believe me—but, what the hell, I was doing a heap better than I was before.) Still, I could make contacts with friends and people who, with their encouragement, pushed me on toward getting my stuff (writing) solicited by this place and that.

I thought the house itself was ugly—and it was: two-storied, woodframed, leaning from the top like the tower of Pisa, with doors that I had hell closing. (I had to wedge them shut, and bam on them like crazy to get them open!) The owner and I had worked at a white hotel downtown years previously, as porters, making very little bread and virtually no tips. There were no black bellhops during *that* time, but a good hustling black could always make himself *some* kind of change. Not always a lot, but some. He remembered me from those days, and when my landlady was about to kick me out of my room at her place—because my latest construction job had played out—it was propitious that he and I met on the street and he asked me to live in his house rent-free, or pay when I could, so that vandals would not break all the windows or steal the family heirlooms that were still left there. So I moved into *that* house, ugly or not! Forthwith. (My mother, Florence Jackson, may have birthed a son that could, at times, be naive or a little stupid and sometimes both, but an idiot? No way.)

So I had me a pad, some comfort and quietude. I wrote a lot, read a lot, and studied my craft a lot. A whole house gives a man a dimension that a mere room cannot. He doesn't have to dress up every time he wants to use the bathroom. And his eating—in a room his meals are too much to cope with. But with a stove and a refrigerator he can plan some eats for days in advance with one rounded cooking. After all, I grew up with a large family. A lot of Mrs. Jackson's recipes stayed in mind. This was cool. I really got to like it.

It was my friends that were the most swell during my post army readjustment period. I had been back home almost nine years then. My army fits of unsettlements had virtually evaporated by now. I could pick and choose those that dug me for me and feel comfortable in their presence and they in mine. Once we got ingrained with each other we gave ourselves a name: the Posse—Texas, Louisiana, and St. Louis, Missouri combined. Lionel, the main deputy, was part Creole, although much of his main family lived in Houston. He had several more brothers, three of whom worked at the paint plant with him.

Zeke and Al from St. Louis, now Texas also, had steady jobs here. Lionel's older brother, Ed, drove the tow motor and had the biggest responsibility for getting paints out on the docks for loading. He, too, was a member of the Posse. I was not only the lone, stomped-down Texan in the group but, being older—and far more traveled—I was the sage of the group, not by election but by *selection*. Because we became as most good friends become—

gravitated to one another. Through many beers, shared half-pints, good movies where our combined Sidney Poitiers, Harry Bellafontes, Brock Peterses, Ruby Dees, Ossie Davises, and other cinematic blacks of our era held sway, we were held in awe by many blacks of Fourth Ward as a "swinging" group (long before any of us ever heard of the term "jet set").

By now our favorite meeting, drinking, and rapping place—Cash Money's—was the supreme headquarters for our Posse. We called this beer joint Cash Money's because the woman who owned and operated it was hell on her cash money for the beer and fish and chicken that we got on credit. All of us felt her hot wrath when Friday, payday, and four-thirty came and we went slippin' and slidin' by without coming there first. Overall, though, it was a swell union. The owner herself, a jazz buff from the git go, had one swell array of jazz records on her jukebox. And we were big spenders in this respect also. Zeke was the biggest. He didn't spend money just on albums, he spent it on *volumes* of albums! Lou Donaldson, Miles Davis, Stanley Turrentine, Nina Simone, Dakota Staton, Aretha Franklin, Shirley Scott, "Cannonball" Adderly, Yusef Latef, ad infinitum. We were so continuous in our fun there that the average customer of Cash Money would do a double take through the big plate glass window before coming in. It appeared that we were of an intelligence or sophistication that stifled their own ways of thinking. (Not true, though. We were of a different breed, yes; but we solicited no members to change their lives for ours. After a bit their attitudes accepted ours for their worth and things went on as usual.) We were one helluva together bunch. We attacked everything, black slaveries, black put-downs by whites, culture, academics; we embraced new knowledge, not letting anything rip us off. We were after it, we had it, and we wasn't about to let go! We were hipped, turned on, worked hard, and were willing to work; we enjoyed life and fun and aimed at moving upward all the time. Simple as that. And I, with my now stabilized maturity, ever looking forward to the company of good friends, had gained a new lease on life that I thought I wouldn't have found here. This was beautiful. I relished it.

It was a white bigot that destroyed my illusions.

With a word.

How strange, that a human being can come from nowhere, from out of the blue, the beautiful-God-Jesus-infinitely painted blue at two-thirty in the afternoon and kill, with one vindictive short sentence of three words, that which another human— black—had prayed secretly would not happen, should not happen, must not happen in a civilization where a majority of decent caring human beings of both races were voting, thumbs up, that this one should live. How strange indeed.

And what of the listener himself, the first to hear the sound gleefully uttered by this human bigot's voice. That human bigot emphasizing it with loudly clapped hands, uttering: "We got him!"

And me, loading the last big tractor-trailer of paint that all of us had pitched in to get out for a new client in Savannah, Georgia. Beginning at seven that morning instead of the usual eight, working straight into noon, past the lunch hour, each one of us, one at a time taking off just long enough to gobble our sandwiches, washing them down with cool tap water, then returning to the processing table. Finally getting the huge order through, feeling relaxed now, because the unity of this minority-ethnic group of Blacks and Chicanos had put together several hundred one-gallon buckets of paint. Now mixed, poured, sealed, labeled, and boxed, now being loaded for its Georgia destination.

And me, the loader, stacking the cartons that Ed—"Mr. Ed, the Talking Horse," we called him, because he talked all the time—brought to me on wooden pallets with the tow motor, saying: "That's all of it, Jack! It's all yours!" And me answering: "Righto! And in a few ticks it's all gonna be the property of the man in Savannah gee a!"

"In twenty minutes, Beer Bust!" Looking at his watch. "I can taste those suds right now!"

"Tell the truth!" I answer, as I work at a more furious pace. "I intend to be there when the first beer cap is pulled!"

"Amen, brother Jay Tee Jay. Will see you there!" The tow motor's blatant sound thinning in his wake back through the plant. Black repartee resounding in my ears The day is nearing its end. Mr. Smith, factory foreman, has had several cases of bottled beer icing in a number two tub since early morning—Texas Style—by now they are frothing. All work stops at three, rather than our usual four-thirty. Then pay and, as Zeke has proclaimed earlier, "Sip time." "Sip" it is.

But the white bigot says: "We got him."

I say: "Got who?"

He says: "Kennedy. WE GOT HIM! In Dallas. . . . They jes' released the news. . . ."

Not possible. Our biggest fears were of the white bigots in Houston. He had come through here unscathed. Yesterday, Thursday, was a long day of sweating—particularly among black folks. But nothing had happened, and we were relieved. But Dallas? The Cotton Bowl, SMU, Neiman Marcus, the biggest thing people in the big "H" knew about . . . the Cotton Bowl in Dallas!

Only a few more cases to throw on the truck, subconsciously, as the impact of the man's words swirled around my brain. The last layer of cartons more hurriedly unloaded and stacked and then my following in the bigot's wake. Even as I left the loading dock to follow the bigot the PA system was blaring: ". . . the President has been *shot*! . . . in his motorcade . . . here in Dallas . . . the President has been shot !!! . . ." I saw Zeke filling a local paint order for the S.P. express truck. He looked at me, wide-eyed, incredulous. Lionel, in another row of paint shelves, turned a corner, approaching Zeke and me, his hands outspread in questioning, his paint order falling out of his hand. And then, the buzzing, squawking of the PA system; then, the only coherent sound of humanity, the sound of the bigot: "We got him!" Then loudly, emphatic, frenzied: "WE GOT HIM !!! . . . WE GOT KENNEDY !!! . . . WE GOT HIM IN DALLAS !!! . . . right in front of everybody !!! . . . He'll never try changing our ways again!!!"

Then the PA system again: with muffled clarity . . . with greater clarity, with sobbing unclarity, followed by sketchy details, the sounds of unmistakable sobbings . . . and more sobbings. . . . And more unclarified sounds of babbled networks . . . and more incredulity . . . and more astonishment . . . and more confusion . . . and less and less pained belief . . .

And the continuous preachment-declaration of one promethean-sized white bigot, now tramping down rows and corridors of carefully stacked paints: gallons, quarts, pints, half-pints, fourths, less; packages, tints; cleanly swept aisles, freeways for tow motors, walkways, points of distinction, radio statics, emotional voices choked with sobbings of disbeliefs while one six-foot-five or -six illiterate, black-hating white bigot went from maze to maze of paint rows, seeking an audience, proclaiming: "We got him! . . . we got the nigger-lovin' sonofabitch, we got that lib'r'l loving sonofabitch . . . we got him ! ! ! . . ." Strutting on, on, through the entranceway of the factory where paint was made, into the huge room of processing, past stupefied Blacks and Chicanos, past the area and amidst the aura of conjoined labored camaraderie not too long before. Past the iced-cold beer frothing in the tub, this something special for us in this week's labors. Past all and through the factory to the outside dock, by an unloading railway siding, where blacks were unloading powdery sacks of paint mixes for the coming week's work; they hearing this crazied Town Crier shouting toward their black faces his hate of an aid or change that this now mortally wounded white knight will nevermore render. Down, down the concreted dock, down the concreted steps, down the railroad tracks toward other white plants, other warehouses, until the voice is lost in our isolated distance. . . .

And then there was all the silence in the world.

The bell for three o'clock rang. The promised early quitting time, the checks already made out, the iced beers in the number two tub sat forlornly with bubbly beads forming thickly about their brown necks. Plant and Factory crews, those from the nearly unloaded boxcar, were standing near and about it, each with a bottle opened. Drinking lackadaisically, looking wan, shocked in disbelief, in deep ponderment, the occasional shaking of a head the only needed sentence for a communication without sound, without words I, too: a great lover of beer, noticing the first taste flavorless, so unlike beer, so unlike the thirst-quencher beer ought to be. There was nothing to celebrate, nothing at all. Not the three weeks of steady work, the good friends I had worked with here, the money I had earned that would pay my debts and leave me something to buy, something nice for one I dug and who dug me; no, nothing at all. Only unanswered questions. Dallas. Of all places. Now, the confirmed KNOWLEDGE: knowledge hanging like a black cloud over our brightly lighted warehouse, trying to accent the brilliant blue and the thick, white cumulus clouds outside our huge warehouse door in our view.

Paychecks being passed out by the two foremen: from Plant and Factory. The checks hardly observed except by a cursory glance, before being rammed into pockets. Then leaving for home—was there still such a place? Leaving the more than half tub of beer untouched. Leaving the previous joy of having done a hectic job for a new client and the knowledge of good work done in an unapproachable limbo. Leaving the day well behind, for its earlier hopes and plans would not mean the same to us now. For the long weekend would be upon us and the strain of bearing up under it would be too great to be borne. Because these people gathered here and those we were leaving to meet would unwillingly and unwantingly be compelled to share a weekend of sorrow and shame for the innate concerns for our lives, our future fortunes, and our—still remaining—sacred honors. Our country, our state, our cares, our colors, our race, our everything within the should-be noble strata of humanhood was as much in jeopardy from the one who fired the bullet as from the bigoted Town Crier who insanely hurled the news. This we would ponder, this day, today, tomorrow, and the day after that—all—for now and the rest of our free afternoons.

Welfare and the Single Man

 T he doors open at 7:30.

It is a quarter to seven, the number three bus has deposited him at Sixth Street and Central Avenue and is now heading south to Manchester. He embarks, pulls the tweed overcoat collar up about his neck, immediately feeling the contrast of the early morning chill as compared with the warmth of the bus. The sidewalk is alien and so is the area.

He is forty-four, black, clean, broke, an obvious student of life yet still ambitious, although needing some kind of aid and/ or assistance in a most desperate way. There is just enough "correct" change in his pockets to get him back home in case the "rumors" he's heard about this place giving aid and sustenance to single men is not entirely true. If all of his quest is a complete bust then back home in his room he can plan tomorrow's foray into the conventional employer-employee gambit that, for lack of jobs, has brought him here in the first place. He gets a bearing and starts walking.

The "place" is not too far from here. Find Alameda. There, next light. Turn left, go north to Fourth Street, turn right. Keep going. Fourth Street veers a bit, becoming Fourth Place. There it is, there: at the light. A one-way street going north. All those men over there. This must be the "place."

The crosswalk is angular, the street is wide. The sun is rising. The big orange ball blinds him as he tries to cross. He shields his eyes, yet fascinated by the beauty of its might. Dangerous. The flowing tide of automobiles sit poised, ready to spurt at the change from red to green. Safety is foremost. There. Made it. Now, to find his place in line.

To the north the numbers are from A to J. To the south from K to Z. His legs are already a bit stiff from the walk but he finds his way to the end of a disheveled line, nearly 100 feet from the next street—or cul-de-sac? The other line beyond the doorway looks much the same, and reminiscently familiar. Didn't lines look that way down South, during the Depression, when he stood in line with his father to get Relief through the National Recovery Act? Being a follower of rules and orders, he takes his place behind the last man in line and waits.

It is probably near seven now and he silently commands his body to wait out the travail. So many men! A raggle-taggle line, with men ever coming from dark enclosures between warehouses situated about this bleak, depressing street. The sun rises higher, burning off the smog that was, autos whiz by hurriedly, daylight manifests itself yet does not erase the desolateness of this skid row area. There is nothing for him to do in this interval but observe, reflect, ponder, speak softly to the man in front or back of him, and listen. The line behind him increases. Time is nearing. To him—as perhaps to others, also—this is a sacrifice of pride. Why is pride such an inherent factor in a man?

Give me your tired, your poor.

You've got 'em lady. (Emma Lazarus on his mind this morning. *The New Colossus*.) Look at them slobs, me included. Men of every stripe, shape, size, color, dimension. The hard-core bastards of the world, the OVER thirties, jokers who have built this country forty times over: forty times forty times forty. All here, checking out the "rumors" that this particular branch of welfare programs gives aid and assistance to single men.

The idea had always seemed fantastic to him, unbelievable,

even when he was working steady. Even now it seemed impossible. Yet it was worth a try. Jobs scarcer than hen's teeth. Rent overdue. Threatening letters from the gas company (with winter coming), the water and power company, demanding, tactful but firm. Those few marvelous friends issuing a small loan here, a smaller loan there. If aid was forthcoming it sure had better get to steppin'. Must be close to 7:15.

A man was squatting on his haunches who looked to him like a white version of James Baldwin. Very near to him were a pair of lovers: a woman with extremely skinny legs with an extremely pretty face, wearing the briefest of a mini-skirt on such a cold morning. Her lover, an extremely attractive male with lengthy sideburns and a heavy shock of brown hair, looking every inch like a movie matinee idol. One fellow, bony, with hair flowing like Jesus Christ, was squatting just ahead of him with a handsome FM radio, looking dreamy-eyed and far away, listening to Miles Davis' "Walking."

The sun was rising higher. A big ball of orange lighting up Fourth Place. The desolateness of the area was still just as stark.

Your huddled masses yearning to breathe free.

The lines were getting thicker as more men came from holes in between warehouses and from streets before and behind, most heading for the point nearest the door, causing the mob to spread over the sidewalk, near the curb. The normal pedestrian traffic going to their jobs had to veer around them. At this point their free passage was impossible.

An official from within the building appeared to admonish the men from ganging up at the door. He had to repeat his request for orderly lines over and over with a tactfulness that, at least, seemed natural to him. Bit by bit with much backing up—and still some continual "cuttin' in"—the long lines stretched nearly to the streets from both directions. The doors finally opened and the human sardines pushed forward, ever forward until they were over the threshold of their intended sanctuary. At last he was in. Now to see what he would see.

The waiting was the galling part. Once inside the room he had received a slip with a number on it and was told to wait until it was called. All the seats were taken and thick rows of men

106

formed a veritable U-shape all about the room. The room at least was warm, although stuffy. The horde was still pouring in. There was noise aplenty and continual movement. To those standing (of which he was one) there seemed only six inches of space to the shoe heel in front of him and six inches to the toe in back of him. (Don't tread on me!) A man closely resembling Moe of the Three Stooges brushed past him as green cards with numbers one through twenty were called. He was in the thick of the line in the aisle to get one of their seats. They were gobbled up hurriedly. He distinctly heard a veteran axiom: "When you move, you lose." Very true. At least he was getting "hipped" to some of it. It was hard to see a great deal because so many heads and shoulders were in the way and constantly in flux; all fidgeting, waiting and listening. Firsts for many like him, seconds and thirds for some others, depending on the number of case workers on hand.

He saw four security guards in all. Two had guns and billy clubs, one had a gun, one had nothing. Endless repeated calls of the green or gold cards sounded through a mike or out in front of the registration cubicle. One of the security guards was unerringly blatant about his calls for order and decorum. "Move out the doorway, let's keep this area clear. Move on down the aisle to your right and to my left. . . . You, mister, you with the blue sweater and the HAIR"—(a loud guffaw from the crowded room)—"please move on down the aisle, towards the rear. We've got to keep this area clear." Blue Sweater and Hair shuffles down the aisle, a surly look on his face. "All right, the rest of you fellows follow him. That's right, all the way down to the rear of the building." The throng follows reluctantly. Blue Sweater and Hair halts midway, a menacing look on his face.

The throng sidles around him, many of them all the way to the back looking like tightly packed human sardines. The aisle is now jam-packed with masculine bodies. "Thank you, gentleman, thank you. Now let's keep it that way. Let's keep this front area clear. We still have lots of people to come in here yet. All right, pay attention to the color of your card and your number . . .

"If you have a green card with numbers one through fifty, come to windows three and four. That's windows three and four." The call is redundant and, seeming more confident, the caller speaks more explicitly. He is in that group. He edges his way forward, chooses his line and, after the interminable shuffling towards the window, registers. Like the others he is told to wait until his number is called again. Nearly relaxed now he returns to what he hopes is a vacuum even for "standing room." Luckily there is a seat, albeit close in, but a seat, nevertheless. It feels so good to sit, for God's sake. "Have your identification cards ready. Your driver's license, Social Security card, hospitalization card, anything with your name on it . . .

"Now, brown/or gold cards with numbers twenty through seventy, brown cards with numbers twenty through seventy come to windows one and two. That's windows one and two. Have your identifications ready . . ." Ad infinitum. He flexes his shoulder muscles, the relief to just sit is heavenly. Not as young as he used to be. There was a time when this waiting was a breeze. "The meek shall inherit the earth." A voice from someone standing behind him, three rows back. "Yeah. All six feet of it." Solemnly. Embarrassed laughter follows. A fool joins in: "Come unto me all ye that labor, and I will give you rest." "If it'll make you feel any better I'll give you my seat." And "I'll take it. I'm tired of standing up."

"Numbers one through fifty, numbers one through fifty whose names I call will go to Room Two at your right, Room Two at your right, numbers one through fifty. . . ." The names are called from a pleasant female voice. The gathering is orderly with profusive "pardon me's" and "excuse me's." They huddle to the room and sit at classroom chairs. At least there is momentum.

The lengthy application is explained in detail, repeatedly, line by line. Like all applications of this sort, it is simple yet involved. Birth, origin, employment history, mother's first name, first husband, town, city, county (he expected them to ask what planet), why this, why that, next of kin. Some fairly easy to answer, some difficult, yet all part of that which he was seeking. He answered them all as truthfully as possible. Not lying, of course. Only not giving them *all* the truth. Besides, the answering lines were too short.

One question befuddled him—and others too, perhaps— would he be willing to work at the county hospital for seven days? Why not? No pay but he would be credited with four weeks on the CALENDAR. *What* calendar? Why? This sounded senseless. Somehow the question did not get answered. He answered "yes" on the form, more from curiosity than from fear of rejection. It would be worth it to see why he must "pay back" seven days of labor doing menial work for whatever they were going to give him. And what were they going to give *him*? He would have to talk that over with his case worker. Okay. He had all day.

More waiting. Easier now. They had his name. No longer a nonentity; all he had to do was to be patient.

A white youth was studying algebraic equations. His friend, a black, was perusing a pictorial book of Los Angeles. One man was going down row after row seeking someone who had a car. Most everyone within earshot was wondering why a ride was so important to him.

(True, this place was a long way from everything.) No, he didn't want a ride. He wanted some Blue Chip stamps. He needed enough to fill three pages. He figured that a man with a car had some in the glove compartment. He could sell the book for $1.50. What would he do with the money? "Aw, you know." And made a drinking gesture with a closed hand. Men looked at him sadly, or, even pitifully. He passed on, into a masculine sea of oblivion. Surely, the men thought, he had enterprise. So there was hope yet—for some.

The waiting was interminable as is all waiting. Men who had been processed passed back to friends the fruits of their ventures. He kept silent but kept his ears open to hear their results. Two dollars for transportation. Come back tomorrow. One man was given five bus tokens and eighty cents to go to the Human Resources Development Center in continual search of a job (all of a sudden the unemployment office had a fancy name!). It made no difference. Jobs were hard to come by anyway. He learned— just by sitting there, listening, that they paid for a week's hotel room for one without a place to stay; that they gave a food voucher for $7.25 for one who had a place to stay.

He learned that a work project bus came to this place to pick up those who answered "yes" to work at the county hospital. And when he was finally called to meet a case worker he learned that he was not to get the assistance that he sought in the first place. The one question his case worker specifically asked was: "Was he *able* and *available* for work." Naturally he answered "yes." And then they told him that unless he was physically disabled or unable to work he was not eligible for assistance. He blew his stack, of course, contending that it was unfair and, why all the paper work and why bother? Indeed, why bother?

They gave him a voucher for food worth $7.25. (Most welcome, though. His ice box and cupboard were really empty!) But at least he knew there was no something for nothing here. That only, in all analysis, he was still the same slob who helped build this damn country forty times over, times forty times forty times over ad infinitum. That the "families" were better blest and he was still the old sage at forty-four, usable only in a damned emergency that fought wars for its country's keeping and, there for the Grace of God go I and I go alone and that is the sum total of it. He came with nothing and he left with nothing.

The sun had dipped over towards Palos Verdes when he entered the street. The desolate area still hadn't changed. It looked more bleak now. At least he knew. But there was one thing he knew most of all. He had paid his dues. And he didn't owe America a goddamn thing . . .

He buttoned the last button of his overcoat, cleaned his pocket to make sure he had the right change for his bus and walked purposefully towards Seventh Street for the long ride home.

Not a Bad Dude

We talked to this cat like he was a soul brother going astray. Like we were all off on a tangent or something. He sat there in Harry Dolan's cramped office, in Harry's Buddha-like chair, in this ghettoed house turned dormitory, turned school for black writers, at the Watts Writers' Workshop. He interlaced his fingers and listened to us writers-to-be blow our minds and possibly his.

I told him he was a "boss cat" and that we dug his brother, also. I remember Vallejo Ryan Kennedy, one of our young poets, asking him a very curious question: "What street did you come down?" At first I didn't get Vallejo's point and the Senator didn't either. The Senator looked at him curiously. Then it dawned on me. And the Senator also. Because Vallejo was merely asking him if he had come down the main drag where everything was spit and polish as befits a person of his stature, garlanded with roses, the usual protocol bull, or did he actually, ride *through* the ghetto. It was confirmed that he had done both. Then, I said to myself, he had come through Charcoal Alley, which is ever garlanded with the good, the bad, and the ugly. He answered mildly, yes, he had come that way too. That he had wanted to see Watts in the flesh and some of the things that we had been bitching about since the

August revolt of 1965 that had been manifested to him were more or less true and correct. I felt from the way he answered us the possibility existed that he could be interested in our cause.

Budd Schulberg was there. A couple of other Senators, Clark and Murphy, I think. And some dudes that might have been security guards or something. Anyway, they were awfully quiet and they should have been because we were mad as hell and it was our time to bitch anyway. So, for an hour and a half we sat there and shot the breeze, talking to this man about things that sorely needed talking about.

We batted things around a bit. What was this writer's workshop? What was this bit with Watts? Did the people know what they really wanted? And were we the ones to explain it? He had heard of our strange, never before heard of black organization, making so much noise to the written words of poetry, novels, plays, our television programs, Losers Weepers, Jeepers Creepers, and all the rest that he had to see for himself. He convinced us that we were a novelty to him, and his entourage was convinced also and showed it in their expressions. They were quiet as mice when the cat's about, and didn't interrupt us at all. After all, this young bloke with a tousled forelock was having his day at our place, but in our groove, in our time, in our way. God knows we had gone their way—the villains—long enough. But, he was listening. And he was concerned. Groovy, babe.

How were we to know that this brash young man would reappear twice more to our establishment and in Watts—period—helping to champion our causes, and in the doing making him dear to our hearts, keeping him ever gentle on our minds.

He wasn't a bad dude. He spoke well, articulate, eloquent, the average American digs a family. Man, this cat was boss family—ten crumb crushers and one more on the way makes us think that he was taking care of business—and that makes for a good dude, fully acceptable in our society. For whatever that's worth.

This dude that shot him—who is he—who was he? What possible aims could he have had in killing this young valiant out to fight our present wars? So, with the death of a hero we gain an anti-hero, a nonentity and an unknowledgeable bastard and the world is worse off for its loss.

This is a salute, a praise, a benediction, a farewell; this is a letter to a soul going home; this is to a not-so-bad dude who took the time and the patience to sit and listen to a few would be writers at Douglass House those few moons ago when he came down our street, Charcoal Alley, and vowed to do something about our li'l old problems. This is forever, eternal, everlasting unto everlasting. I will miss you, baby. This is not the end of life, not the end of Douglass House. You came down our street, Charcoal Alley; white folks, black folks, people who dug you and your fabulous brother. We feel that we had something, somehow in common and you weren't such a bad dude after all.

Watts Workshop:
From the Ashes

Had it not been for an ex-World War II confidant, David Westheimer, I might never have become involved. A Houstonian like me and a prolific author, Westheimer's encouragement sharpened my perspectives to face the literary odds after my last enlistment. I followed his progress to Los Angeles, and then to his writing office in Beverly Hills. After arriving here, I was apprehensive, wondering what I could do as a struggling black writer to answer the establishment's charges of vandalism, burning and plunder that marked the black deaths and jailings of the upheaval's participants.

David strongly suggested I attend Budd Schulberg's then just beginning Creative Writers Workshop—predominantly for blacks. No joiner, I balked at first, twice, but the memory of my 10 years failing as a writer in Houston turned my thinking around. Worse, I had turned that dangerous corner of 40, and job-wise, the future could be pure hell if my attempts at writing *never* materialized.

So, with all the trepidation in the world I entered the unknown portals of Budd Schulberg's Watts Writers Workshop.

And to this day, fifteen years later, I feel it was the most sensible step I have taken.

It began in a condemned building on 103rd street, near the railroad tracks, in Watts. The Watts Happenin' Coffee House was a two-story, condemned stucco building. The floor trembled under our feet, more so when a train passed. The supporting interior columns shook; the already jagged window panes were dropping out one by one but, blessedly, not one fell on us.

But it was our guru who got every black writers' attention on those Friday afternoon meetings, 3:30 to 5 p.m. Schulberg was a robust white man in his 50s with graying hair and a disturbing (at first) stammer in his speech. But no writers snickered.

He made notes on every writer's labored, probably fearful out-loud readings to an extremely attentive and thoroughly scrutinizing audience, ready to tear a manuscript to shreds at the slightest deviation from acceptable syntax. We would often ponder, "Who was the most ferocious, Budd or us?"

Budd's notebook was Murder, Inc. It mattered not that he was a gentle man where gentleness was needed, but shuckin' and jivin' could rate the predator late readings, plus being unsanctioned by the rest of us—the severest racial critics. Save the "Charlie Browns" and the "Dadios," this was serious business.

So we listened, were circumspect and used our creative mental dexterity collectively for the first time in our lives. Although strangers, we were communicative. In this new family devotion to our own stylistic and creative literary causes was our beginning.

In 1966, on the first anniversary of the Watts upheaval, Budd's brother Stuart, of NBC, came to our little house to make a documentary, "Angry Voices of Watts," the group of seven founder-writers: Johnnie Scott, Leumas Sirrah, Jimmie Sherman, Birdell Chew-Moore, Sonora McKellar, Harry Dolan and myself.

As we arrived that Friday afternoon, one by one we were placed in positioned chairs amidst the cable-cluttered floor. The bright kleig lights fairly cooked us. On a slightly elevated stage we took movie "takes," over and over on film-less cameras. We read our missives, for sound, for clarity, for projection. By the time real film was rolling in the cameras, we were loose.

No one had to tell us that this was our moment: to issue our testaments to the world, of why an upheaval—or riots, if it suits you—occurred in this tiny corner of the modern world. We felt we knew and we *would* articulate it: in our poems, our essays, our articles, our stories long and short, now briefly cut to 3-, 4- and perhaps 5-minute typed pages. We were students, maybe even scholars, of almost unknown universities, holding in our lifetimes' grip the most immutable degrees of all: those of inequalities, injustices, discriminations of every stripe.

In that respect, and with Budd Schulberg at the helm of our expanding Writers Workshop, it was destined that we became "family," just as solidified as the photo of that group in the *Reader's Digest* that I had observed for years and wondered and wondered would there ever be a group like that in our race? Beautiful.

After moving to a refurbished rental house at 9807 Beach Street—just a short walk from our 103rd Street building—other opportunities for visibility were presenting themselves to us. Harry Dolan (the rotund director of our workshop) wrote "Loser's Weepers," his first teleplay, which was filmed entirely in Watts, using black natives of Watts as "extras." Later his "Julia" became a popular, long-running series, starring Diahann Carroll.

"Loser's Weepers" helped to launch the film acting career of Yaphet Kotto. Sonora McKellar, our versatile social activist and writer, was also Dolan's strong and dominant female lead.

Concurrently, our Watts Workshop Theater was begun and Dick Williams initiated its first full-length satirical play, "Big Time Buck White," held nightly at a burned-out supermarket, refurbished and right next to the railroad tracks.

Once a theater group was established under the Watts Writers Workshop aegis, it spawned the acting careers of Paris Earl, and three female actresses of immense and intense brillance: Odessa Cleveland, Thelidra Calhoun and Joann Bruno.

Another thirty-minute televised documentary, also by Stuart Schulberg and NBC, "The New Poets of Watts," presented yet other black voices from the Poets Corner at 9807 Beach Street. Quincy Troupe was the pride of black soul; K. Curtis Lyles, the social, street and manifest essence of our everyday black lives; Emmery Evans, our "love" poet, was the romance of soul emanating from our black skins.

Other names inundate my memory: "Ojenke," Eric Priestly, Toby Hopkins, Bill Jackson, Jimmie Sherman, Fannie Carole Brown, Leumas Sirrah, Johnnie Scott, B. Norton Olive, Ellen Brown, Jeanne Taylor, Marguerite Terrell, Blossom Powe, wife and mother of a brood of five, was ever taciturn, more inclined to listen than to participate. Her epic poem, "Black Phoenix," served as a catalyst for our second anthology, published by *Antioch Review*.

Special tribute must go to Birdell Chew-Moore and Sonora McKellar, both Watts residents, both with a fiery passion for stinging social oratory that worked so well in cementing the Watts Writers Workshop together. These two female firebrands composed with their lives the very epitome of justice, equality and black pride/dignity in their treatises. Theirs was the black woman's mystique at work.

Guadalupe De Saavedra, the lone Chicano, entered our portals with perfect timing to get his poems printed in our hardcover (New American Library) book, *From the Ashes—Voices Of Watts*.

Louise Meriwether, a late comer, published her book, *Daddy Was a Numbers Runner* through the aegis of the workshop. Mildred Walter and Lillian Tarry followed with their individual works. Writers went on either to free-lance or pursue related occupations to their initial starts.

But the biggest dividend of the workshop—after the publishing of our two anthologies, *Voices of Watts* and *Black Phoenix*, must be the experience of the traveling poets, who journeyed from one school, college or university to the other, reading our works of the "black experience." It was our workshop's first extension beyond the Los Angeles area.

At each school, our gatherings were the greatest—in our mind—ever afforded any writing group from my wildest imaginings. They hung on to our every word. But we all felt strangely prepared for the adulation. It was as if a literary soul-seeking magnet from nowhere had drawn us solidly together.

Today, fifteen years have elapsed since our literary mentor, Schulberg, took in his first student in 1965 at Watts Westminister Neighborhood Association House to talk about creative writing. I look back with a good feeling.

I remember the readings and the fear that our colleagues would tear our precious and labored manuscripts to infinitesimal shreds, as well as the pleasant uplift we felt when everyone *knew* we had it all together.

When the curious and devout came from the "far away" capitals of learning, affluence and influence—Beverly Hills, Van Nuys, Sherman Oaks, Encino, Brentwood, to name some—our image became enhanced overnight. Soon perhaps 125 established writers—some of America's best—had pledged $125 per month for our Writers Workshop House and its needs, which included occupancy for some who had no such residential havens. Then there were staff writers from *The Times*, the *Herald Examiner*, the editor from *La Opinion*. To say the least, a myriad of top name Hollywood actors and actresses journeyed to our small hamlet to nourish the seeds of budding black thespians who had been without professional counseling as we creative writers once were, now exposed to lighted elements. Between the two divisions, there isn't enough this humble writer can say of their efforts to open a way for some once-repressed talents.

No matter that our Watts Writers Workshop ended after its six-year life, there are those of us still pursuing our writing goals, who look back upon those days as days of some glories, of some gains. True, there was fire in our works—just as there was fire in the Watts upheaval. There were reams both written and unwritten of inequalities, repressions and a more than 200-year-old "hurt" our penmanship yet cries out to avenge with our testaments.

It was anger all right, a mottled anger, but the anger became beautiful, to me, because none of us was alone in his presentation.

That thought alone, of a beautiful anger, coming from more than just a single black would-be writer who adorned his walls with publisher's rejection slips in a little dinky room in Houston, to this day makes me proud that I was a member of such an elite group. In that regard, it is more than thanks for the memory. It is right on; those two words are far more enduring.

Some Notes on the Frederick Douglass Writers' House

It took me forty years to find this house.

From my lusty, infantile wailings at the foot of my mother's cotton sack in a long, dusty, cotton field in Temple, Texas, to a "suburban" ghetto section of Houston's Fourth Ward, to a riot-torn area of Los Angeles' South Side, often unaffectionately called Watts. It's a good thing, I suppose, that I was a wailer then, because the time was going to come when I would put all that wailing to use and be a writer-to-be among writers-to-be, virtually nesting in the same sort of house in which I was born, and similar to the one in which I was raised! If this is poetic justice then, the justice—delayed as it is, to me—must somehow be fitting.

The first few years were kind of normal: that is, for a black kid, being poor and what not. Doing chores at home after school—and were they many! Reading storybooks and the Bible and poems from Whittier, Poe, and Robert Service, to the aged and infirm as well as to many illiterate, direct descendants of slaves, plus making damn near any kind of hustle to get a few bucks to help keep our family going. Shining shoes, for instance, at five cents a pair (I made a young mint on weekends!), throwing handbills on Friday evenings for grocery stores (now such things are corporations), selling the *Houston Chronicle* and *Houston Post* on a secondhand bicycle—bought with extreme thrift—on Saturday nights and early Sunday mornings. Always keeping one eye open for malicious white drunks in speeding cars, threatening to run us over; young white boys, our own ages, who traveled in gangs and beat the snot out of us when we were too slow of foot or wheel; and the ever-prevalent "boys in blue" who called us "nigger" with varying timbres of voice, which, by knowing, and by knowing how to "act" in those strange, unfamiliar white areas, prevented some severe head-whippings.

Then I was eighteen and off to the wars—bless the Saviour—although in a segregated army, company, battalion. Having a freedom that was not really a freedom but which contained some helpfully lusty incentives within the interlude and the varied climes where it was my fortune to be stationed. Here, in my ever-searching solitudes, did I become more associated with books, thinkers, and writers of books. Even here, my old adolescent processes of reading and knowing and remembering stood me in good stead. There were many I met along that way, in that war, who desired with all their hearts to know what there was to be known. Many who had "escaped" their own miserable Southern hamlets, even as I; many from the canebrakes, the cotton patches, the eternal "sharecropping," the muddy Mississippis, and the aloof and lifeless ghettos, who came, *willingly*, as conscripts to serve—however, supposedly, "utilitarian"—as soldiers in this war that was to end all wars. Now I had a built-in, within-me sort of freedom: some call it perspective. I *still* call it freedom. *I* could help those who wanted to caress words, sentences, paragraphs— their meanings—to their bosoms, and to feel that they walked in a knowledgeable light and that once they learned, they possessed a power that prevented them from ever returning to the yoke of ignorance and a borrowed plow simply because of ignorance alone, and that they could go on from there in pursuit of other greater knowledge and, consequently, more comfortable living.

I must have been the most "natural" teacher the world has ever known. I sure didn't have any degrees. Didn't have a diploma, even then. (That came later, via a lot of correspondence

121

courses and things.) All I really had was zeal, interest, enthusiasm. I guess *they* needed *that*. I had a good memory. I wasn't afraid to face a class and give a lesson. I suppose necessity overrode fear—in this case. And I was young. That helped. My reputation for studiousness always seemed to precede me somehow from camp to camp. I wasn't a catalyst—I don't think—but I was often called on to work in anything that *taught*. As a consequence I continued to seek out more knowledge, to know and to observe.

My horizons broadened with these now anchored-in incentives. I even stayed in the military longer because of the continuing traveling, because the desire to know things seemed to ever rekindle itself. And, like the Big Bear making his big strides across the Milky Way, I felt like the baby bear making some baby strides across continents other than this one—with the help of a journeying, military mendicant. I was its foil to hawk her wares. I was one of its musician sentinels, who often doubled in brass, from trumpet to trombone, it seemed, from one coda to the next as the symphonic pages were turned. Because for every area we halted in to hawk our military wares I found or established a symbol of learning for those other black masses in my midst who wanted to improve their minds and thereby destroy the myth that intelligence and learning only favored a few.

In this all-black, military world with which I was associated for nearly eight years was another, historical black world that existed in musty, black-imbued books in segregated camps, in post and station libraries. We found many black heroes there: Harriet Tubman, Frederick Douglass, Booker T. Washington, Alexandre Dumas, and many, many others. They were fiery spokesmen, natural-born rebels, lovers of freedom, abolitionists. I wrote for, of, and about the comrades in my midst because there was seldom anyone else in our immediate group who could do so or who *would* do so. It boosted my morale while elevating theirs. It established my ultimate aims while infusing them with a status quotient to their immediate worlds that were so many-faceted and important—just like their own white brothers in their many white camps. Suddenly, reading and knowing and the desire to impart knowledge of things that were, that came before, that came afterwards, became all-encompassing. Suddenly I *knew* what I wanted to do most of all: I wanted to communicate. Dammit! I wanted to write!

Then I was back in Houston again. The traveler at home to rest. The chicken to roost. Now for the assembling of thousands of notes and minute impressions. Now the collecting of past fires and often repressed heats. Now the aura of various syntaxes abounded before me, above the clouds, beneath my pillow, in the demeanor of people in my midst, in the trouble of black folk everywhere. In an Alabama bus-boycott, a poem; in the merciless slaughter of black innocents in Sharpesville, Africa, a poem; in a white youth's spitting in a young Negro girl's face at a university, a poem; in the senseless lynching of a Negro man, a poem; in the senseless castration of a Negro man on a lonely Southern road, with his love, his woman, a poem, an epistle, a decree; in the wanton killing of a Negro soldier in a German field a story: in a collective round-up of many incidents, involving many colored people and many people of color, from many provocations, many aggrandizements, many frustrated attempts of many black people to rise above the now stereotyped status of the lowly, a book, a huge book, to ever trumpet to the world. And more stories, a play, an essay, an article. The written word. The word. I*m die eingang vor dass wort.* In the beginning was the word. A surfeit of impressionable tidbits that flit across my mind's eye from time to time, and I feel the need to commit it all to paper.

The rejection slips come back almost faster than I can send these missives out. Too late. Too early. Doesn't fit in with our current needs. Sorry. Sorry. Sorry. Some, never to return. Some irretrievably lost. Other bits of knowledge gained from bumming around so many libraries flash across my mind's eye during these last ten years at home, causing me to ponder: Writers' Conference, Breadloaf, Martha's Vineyard. Places so far away. Writing groups that are held together by one common bond: to communicate. The wonderment if such places are exclusively *white* or if open only to *published* Negro writers. An impasse looms.

New Negro writers on the horizon: now here, now there. One, extremely gifted, each new work of his better than the last: *Go Tell It on the Mountain, Notes of a Native Son, Nobody Knows My*

Name, Another Country. A sudden glance in a bookstore reveals yet another racial face on the cover of another epistle, some ten years in the doing, with a highly provocative title: *A Chosen Few.* There are others, yet distant from here. How did they start getting *their* works published? What simple quirk of fate turned their blinking amperes into blazing kilowatts? What the hell did publishers want?

The laboring goes on. It has to. I am too much past the point of no return. I am too deeply committed to my calling. The little construction jobs that perpetuate my existence are few and far between. They don't pay enough, nor do they last. Where I was naive and subservient in my formative years, I am belligerent and filled with aggression now. I've got to help kill the cursed stereotypes rather than docilely sustain them. Nip them in the bud at the outset. This is dangerous because it is believed to be anti-social on my part. So I often lose that which I urgently need more than the mere publishing of a manuscript.

The years pass. The people die. Both of them. The mother and the father. Their youngest son's only accomplishment before their deaths is a full-page, complete-spread story and photo of me and my frustrating attempts at getting my work published. They read that an excerpt from my play, *Bye, Bye, Black Sheep,* has been put on in a local theater. They read of my numerous other works and are startled because I could never issue these declarations before and truly *convince* them. At last, at least, they are proud of this. Because writing is an intangible thing. No one can *see* a writer *writing* like they can see a sculptor *sculptoring,* a painter *painting,* a pianist *piano-ing.* Writing is a gift that completely envelops the intellect and keeps it hidden, until the testaments are blazoned on papers of the world, if the penman is thus lucky. It keeps its adherents studious. Some may prefer a beard to build an image, but on me it scratches. I'm an introvert and easily touched anyway: for true impressions or false ones. My successes or failures have to be worked out by me from there on.

Finally, after ten years of this futility, my first cousin, who has longed to see me in the twenty years we've been apart, sends for me. I hesitate, dreading to leave home, and especially those that I hold dear—the midway mark of forty fairly whistling around the corner—to come to this place, to L.A. And, ultimately to Watts. Reluctantly, I go.

Here my chances for survival alone are eight million to one. Seven times greater than at home. Gregariousness abounds. In a sea of people is a man alone here. They rush to and fro. The forest is too thick to see the trees. Jobs that appear on the surface to be magnanimous and lasting fade out before I can get solidly entrenched. This is a big town, with big-town ways and with big-town temper. I arrive here on the last night of the Watts upheaval. A terrible time for a Southerner with limited laboring skills to be job-hunting. Occasionally I ride a bus out to Watts to view the havoc's remains. The ghetto that still exists reminds me of the one I left behind; only mine was infinitely smaller in size—but not degree. Actually I feel a kinship, an almost natural metamorphosis, as though I've been here all along. In spirit I have. I know I'll be back.

During my ramblings while trying to establish myself as a citizen here, I locate a former friend from home: David Westheimer. He is doing very well with his latest book, *Von Ryan's Express*, which has now become a movie. He helps me out considerably. (Thank God for the David Westheimers of this world!) He impresses upon me the need to join the Budd Schulberg Writers' Class. I remember this guy's works. I had read *What Makes Sammy Run?* and *The Disenchanted*. Had seen the "The Harder They Fall" and "On The Waterfront" as movies. At the time, it seemed incongruous to me that he was heading a writers' group in Watts, or anyplace else for that matter. I don't know why. I didn't want to be taught how to write. I knew how to do that. I wanted to be taught how to be *published*. Of course I didn't know the set-up. I was in an economic fog. I let David's suggestion ride a while, meantime becoming familiar with Los Angeles and trying to keep the wolf of starvation from my door.

It was a bitch all the way. This place is colder than an Eskimo's nose in the Klondike. It's amazing how the many Southern people that one meets here change so radically within the flux of a big city's momentum. There were more people of the earth here, just like me, who beat me out of my few pitiful shekels from my hard labors, than one could shake a stick at—and who then got swallowed up in the vastly tentacled mires of L.A.! My landlord and I were perennially at loggerheads over *his* rent money. At one point I slept in my car for five nights—straight! (But they were very tolerant, very considerate with me and my shenanigans. I don't owe them as much money now as I do gratitude.) The only collateral I had for subsistence during my acute joblessness was my typewriter, my veritable right arm with which to solicit work. I pawned it—as though pawning my soul!—to carry me over to another hopeful day that did not bring much hope. But I hopped, skipped, jumped, loped over many minor jobs to scrape up that twenty-five bucks to get it back. I think hell itself will have to freeze over before I go that route again.

During another visit to David Westheimer's "writing house" he gave me a copy of his latest book, *My Sweet Charlie*, and repeated the suggestion that I attend Schulberg's writing class. This time I didn't hesitate. From that first day I knew that it was to such a group as this that I had always wanted to belong.

We were given an assignment. "What caused the riots?" and "Would they occur again?"—all in conjunction with our writing skills and the Poverty Program. When our works were turned in and assessed by Budd Schulberg it was considered apt material for filming a documentary. It was titled "The Angry Voices of Watts." Stuart Schulberg, the producer, presented in beautiful, pictorial prose the very essence of the inequities of which we wrote. My works—as well as those of the rest of the class—were at last published.

Then, a house *for* writers was leased, with the prime intention of establishing it as a place for talented writers to live and pursue their craft in, particularly those with "no visible means of support," who are otherwise exposed to the stigma of colossal drifting and the woeful anxieties of repressed communication. I see it in this light because I was once a drifter. And God knows, I've been entombed in that "no visible means of support" bag many times over. But the most endearing part of this gesture by Budd Schulberg, and other men of his stamp, is that of all the Arts, the one that is the *least* concrete especially among members of my

126

race, *this* one, that of writing creatively, has at last been given some recognition.

As for the house itself, it was no fabulous pad by even a writer's stretch of imagination. It was certainly one from my past. It had been thoroughly lived in and just needed some "fixing." Actually, it might have been the type of house that Frederick Douglass himself lived in, pursued his dream of freedom in, was closeted in to learn the alphabet and—consequently—to be a master of the written and uttered word. And I was given a chance to work on it and in it, to help shape it up to some comfortable degree of livability.

This is probably the first house of its kind in history, and I, for one, am certainly glad it's here. Now our present writers' group, to which I am happy to belong, will hold our meetings here, read our works, old and new, and share our knowledge of outlets to which to send our labored testaments across the land.

We are all in accord with the zealousness of that symbolic man, Frederick Douglass, who taught himself to read and commit his thoughts to paper, enjoining us to become equally zealous, now solidified in our unity—and ever hoping by our conjoined efforts to help improve the ills of the world, and of the black man in particular, by shouting our declarations to the world. Indeed, to the whole universe!

Stars in a Black Night—
Beacon for a Black Dawn

Los Angeles—as opposed to New York—has long been a mecca by and for black entertainers.

It's a kind of beacon, flashing its intermittent beam to the Texans, Georgians, Alabamans, Mississippians and others below the Mason-Dixon line. True, the North and East have their bizarre and innate soul talents there too; (chitterlins are sold all over New York, I know: I've been there; I've bought them). But Los Angeles is the home of the spectacular. It's the residence of Hollywood. It is not the most cultural place in the world, but it has always had the germ or bacteria for it. And this covers a multitude of sins, of sinning and success.

As a boy growing up into adulthood in Houston, before I was inducted into the Army, I was exposed to what I thought was the best that West Coast entertainers had to offer our generation. And just about always, the fountain spring was Los Angeles. Growing up in Houston for me and many of my equally young comrades was more of a lark than a hindrance. There was always something or someone to aspire to. Entering our teens, we got turned on to Ralph Cooper and Nina Mae McKinney and never missed a flick when those two superstars were featured. There was also a black film producer named Oscar Micheaux, who produced films like *The Wind from Nowhere, The Adventures of Martin Eden* and a novel titled *The Case of Mrs. Wingate.* (I guess he was black; at least he seemed black to me). With Houston's normal segregations of that period, Micheaux's efforts at piloting a racial course of dignity in film entertainment filled our young minds with enthusiastic expectations from year to year. Always in the forefront of our minds was what Hollywoodian fantasies would come out next. Expecially movies concerning blacks or just having blacks in them. To say nothing about black musical entertainers that were just about always on the West Coast.

We looked forward to seeing them all. Just seeing a black in a movie was ever an inducement to save our money for the day a film with "some of us in it" would come to our segregated movie houses. Willie Best, Louise Beavers, Stepin Fetchit, Mantan Moreland, Lena Horne, Eddie (Rochester) Anderson, many whose names escape me now—we looked forward eagerly to viewing again and again and again. Sometimes we'd be lucky enough to see Butterbeans and Susie doing their vaudeville act at a local theater. They were considered too risque for us young Baptist children. But we saw them anyway, somehow, as children are wont to do with things that are forbidden to them. And laughed like crazy loons at their crazy antics. Or Bill (BoJangles) Robinson—"everything is copacetic"—making those movies with Shirley Temple, wearing his favorite dancing shoes and that ingratiating toothy smile; and she a child actor we knew and loved so well—mostly because she was starring with him—keeping in step with those magic dancing feet brought joy, great joy.

Something happened one year in my youth that stopped me from seeing movies for a time. It was D. W. Griffith's *Birth of a Nation*. All those lynchings of my black people made me leave that theater cursing my blackness, feeling inferior and afraid. And there was no way I could change either. It held me in limbo for a long time. Until I learned to embrace anger, hold it close to my chest and nurture it like it was gold. Anger to fight back. And still hold some pride for the only country I really knew: America. No matter how much I revered my African heritage. Wheels were turning in our behalf: the NAACP and the Urban League were blooming, novels and books and essays by blacks, for blacks, of blacks were giving us hope; and in the hope, courage; and in the courage, incentives; and in the incentives, action; and, bless God, in the action; manhood and womanhood, strength and growth. Damnit to hell, it was great being black!

Youth reaches a plateau; one does not stay forever young. One moves and lives and has his being. One sallies forth. As I and my associates did. The ugly incidents of our past were put in the backs of our minds. Not forgotten, mind you, only put aside as future memories for future courses of life that—if we lived—we could dredge up and thus make our adult lives better because we would be prepared. We would never be hurt that badly again. We would teach our kin, we would show them how to squelch lies, show them how to reveal truths,we would allow no man, no person,to stomp on our culture, our worth, our lives, our dreams, our sacred honors, our desires, our right to be!

And we grew. As all youth grows, eventually. I went off to war to serve my country. Gladly. (God, I was sick of Texas!) I even saw Los Angeles for the first time. Walked Hollywood Boulevard and Sunset Boulevard and gawked and gaped like the average tourist looking for the "famous" to brush against my elbow. Saw and heard Louis Jordan singing and blowing—on that ever famous saxophone, "Caldonia, Caldonia, What Makes Your Big Head So Hard—Mop!" And Eddie Haywood playing "Begin the Beguine." And remembering later Cole Porter's statement that he wished "he could have written it the way Eddie Haywood played it." Being here felt good like a dog. Saw an early Nat (King) Cole trio doing his own "Route 66" and "Sweet Lorraine"—among others—and had myself a ball!

I walked Central Avenue where all the happenings were. And seeing jillions of blacks being busy, busy, busy. And eating juicy, spicy, pink barbecue that was so much like Texas that it seemed I had never left home. And black waitresses that didn't have Gloria Marshall's stamp all over them. And Cecil Gant singing "I Wonder" and playing pool at the Hollywood Canteen with a white soldier who beat me sixteen games out of twenty. And leaving Los Angeles convinced that it was one helluva, swelluva swinging town and someday I just might come back to live; but fearful that it was earth-quake-prone yet grateful that it had so much ocean and so many beaches and a guy—if he was lucky—could take him a flying jump buck naked in one of them sometimes. That's what we used to do in the creeks in Houston when we were kids. Damn near everybody in Los Angeles had swimming pools—even some blacks—and tall, swaying palm trees grew on every other street, and L.A. didn't have Houston's heat and humidity.

I served my time in the war, making my parents happy because my father had served in World War I; and I stayed in longer with two reenlistments because I wanted to get a good bird's eye view of the world, a world I had known mostly from *National Geographic*. And I had seen rivers unimaginable and traversed some of them on ships and got sicker than a dog and thought that more black men and women should leave those sometimes miserable boondocks and take a plane and see the world because there was damn sure a lot of it for them to see.

Now back home in Houston. Getting turned on to James Edwards' role in *Home of the Brave*. (A veteran's preference: any movie with soldiers in it, color notwithstanding, so long as it wasn't silly.) And when my friends and I saw Sidney Poitier and Tony Curtis in *The Defiant Ones*, we rapped about it for days. We were really incensed that this black cat, after being in that Southern prison for so long, now had a chance to make it and gave it up! Later for that jazz, we said. It fair blew our minds. (We loved Sid. That went without saying.) No black man could ever be that big a fool, being cooped up in prison all those years, and checking out those freight train schedules, heading North, to freedom, getting on and chucking that one last chance just to save a hunkie's often bigoted behind. No way. That's a no-no. My friends and I didn't like that worth a damn. It was like the old black joke, I guess where the rabbit is being severely chased by the hounds and men with guns. He passes by a turtle and the turtle asks: "Are you gonna make it, man?" And the rabbit answers: "Hell, I got to make it." That's the way we felt about Sid. He should have made it. We also felt that sometimes black people display the courage of an idiot to save the life of a known bastard.

131

But that was Entertainment; and we lived it to the fullest.

Time moved along and we moved with it. I was not over-joyed when Butterfly McQueen won an Academy Award for her role in *Gone With the Wind*. For what? I asked myself. For being a condescending servant? No way. That's a no-no. But when Poitier walked up there to get his for *Lilies of the Field*, I walked by his side with him. Because by now I had learned to appreciate dignity. And thank God Sid was black—I mean *black* like me—and had taught himself, for the most part, the art of elocution and drama. Now there was a chance that both of us could be heard.

Today I am a tenant here. Almost eleven years of my life wrapped up in this town of sin, sinners and seekers of success. I've gone back down Hollywood Boulevard and Sunset Boule-vard and even in 1976 there are echoes of what used to be. Memories of Harry (the Hoot) Gibson, or Sugar Chile Robinson, the Ink Spots, the Delta Rhythm Boys, white bands or orchestras such as Stan Kenton, Charlie Barnett, Gene Krupa, Woody Herman; supper clubs such as the Last Work, or Club Alabama; the Million Dollar Theater; boogie-woogie; streetcars (whose tracks have gone into oblivion, replaced by screeching rubber of today's twin-belted radials); of hicks from the sticks—like me—who have grown older, with our knowledge of the times and its changes; and a Civic Center that does its damndest to bring us culture both foreign and domestic; and a Hollywood that knows that it cannot—anymore—bring us movies that don't have blacks. We're conglomerate—whether we like it or not.

Ned Bobkoff and Me

For almost ten years, in my hometown of Houston, Texas, I was the only black writer I really knew.

Struggling, unpublished, hustling construction jobs, I was determined to one day get my work published. After trying every gambit a fledging writer would try—after submitting manuscripts, getting rejection slips back by the boxcar, posting them on a 4'x4' plyboard on my wall—I thought I'd try yet another tack. I started paying attention to a young man, who happened to be Jewish, who was writing and putting on plays like a horse trot, in a small theater in Houston called The Hamlet.

My new friend was Ned Bobkoff and I took to him like a duck to water. Mostly because he was an underdog like me. But more than that, because he was putting on avant-garde plays in the Richmond Avenue neighborhood, which always—especially in my formative years—had been staunchly secessionist, which fairly reeked with antebellum mores, regardless of the changing times. I thought Ned Bobkoff was either brave, foolhardy, or the most intense idealist that Houston had ever known. He was probably all three, and enjoyed every minute of it. In some ways we were two of a kind.

At this point I had written darn near every type of writing around: chapters for my novel, sixteen short stories, essays, a book of poetry, news and feature articles for two of Houston's black newspapers. I had tried the local yearly creative writer's contest for three years running. And had lost out each time. (I'm black, my experiences are black, and I incorporate them in my writings within the scope of a black-white world. But *that's* no guarantee that I'm supposed to make it.)

Worst of all, I was no spring chicken. Hell, I was nearing forty. One should have made it by then, our elders had taught us. My friends and associates were *eagerly* looking forward to my success. So was I. My father—alive then—was wondering what I was putting down, for I was always seeming to him like a down-and-outer; he was forever admonishing me to "get a decent job" and "settle down." But I was living alone and making my own hustles, so I didn't have to listen to that mess every day.

But I had always felt that I was cut out to be a writer. As a youth I had read to the blind, the bedridden, the moribund in our ghettos. (Mostly I read them the Bible, our mainstay; readers were few, to say the least.) Writing was lonely, but I was tuned in to words and her winged creatures fluttering and screeching past my window in pondered great books—creatures that would fill my life with meaning. I knew that the study of writing would be a long and lonely crusade, but I could live with that. My biggest hassle was in keeping a steady job and a roof over my head. I never liked writing in the gutter.

* * * * *

It was the marvelous "Naked City" that inspired me to write a TV play. That series was *too* much! The voluble intensity of Paul Burke was just what I wanted an actor to do. I knew I had stories like that in my mind. And I worked at it like a dog. I also knew that Houston's *cultured* mores wouldn't let blacks enter their theaters for play viewing just like that, without a hassle. "Sorry" this and "sorry" that and "no night for nigras to see this play" were standard excuses. (It would be such a big help to see a good play every now and then.)

Yet every week, when I bought a *Houston Post*, I could read something about Ned's theater. I followed him religiously for over a year. I kept viewing "Naked City," and getting moved. Then I tried my hand. It was a great idea, I thought: an ex-GI transplanted from the South, and a good cop who more and more understands the dude. But it got too long . . . and too strong! Then the teleplay became a play. Acts I, II, III. . . .

I worked into the Texas summer nights. Sweating profusely in the one room of my Louisiana friend's apartment upstairs. Working my behind off as Hurricane Carla besieged us for three days while live power lines swirled about our downstairs porch lintels. It didn't matter. I was in heat, in love with my writing. I pounded away on my monthly rental Underwood and my play was born, by God!

Then it was done.

But who could I give it to?

There was only one person handy. . . .

II—I was working with an independent contractor, installing kitchen cabinets into new apartments. I had only recently gotten the job as a helper, and was hoping that it would stretch out long enough for me to make some financial waves. My paycheck wasn't magnificent, but it made for a living. Ned Bobkoff's Hamlet theater was around the corner and a few blocks down Richmond Avenue from my job. After getting a hot sandwich from the segregated eatery, I decided to get my play into his hands. (I had it tucked between my t-shirt and my outer shirt.) It was with trepidation that I approached Ned's living quarters, down a brief sidewalk adjacent to The Hamlet. Me, my play, my grease-stained cheeseburger and all.

Ned's father answered the door. A Houston taxi driver, he looked about what I thought a Jewish father would look like: a little gray around the ears, baldish, not too short. He had that no-nonsense "I'm-used-to-meeting-people" look. And that spoke reams.

"I'm a writer," I stammered out, feeling foolish and looking like the working man I was, soiled clothes and all. (I felt like an idiot. A fledging writer could try a stunt like this in the East or on the West Coast; but this was Houston and therefore Home, and I was a nobody, even to my parents.) "I know I don't *look* like a writer"—not having the faintest idea what a writer looked like. "But I am a writer and I want Ned Bobkoff to look at this play of mine." With that I thrust the manila envelope in his hand and started to walk away.

"Hey! Wait a minute! . . . What is it, Dad?" It was Ned, even shorter than I, his face more bronze than his father's, with a smile of surprise a mile wide.

"He says he doesn't *look* like a writer," the father mimicked, making me feel even more like an idiot. "But he gave me this script to give to you."

"Well, let me see it," Ned said eagerly, surprising me for some reason, taking the envelope from his father and pulling the bulky script out. I was fidgety.

"Come in, come in," Ned said, glancing at my name and address on the top page and at my opening narrative.

"I can't," I stammered furiously. "I've only got thirty minutes for my lunch break. Just read it when you get a chance. My phone number is at the top there. I'm at home nights. I've just got to go."

And I moved out smartly, walking a block down the street. Then I ripped open my sandwich bag and began to gobble my sandwich. Out of their view, I was just another black nonentity, eating my lunch as though I had no cultural value whatever, no sense of decorum. Just another nigger hurriedly masticating his food so he could get back on that white man's job. In the meantime I was smiling to myself because I had put my masterwork in the hands of a writer-director to read when he got the chance. I didn't give a damn if he took all year. I had broken a barrier in Houston, some "gentleman's agreement," with a last-ditch determination to get a reading at *home.* I chomped on in relish. No cheeseburger ever tasted so good.

III—It was nearly three weeks later that I found a free day to go to The Hamlet and talk with Ned about my piece. We sat in his comfortable home. Although he went at my play with hammer and tongs, his criticisms were helpful. (God, did this man know theater!)

His theater-in-the-round staging wouldn't seat too many people. (Just enough to pay the rent, I'd say.) But Ned was happy with striving to attain his goal. His father carried much of the financial load for both the theater and the home. A huge keg of dark beer was the main concession, which patrons bought throughout a performance, contributing to the "survival" kitty. I thought Ned was a stone genie, the way he gathered his actors and actresses to perform his plays. Most of them—black and white— were struggling like him to keep the wolf of starvation from their doors. Ned was a showman. Writers had things to say. The Third World was here already and he was engrossed in it.

Events moved swiftly after that meeting. My cabinet-helper job had played out, and I had been recommended to a new contractor-builder who had just finished a sixteen-unit, studio-type one-bedroom; I was due to start cleaning them up soon. But first I was aroused by a loud knocking on my door from a *Post* writer, Charlotte Phelan: "All right, Jackson, come on out of there!"

Believe it or not, I was ready to chicken out. The idea of suddenly becoming a celebrity in Houston was scary. But I wasn't so ungallant that I'd keep a lady journalist waiting. So I chested up and went out that door.

I sat in the front seat of her car, trying to seem aloof, and oblivious to passing, curious blacks who lived in my neighborhood. "All right," she said. "How long have you been writing? Is this your first play?" All business, this woman. I felt uncomfortable, simply because she *was* white, and we were in my ghetto. And a patrolling white policeman—even on a bright spring morning—could read all sorts of things into that union.

"How long? I don't know. Forever, it seems. Since I was eighteen and in the Army air force. Writing letters to my comrades' folks and girlfriends. I got so good at it that I began to charge them for it . . . especially when they came to me at oddball hours of the day or night—even when I was on pass or at the USO.

The money wasn't much; but they paid willingly. They thought my writing was more imaginative and colorful than theirs. Who knows? I was there, we all had oodles of time, and deep within, I was happy to do it."

And it just all poured out. About keeping a daily diary on the Liberty ship, going to Italy. About being a feature writer for our mimeographed battalion newspaper, and covering a disabled B-25 bomber that was threatening to crash. I took a jeep from the motor pool without permission and picked up each crew member as he bailed out; I put men and parachutes in the jeep as we jogged and jumped over the Italian field. The special interview with the pilot, who made a safe (but scary) landing after all, saved my bacon (for stealing the jeep).

About being stationed in Austria. "You think the Peace Corps is new?" I told her. "We had our own Peace Corps. A Negro's face goes before him, and it took plenty of kindness, patience and understanding for him to make friends. Those people in those little hamlets way back there behind those hills would take one look at us and disappear.

"But we would go back in there Thanksgiving or Christmas and pitch a party for them. We gave them tobacco, snuff, goodies, food, necessities. Wherever there is a Negro, there's a Peace Corps."

On and on, spilling my guts, letting all those repressed memories hang out. Repressed because many black people—especially women—did not want to hear of the black soldier's exploits overseas. And the southern white man for damn sure did not want to hear it at all. No wonder I was paranoiac! My society had clamped a strong lid over my talent, and I had failed to break its bonds.

Charlotte Phelan looked at me with an expression not usual to reporters—a look more in awe than anything.

"I suppose this could go on?" she said. "That there's more? These things happened to you?"

I looked at her squarely and said, "Yes. It certainly could. There are too many stories about black people that look like they will never be told. That's why there's a need for writers like me
. . . .

"It looks like here I am. Everybody says, 'You've got great potential,' and pats you on the back. But you've got to start somewhere, but how?

"Day after day, year after year, there's old James, still on a job like this. Those people around that neighborhood where I live, where I grew up—my friends—they want me to succeed.

"They don't want you as a failure... I may give in sometimes, but I don't give up."

Then came the photographer. On the third day of my cleanup job, he walked in the apartment room amidst my swirl of dust. "I want you to do as you do every day," he said with perfect ease. That was easy. I just grabbed my broom and continued sweeping—though not as vigorously as I usually did, out of respect for his lens. He took several pictures. Then just as suddenly as he had come, he was gone—"Thank you very much, Mr. Jackson." All of sudden I was a *Mister*.

In his wake were the puzzled white contractors and laborers gawking at me as if to say: "Who in hell is he? What was *that* all about?" I was beginning to enjoy the notoriety. After all, it wasn't *how* a writer got started; it was the fact that he got started at all!

Of course, as a double safety, I displayed more vigor than usual—though not too much; this was still a job that paid by the hour, and I had to make it stretch as much as possible.

IV—The whole thing was beautiful. Charlotte Phelan sure let it all hang out. The photographer got the real me: broom and all. Only the title bugged me: "DREAMER." I hated that. It was the damndest truth, but I still hated it. Yet it was there, my photograph was there, and my life's dream was there, exposed for all of Houston's readers. I was both elated and morose. I didn't want to make waves through this kind of media. Not really. Literary blacks weren't always in abundance and how would any of them react to my being singled out to represent our race? (That inferiority feeling again.) But who can pick his entree for success? Be glad, stupid, I told myself. You're in: a nonentity no more.

* * * * *

139

When I arrived at The Hamlet that night, I was late. Outside the closed doors of the inside corridor, I heard snatches of dialogue. They sounded so familiar yet theatrical. Then it dawned on me that those were my words, my thoughts.

"That's the very reason you're in this trouble today," said my character, Jean, on stage. "Getting mixed up in somebody else's problems, and with a woman that's not even in your own race. What's so killing about it, she wasn't nothing but a street woman! That's what all your smooth words did for you. All your knowledge, all your education, all your books. In the end (she points to Dusty's jail cell), this is all you end up with!"

(Dusty stands and stares at her, seeming a little shocked. He gestures in seeming resignation.)

"And don't tell me that old psychology stuff about 'Nobody understands me,'" Jean continued. "Phooey! I've heard that gawk so much I could vomit. You're not a baby. You know right from wrong. You should have stayed in your place."

"God Almighty!" said Dusty, smiling through it all. "Why are women so beautiful when they're angry?" He paused. "I knew you were feminine all along. I like that. . . . Got doggit, I sure do!"

Then he turned serious. "Don't kid yourself. People understand me. I've gone to a lot of trouble to *make* people understand me. Don't forget: I'm a Southerner and white folks used to use us for playthings when I was a boy. They might bring one of us into a white-filled room, and we, or I, would sing at their commands, strain those incredibly stratospheric notes of *The Star-Spangled Banner*. And do you know what? None of them ever asked us to sing *The Negro National Anthem!* No, no. Not once!

"Then they would applaud in the most perfunctory manner, as if they didn't want to abuse their tender palms. We were sent scuttling back to the kitchen then, where my Great Aunt worked. There I'd sit in the lovely white kitchen, immaculately scrubbed and shining bright. A kitchen that both my Aunt and I scrubbed like crazy. I'd sit on a stool or something—not on the 'good stuff'—and watch my Aunt work.

"I saw something else, also. I saw my Aunt's eyes brimming over with tears as she did her work. Crying because my little early-acquired talents were abused and stepped on and mocked by all those grown-up, 'superior' white people in that living room. Much as she loved me and as much as she loved to have me come over and visit her on her job, she never again attempted to get white people to let us sing or recite poetry in that house. Or any other white house. Believe me. My Aunt understood. And not too long afterward, when she died, I understood. And I have been making people understand me ever since. . . . "

I tiptoed through the aisle in semidarkness to a seat near one of Ned's paying customers. Ned was in the middle rear, to my left, standing, in that intensity that so easily enveloped him, signaling cues. Save for the sporadic noises of cars on Richmond Avenue, the tempo and sound of the actors held us in rapt subservience. Of course, I was more moved than most, I thought. Ned put on only one act from my play, but it was one of the meatier ones and his kids really put their hearts into it. God Almighty, I was moved!

Things fell back into their normal pattern. I held on to my cleanup job. Ned continued to put on his nightly one-acters, most of which he wrote. I continued to follow his exploits in the *Houston Post*, now my favorite Texas paper. Then, just when I thought I would be seeing more of him and working with him to revise my play, Ned left the city.

Fall had set in, and our Indian summer was giving ground to cooler evenings.

V—In his letter to me, Ned described the lack of patronization for The Hamlet. He had had it. He *had* to get into the mainstream. He was going to hitchhike to New York and then to Edinburgh, Scotland! He wanted to attend the Edinburgh play festival, to stage and direct his plays as well as an excerpt of mine. Then he would go to Israel to do the same thing.

What an adventurer, I thought. If I had had that drive, I would have gone with him. But loner that I was, I would do my thing my way. After all, to the eyes of the world, he was a white boy: My blackness would be a liability to him, and his whiteness would be a burden to me. I couldn't have stood those crosscurrents.

So I bided my time in the big H. I worked on my book of short stories, on chapters of my novel. I saw both of my parents buried. My jobs got scarcer and scarcer. And finally, like Ned, I'd had enough of Houston, a place I loved and where I had so many roots. The age of forty was whistling around the corner. The age where black Houstonians expected to be *there*. The call of the wild geese beckoned me; and like the wild geese, I felt sure that there was a better lake farther ahead, and that I would spot it in flight. So I felt I had to go.

Then Ned came back.

VI—We went to a bar and sipped beer and talked—that is, Ned talked; I listened eagerly. He still looked lean and trim and brown, and his brown eyes behind his horn-rimmed glasses were sad and impish. He told me of hitchhiking to New York; finagling a plane ticket (one way) to Edinburgh; then waiting, waiting in line, waiting to go through Customs.

"James, there I was in line, only three or four people in front of me. I was elated, I'll admit that. Look at how far I had come. In my bag I had a bunch of scripts, including yours. I could see myself walking the streets of Edinburgh, observing the theaters, meeting the people, planning the plays, casting the actors. And all from my shoestrings and some help from my friends.

"The tall, lanky guy in front of me was a *stone* hippie: scraggly beard, hair growing down to his behind, looking every bit like Jesus Christ; I'll bet he didn't have five, six dollars in his pockets. Hell, neither did I, but at least I wasn't dressed like a bum.

"I heard the customs inspector ask him what was he—meaning his visitor's status. I heard the hippie answer, 'A tourist.' The inspector passed him on.

"Then it was my turn. He looked me over, at my passport, my luggage. He asked me what I was.

"'A director,' I answered, feeling a bit smug about it all.

"'Where is your work permit?' he asked.

"'Work permit?' I answered, suddenly feeling a fear of failure creeping up my spine. 'I'm . . . I'm only over here to direct some plays. I . . . I don't see where I need a work permit to do that.'

"'I'm sorry, sir, but you must have a work permit for that, I'm afraid.'

"Boy, was I in for it. This was something I hadn't counted on. Back in New York the biggest worry I had was getting plane fare over there, and having a place to stay after I got there. But that work permit thing really got to me. And just minutes before, I'd wanted to kick that hippie's behind for looking like such a disgraceful emissary from America. Now I wanted to kick mine.

"For a long minute, me and the customs inspector stood eyeball to eyeball. Of all the powers-that-be that I had bucked against before, this was one that was totally out of the question. All I had to do was what that hippie did—say 'I'm a tourist.' Now I was hung up after I had scuffed and scrimped and begged and saved and did without, and got stopped right at the door of the thing that meant the most to me. I was losing confidence fast.

"The inspector asked me to wait over to one side. It was the first of many long waits I had in that country. I was *interned*. In some dank cell while they checked and rechecked my status. I made numerous calls to the house where I was supposed to live, to no avail. This wasn't America, where a man could bum and bluff his way through. Every phone call I made to the states, I had to call collect. You can imagine what a cost that was to the people on the other end. It was maddening. The agony of my failure—which was now a certainly—was almost more than I could stand.

"After three days of that hassling, I got the news that I was to be deported back to the States. Someone finally had been reached to pay my plane fare back. If I could have made it to Edinburgh itself, I could have worked out my finances regally. But this way made everything about me a question mark. It was a mix-up that would take too much time to unravel. . . . If only I would have said I was a 'tourist,' like that hippie.

"Finally I was escorted to a plane. I got aboard. You can only imagine how I felt. I had gone through hell and high water to get that far; and a little too much ego at the wrong moment had robbed me of my most precious ambition."

We were both silent then. I was making rings on the oil tablecloth with my beer glass. Ned was rotating his beer bottle, his mind still back at that Edinburgh airport. I was nowhere near as disappointed at his failure, nor angered at its cause, as I was saddened for his brave attempts. His trek was historic in my mind, failure or no. I told him as much. And I gave him more: my thanks. After all, he had cared enough to put a segment of my play on in a barely-supported theater in a city that had not yet learned to come of age. Hell, I was *proud* of the guy. My nine years of knocking myself out, striving for literary recognition, hadn't gone for nothing. Not so long as there were men with pluck like his around. . . .

"The last thing I remember," Ned continued, "was as the plane was taxiing down the runway for takeoff and, turning, stopped for the go-ahead from the Tower. I looked out the window and saw a city bus that read: To Edinburgh. My dreams, in that instant, went up in smoke—or at least in the plane's exhaust. I thought about you, then, and I wondered what James did when his dreams got away from him in an instant's foolishness or ignorance. I thought about your waiting until I got back with some probable 'good' news; and I wanted to watch the expression on your face when I told it to you.

"But that wasn't to be. Not then. Who knows? Perhaps not ever. I could only share with you my failure, not our success. Anyway, I came to New York and started to pick up the pieces and begin all over again."

I could believe it. I *did* believe it. Lord knows I have had my share of troubles. Only I'd felt that I had a monopoly on them. Mainly because of my blackness. And my writing. (Got to be fair about this: I had to get good before I could be published.) But to meet and *know* a struggling white writer—both of us from the same hometown, entertaining similar losses—was more shocking to me than my everyday travails. The man was a marvel. Imagine: a young David, armed only with a slingshot and a few smooth stones, out to slay an impersonal Goliath. *How* could I help but admire him?

VII—Ned helped me pack my bags. I had already learned to travel light. The bulk of my stuff was books, notebooks, manuscripts. My clothes were in threes: underwear, pants, shirts, socks, handkerchiefs. Two coat jackets and one topcoat without lining.

Ned took me to the Greyhound terminal in his battered old car in the middle of the night. He helped me with my ticket money. We drank coffee while waiting for my bus, and talked about our futures.

Ned was going to try again after he had gotten himself together. We would keep in touch through his father. I was going to Temple, Texas, my birthplace; my sister was there and I would hustle work until I'd decided where to go next. Fortunately, I had a beautiful cousin, Robert Lee, who remembered my potentials and saw to it that I came on up to Los Angeles. From there I went on to Budd Schulberg's Watts Writer's Workshop and to some degree of fame that I doubt I'd ever have acquired had I stayed down home. (Two of the pieces that had lost out in Houston's creative writing contest won stature. One appeared in an anthology, *From the Ashes—Voices of Watts*. The other was presented to millions in the NBC documentary, *The Seven Angry Voices of Watts*. It was my voice that the nation heard, and my face that it saw.)

It was cold outside the bus station. February. To me it was like a winter day from one of O. Henry's stories. Two *significant* failures drinking coffee that seemed laced with a stimulant of knowing which mistakes *not* to make again. The biggest thing I had in my favor was a backlog of experiences that would become stories of many dimensions. Ned plotted confidence, too. Hurt and disappointment were etched in his voice, but they weren't killing him.

Four a.m. The bus was sparsely loaded. I sat near the rear. Leaving Houston—possibly forever. I didn't sleep.

But I didn't have any compunction about sneaking away like a thief in the night. I didn't owe this city anything. My only debt was to my young upstart Jewish white friend, who had reaffirmed the dignity that had always been in me anyway; who had taught me that though we came from two houses, two ways, we both could win. And that was cool enough. Swell.

145

The winter outside my bus window, kissing the cedar posts, the Austrian pines, the cyclone fences, both chilled and warmed me. It felt good, challenging. I was going to forty and I was turned on. All my roads were new, my compass was pointing due North—Freedom, by God!

How many, bless God, how many aging dreamers could have such luck? How do people get married? Or friends meet? Or cross rivers, ford streams without the hand that comes suddenly out of nowhere?

That, all of that, and God knows how much more, swept across my mind as the Greyhound whisked me farther and farther away from where I had been to where I was going. Now. That was where it was. Now.

Wadsworth

His first visit had been to the Eye Clinic Waiting-Treatment Room. Fused with much light, his eyes couldn't help but follow the sound that transcended the muted but mundane voices of those in his midst to its source. It was too purposeful a drone to ignore completely. Far, and placed high above his standing six-foot frame, the little black box's voices poured out the woes (mostly) of people from a celluloid world. The daily world of the Soaps. The channel knob was fixed to one station only—the height saw to that. And, seemingly (to him), for hours on end, the tiny sliver of metal in his right eye would throb with alternate intensity until his name was called, much to his relief. But, God Almighty! In the meantime, would this mess ever end?

One floor above, four hours and many Soaps and Soap-selling silly Coms later, he had made it to the Pharmacy Room. Here, with the sliver of metal out, the huge eye patch feeling like a giant cloudy pad, the waiting held a different agony. Four huge boards flashed numbered prescriptions, from 1 to 300, soundlessly yet distinctly visible. Numbers ticked off (at long last to everyone concerned) of prepared medicines to a good-sized group that played an endless game of non-musical chairs. The black box (here, too!) droned on with its afternoon shows, station breaks and minute newscasts. Individual interests, tastes and preferences now kept in the pits of breasts without vocal comments. Here, numbers were Kings. He could cope with that. It was how to avoid, during the temporary inconvenience of one "good" eye and one bandaged one, going through the spate of magazines that glowed out so brilliantly from wall racks. He would cope, though. All part of being a veteran. And a veteran of any stripe could cope with just about anything. Given enough time. And that was the essence of this wait: Time.

Seven months later he was an inpatient. Only this time it was for something far more serious—and far more critical. (Illness does have a way of coming back at one with a seemingly oblique thrust.) Now, after twenty-five years of "tap dancing"—as he called—that time was now. And it would in no way resemble plucking out a metal sliver from the eye or sweating out a follow-up prescription.

In Building 500—and throughout the Wadsworth VA Hospital area—every ex-GI is addressed as "Mister." This is the place. In this six-story monolith is a veritable montage of rooms that include clinics, surgeries, research, and treatment, to name just a few that stagger the psyche of the incoming patient. It's a white world, and a bright world, an antiseptic-impressioned world, and its inherent human denizens-in-white who are more than capable of laying siege to the flood of illnesses that brings one here, both the benign and the malignant.

To someone who has barely set foot in a hospital in twenty-five years—except to see an ailing friend or relative—the odds on that possibility loom enormous indeed. Since the inevitable has at last presented itself—and now—as an immutable entity, there is absolutely nothing one can do but go with the flow. There is no more wishing or willing that incipient, oft-ignored, now implacable illness away. The "dot" on the X-rays stands out more starkly than points on a compass. Heretofore unseen—particularly by its possessor—now it clarifies everything.

Now, the Fourth Floor and the Ground Floor (Basement) are my primary areas for treatment. Vitals, Diet, Interviews, Medical Histories, Bed, innumerable examinations are ladled out via those two centers. The Ground Floor (Basement) will explore my body with countless X-rays—many with the liquid Barium: an unwanted vanilla "milkshake," that with cloudy filming identifies starkly the exact area of him. Much thumping and poking, pressing and prodding will tell my many examiners what they want—or need—to know. I am both putty and guinea pig to their strokes. Willingness or unwillingness has damn little to do with it. I am bled (weekly, sometimes) temperatured, thermometered, blood-pressured and pulse-tooked. A thin wrist-band with my name and Social Security number is instant identification to any night or day nurse who keeps my chart. I am in, bedded, wide-eyed and full of wonder about this new white world about me.

The decision from a phalanx of doctors' diagnoses is rest, a tricky diet—("icky" is a better word since *all* my food hurts going down to my stomach)—and radiation treatment: 4,000 "rads." That alone will cover four weeks. 1,000 "rads" per five-day week. Then more examinations—follow-ups; with a surgical operation set for three weeks after.

Having all this fantastic and disturbing knowledge in my head, I simply go forth like an automaton, and observe the comings and goings of those about me. That and catching up on a lot of reading and television watching—when I'm not looking askance at good-looking nurses and LVN's in crisply-starched linen.

On my floor—and especially in my ward—vets whose ailments cover the torso of the body from the throat to the liver—thoracic among other new words—enjoy the TV-Smoker Room most of all. (Smoking is forbidden elsewhere in the ward and even I have been advised to quit. Yes, me. One herculean task after forty years of being its addict.) In our little corner of this world, the lengthy morning newscast—Channel 4 is dominant with this group, although 2 is an easy runner-up—holds us in its tentacles, while we listen with half an ear for the wheels of the food wagon. In sitcoms, the Jeffersons predominate, and sometimes Alice, maybe Flo, but for pure macho, the wry wit of Bill Cosby and the dry wit of Robert Culp in the "I Spy" syndications has a firmer hold to our "action" interests. This group—yours truly, included—is death on Soaps. Sorry about that.

149

In the afternoons, our group remains steadfast in the macho mold relative to our being. We screen the "Big 3" in succession: "The FBI," "Ironside," "Barnaby Jones." An impasse looms among us one day: even though "Barney Miller" is everyone's favorite, Barnaby's continued hour of story line somehow just plays itself on through. The next day it happens the same way—and one day it does not. We accept that too—when a change is made—hurriedly switching back to catch a last befuddled 30 minutes of Barnaby's unflappable triumphs.

Weekends are anyone's toss-up. Sometimes devoured by reading books and periodicals, or going to the Canteen for coffee, or to the PX for souvenir-gifts. And/or waiting for visitors. My first Saturday, though, turned out less than a drag. Starting out at the sixth-floor library (closed on weekends) and working my way down, "nosing," seeing what the floors contained, I had made it to the 2nd before I thought it best to hustle back to my floor for "Vitals."

My common sense must have been working overtime, because a Vietnam veteran was staging a commando raid in our first-floor rotunda lobby, shooting up the place. Very coolly, the nurses ordered us to remain in our rooms until the crisis had passed. Fortunately, no one was injured, not even the "commando," but we kicked that story around the Canteen and TV-Smoker for days.

Early Sunday mornings, TV fare is rife with religious platitudes, so some prefer the chapel on the sixth floor. Our padre had made his stroll through our ward earlier with gentle solicitations. Sunday visitors come both early and late in the time allotted—from 10 A.M. to 8 P.M. Even patients with their vertical IV "trolleys" sit in the Smoker-TV room in family harmony. The color television set—which I've never had, and seldom viewed until now—blazes on in all its vivid colors, unendingly. Although there are sets in almost every room, most prefer the camaraderie in the Smoker. That is the second phase towards getting well and going home.

Another section of Wadsworth VA Hospital is the one called The Dom, for domiciliary patients. It houses many veterans with service-connected injuries, disablements and illnesses—some that date back to World War I, particularly those who were "gassed." More than a few of these are wretched living reminders of wars in which America has been embroiled. Were it not for facilities like the Dom—whose inpatients are screened thoroughly—more debilitated ex-warriors like these would be packing blighted areas of greater Los Angeles. It is both a haven and a half-way house for ambulatory patients with serious ailments, prior to eventual and/or continued surgeries at Building 500, the main hospital. Inpatients here are thoroughly examined, civilian-clothed (all new) with arrangements made for disability payments and SSI supplements. The four-story edifice averages four men to a room, with excellent and creative menus shared with other civilian-clad (although much younger) patients at the Brentwood dining hall.

Spacious, well-kept grounds and greenery offer a pastoral view of the Westwood-Wilshire fringe, just over the San Diego Freeway. Similar to what I've seen other places where the aged gather, multitudes of pigeons, blackbirds and sparrows abound in rest areas between buildings awaiting daily handouts. At the PX, Cafeteria and Post Office Mall-Patio, a small group of fearless squirrels almost daily stand on their hind legs and beg shamelessly for Planters Peanuts from any proffered hand. Conspicuous by its absence though is that most favored of man's friends: the dog. A coyote (or two, or three, maybe) comes down after twilight for a surreptitious feeding from some equally surreptitious feeder.

Pocket transistor radios (earphones required) abound among us also. The library, with its extensive stock of late and early tomes and its impressive array of out-of-state journals and periodicals, draws many of us. Bingo-winning chits for purchasable items in the PX are fought for eagerly, as the popular game is held most nights. Two or three movies a week are not uncommon. Several are first runs. A clearly mimeographed—with art illustrations—news organ, *The Signal*, by and for Dom patients, is issued and distributed room to room. At least two TV sets are on each floor. (Some, privately owned, are in patient's rooms, but the volume must be controlled.) A contingent of nurses is on duty around the clock, making periodic checks not only of aids and treatments, but also of patients' nocturnal wanderings or smoldering cigarettes after "lights out"—which is verboten, anyway.

Recent national events have had a profound and extended effect on the interests of GI's living in the plastic-windowed Dom buildings. The attempted assassination of President Reagan, his Press Secretary and protectors was no less felt and reverberated here—where we kicked it around in impromptu discussions— than anyplace else in the "civilian" world. On the one hand are memoried aged voices expressing concern about whether the Reagan "ax" will fall on continued GI benefits. On the other are voices speaking about film titles like *King's Row, John Loves Mary, Death Valley Days* or *Knute Rockne—All American*. One for the "Gipper" suddenly becomes a study in contrast. And then there is the blatant act of ex-Marine Hopkins, the one-man commando "raider" whose assault on 500's lobby entrance weighs in every GI's mind. Whatever our ages or wars, the GI mystique lives inexorably on in all of us and is of everlasting concern.

Meanwhile, our tenures at the Dom go on, awaiting our treatments, our surgeries, our hoped-for cures. One pair—an aged blind man with a cane, holding on to the coat tail of another aged man with impaired motor coordination—shuffles inexorably on as day goes on into night. The sighted one's mind is quick and alive; and to see them seated together on a bench in the warm sun, while one reads aloud softly from Keats, is positive assurance that life does go on, no matter what. Comrades. Conjoined and inseparable. Suddenly Tim Conway's skit of the shuffling old man does not seem funny at all.

This is "Sam's" country. All of it. And thinking over the enormous cost of curing our various and wretched ills, makes me wonder how many of us could afford to carry the freight. And yet the thought hangs ever in abeyance: which is the most enormous—the cost, or the human balance? Like everything else, only time can answer that. But not today. Certainly not today.

James Thomas Jackson as a soldier stationed in Europe.
Courtesy Connie Campbell.

James Thomas Jackson, in California in the 1970s. Courtesy Connie Campbell.

James Thomas Jackson (R) and his nephew Clifford Campbell (L), about 1955 in Temple, Texas. According to his sister, Connie Campbell, James Thomas "was very interested in young people and spent a lot of time with them." Courtesy Connie Campbell.

James Thomas Jackson (foreground) in front of the Frederick Douglass Writers' House, home of the Watts Writers Workshop, ca. 1968. Behind Jackson are Budd Schulberg (R) and Robert Kennedy (L), shaking hands. James Thomas helped restore this house, which had been partially destroyed in the Watts Riots. At this time, he was a janitor at the Eagle Bar, where he would often be cleaning up after closing time when Budd Schulberg stopped by to pick up chapters of his novel. Courtesy Connie Campbell.

James Thomas is seated on the couch (R) among the other members of the Watts Writers group. Courtesy David Westheimer Papers, Woodson Research Center, Rice University Library.

James Thomas Jackson, undated photo. Courtesy David Westheimer Papers, Woodson Research Center, Rice University Library.

PART II

Fiction and Poetry

Gasthaus

Paul Merritt left the personnel office feeling light and feathery. Up to now his body had been taut as strong twine but now he felt loose and cotton stringy. Perhaps because this was Saturday afternoon and the *kaserne* so deserted, he extended what would have been an ordinary brief walk to his billets so he could think about what had just happened. It was something akin to success. A personal gain. Being black, he couldn't help comparing this initial literary entree with that of other blacks, like Richard Wright, Chester Himes or an even more recent soldier-writer, William Gardner Smith, whose description of black soldiers in the previous war was titled *The Last of the Conquerers*.

Of course, his own five vignettes, which Sergeant Moment had praised today, were not in the same league as those authors had been. They did not appeal to as large an audience; his work was not an issue nor was he seeking a forum. This was still the Army, Mr. Jones/a.k.a. Merritt. He had three volunteer years to get along with it. If he fucked up it would be a long, slow dance on the killing floor. (Sergeant Moment was right: he had damn well better stay away from politics; even though deep down within him he knew politics were at his stories' base.) But first he had to get going. Sergeant Moment had fired the starter's gun. Merritt was off already.

He knew he would like writing for the *Argus*. A beautifully printed paper, the back issues he'd read were challenging, neat, brilliantly legible. Not as large as a back home newspaper— actually it was the same size as the *Stars & Stripes* only glossy in format—but full of condensed world news, predominantly Army features, a lot of variety and humor fused in among Army credits, commendations to units and announcements. The *Argus* office was obviously well staffed, but "Spook"-less. The paper professed high standards, but Paul concluded that if the Bat had not come directly under headquarters, it would not have gotten any space at all! That would change now.

He decided to stop at a *gasthaus* near the *kaserne*. He had been in the Bat long enough to quit being stand-offish. There was a limit to how long one remained a stranger in a battalion. He thought back on the oceans of braggadocio from Bat members at the mess hall and at the Post Service Club. Even though a good bit of their talk was saturated with what all accepted as "Negro bullshit," he felt he belonged in their company. They were loud, boisterous, excessively vulgar—but then where was the Army that wasn't? Besides, he could raise a little hell, too: he hadn't completely forgotten that fiasco with Rose and her boyfriend in Boston. . . .

An aura of *deja vu* pervaded his consciousness. The *gasthaus* he was entering now was red-bricked, two-storied, with the owner's name across its upper face with huge Germanic letters: *"GASTHAUS zum HEINER."* He wondered what the *"zum"* meant. The wooden door was wide open and braced itself against the wall. The brief hallway leading to the rear looked dirty. A huge mongrel of a dog, looking aged and badly in need of a Saturday bath, blocked his path. A small sign above the door read: *Gastzimmer.* From within he heard the flat vowel sounds of Army buddies, along with the half-English, half-German guttural utterings of female patrons. He stepped over the prostrate hound. The staccatto voices stopped abruptly but the men continued speaking as they looked him over. The *hausman*, a short, portly man with a happy round face, spoke to Paul in broken

English, then seeing the dog crowding the doorway, waddled over to him, fanning a heavy bar towel and yelling angrily, *"Raus, raus, du blade hund, du! Raus!"* The mongrel jerked up as though his bones were too ancient to escape the wrath of his angered lord. He hobbled away, looking back with sad brown eyes at the *hausman* in faked hot pursuit. The group inside watched the action and laughed uproariously. Paul walked up to the bar and waited until the bartender returned.

He ordered a beer and drank. It tasted good. Not cold but good. And strong. He looked about him at the sea of faces—the Negroid hues: black, brown, in-between brown, ebony. His eyes cast slow, sweeping glances at the women who sat beside them: all white. At home, this kind of social mixing was a pronounced taboo. But what Merritt saw did not make him feel triumphant. The very fact that these white women were in the company of black Americans—and all enjoying themselves, obviously—was enough for him to know that this was only a temporary arrangement. When their enlistments were up, when the Occupation was over, that kind of kissing was going to stop. It was soldier's play, anyway. Color notwithstanding. To hell with it: live it up. Let the good times roll, as Louis Jordan's song still rang in their ears. Let the finger-poppin' and foot-tappin' continue. Ever'body have a ball! They had been weighted down by restrictions for centuries.

"Hey, Merritt!" a voice called. "Come on over and take a load off yo' feet."

Paul looked in the direction of the voice. A short, slim, immaculately dressed soldier with a face like a baby monkey, was beckoning for him to join the throng. Paul turned and smiled, walking over immediately. He sat down in the only vacant chair, next to the soldier's female guest. It was a long, square table, which seemed virtually loaded down with empty dinner plates, used silverware, a few empty beer bottles, some full ones and four tall bottles of cognac, one of which they had been earnestly working on. Paul set his beer down and nodded to the group. Two more soldiers and their female guests sat around him. Another girl, with questionable blonde hair (a line from a Nat "King" Cole ditty—"is black de roots, is blond de hair"—made him ponder) and a pronouncedly freckled face, was seated on

Paul's right. In the one glance he gave her to make certain he wasn't crowding her, he concluded that she seemed out of place.

The three men were from Headquarters Company; Paul remembered seeing them before at breakfast chow. Their skills were considered of lesser importance (to those who believed that) within the intellectual format of Headquarters Bat. They were couriers, but were referred to as truckers. They drove the trucks which were necessary to haul desks, filing cabinets, heavy typewriters, and other objects too large or heavy for the jeeps. They too wore that Headquarter's proudness.

The soldier introduced himself as Bartlett and the other two as Simms and Grant. Bartlett's girl was Anne, the other two were Frieda and Luisa. Bartlett didn't introduce the other girl, and Paul wondered about that. Continuing with the amenities, Bartlett loftily presented the newcomer to the group as a "school teacher" and a "writer for the *Argus*." The girls were impressed and bowed their heads (almost like a curtsy) to him, making him instantly uncomfortable, though he *was* a mite pleased. His fame, such as it were, was spreading.

All three of the girls already with someone were pretty, Paul thought right away. Anne seemed the prettiest to him: a brunette with striking features and big doe eyes. Luisa and Frieda were pretty in ways that might-be stupid women are: not possessed with instantly clever and witty retorts or much general knowledge, but filled with predictable utterances of endearment and acquiescence when they felt it necessary. The other girl was not pretty at all, except, perhaps, in her eyes. They were periwinkle blue; her heavy black eyelashes (hard to hide those with a dye job) gave her the appearance of being easily condescending. Something inside tugged Paul towards her. (An easy lay, perhaps? And hated himself for the thought.) She was too politely aloof and sometimes, when she replied in conversation, her cheeks became pink-flushed; as though angered at some inbecility uttered by the other women. Something about her spoke to him with the sensitivity of a higher order. He found out her name was Ilse.

Bartlett made it obvious that he was glad to have Paul at his table. He provided him with a (reasonably) clean glass and poured cognac in it well past the three-fingered mark. "Drink up,

Merritt," he said, almost apologetically. "We' all jes' folks here. No need to be shy."

Paul didn't much like cognac, but it seemed to be the most popular drink for soldiers over here. As usual, he sipped it first, then feeling that the eyes of everyone at the table on him, drank a huge swallow. He thought he might gag, but he didn't. This brand was milder than he'd imagined bar whiskey would be in this seedy-looking place. The group around the table laughed at the expression on his face.

"It's good," he said. Still, he washed it down with beer.

"You think you gonna git you a room an' a ol' lady?" Bartlett proffered, grinning. All the girls looked at him . . . waiting.

"A room sounds alright." He avoided their eyes as he searched for a cigarette. Then, deliberately avoiding the "ol' lady" question, he countered with another: "Rooms cost much?"

"Naw. You kin git one fer 'bout twenny a month. *Our* money. Or cheaper. Most of the fellows in the Bat live right aroun' here. We call it 'Spook Village.'"

"They do?" He knew that already, but no harm in making conversation noises.

"Yeah," the soldier named Simms cut in. "They ain't bad rooms, and they won't let just anybody have 'em. Bartlett's good at finding 'em—him and his ol' lady, put together." The "ol' lady" remark was taken in stride. Paul was the only one who flinched at someone else using such a personal term in a crowd. "If Bartlett can't get you one, nobody can."

"Well, Bartlett, it looks like you're the man I'll have to see," Paul agreed condescendingly, although he wasn't sure he really wanted one. Especially if Bartlett found something he did not want: too far, too near, too close, too much sameness. That would never do.

"I'll tell you what. If you find something between now and next payday and I like it, I'll take it." Why he had uttered that quick resolve he didn't know; unless it was reciprocal Negro bullshit. Making more noises. But it was expected, and he complied, for the moment. It didn't mean a thing.

Playing the charade of two businessmen, the room was agreed on, and a suitable price was fixed at the bargaining price equivalent of fifteen dollars (*their* money) and not to exceed twenty. Later, the talk became mundane and local; most of it military gossip concerning individuals within units and their "ol' ladies." Some of it was talk of the Post Club: its reasonable prices, its fantastic hamburgers! But no place to unwind (and get loud) like here at "Carl's." Some of it bordered on hopes that the current black market price for cigarettes would increase; some were pipe-dreaming out ways and means of transporting several cartons of cigarettes, coffee, nylons, and other saleable American staples across the border to their ol' ladies' country cousins. This last, Paul knew was a great risk; but the men talked it because it was the custom of talkers to do so. The do-ers he had known had always been sphinx-like. Quiet, you betcha. They had their times, their ways and means to try getting contraband sold, taking fewer risks than running off at the mouth at some open *gasthaus* where even an over-the-hill mongrel dog might be wired for sound.

In the meantime other soldiers came in and went out and returned again—as soldiers are wont to do. A group of elderly civilians came in—six—wearing threadbare clothing, a couple with Hitler-like mustaches, the other four with wheelbarrow or walrus upper mouth adornments of various thicknesses. They slapped their quaint Alpine hats—each with a brisk, gay feather— on pole racks and huddled around a table facing one another. They ordered their own version of the local (and, obviously legal) home brew: a light-brownish liquid Bartlett's girl, Anne, said was named *MOST*. Primarily an apple cider fermented by Carl, the owner, it was especially potent. Paul believed Anne beyond all doubt when, to a man, the group became boisterously high and commenced singing, mostly off key.

"That's the 'kick-a-poo joy juice' coming out of 'em," he said to no one in particular. The unfamiliar phrase piqued the interest of the girls and he had to repeat the phrase to them several times, becoming an accepted wit instantly. Then he had to explain where the name was from. He obliged them by explaining that it originated in one of America's favorite comic strips, adding that it was based on the fact that there were people living back in the Southern mountains who illegally indulged in making corn whiskey and "white lightnin'" brews. He had a time defining "boot-legging" so he compromised with "under the table." They liked it, understood it, and seemed to entertain a sense of conspiracy concerning it. Especially the humorous part when Paul declared that these same mountain folk had to keep one eye on their "pots" and the other on the trails below, to see if the *gendarmes*—or *polezei*—were coming.

They were delighted at his flow of words—once his "shyness" had vanished—and both Frieda and Luisa, trying to talk at once, explained the similarity of the way the beverage was made in their country. With the notable exception that it was illegal *only* if not sold in great quantities or in a *gasthaus* without a permit. Here at Carl's—they explained with some derision—it was legal because Carl was a "freddy-cat" and a chronic "worrier," and because he was "too cheap" to take a chance on being busted.

It was the cognac that had loosened his tongue, as well as being in the circle of earthy friends, the second such since his visit to Kendall's house on his first day there. It wasn't a bad second start, and he didn't have to explain his getting down.

The six civilians were feeling the full effects of the cider now. Their impromptu choral group was drowning out other patrons' conversations. They sang first one song, then another, so loudly that Carl was angrily threatening to oust them if they didn't tone down. The sextette argued, cajoled, feigned hurt and argued some more, until the frustrated Carl walked away in disgust. They continued singing yet another toast in strong, loud, thick basso and baritone voices:

"*In Meunchen steht ein Hofbrauhaus . . .*
Ein, Zwei, X Zofa . . ."

Paul looked in their direction and was entranced by their savage and violent zest. "Talking about letting yourself go . . . about letting your hair down . . . these guys take the cake. . . ." He said it to no one in particular.

Ilse was looking dead at him. When he turned half around to look at her, he cocked his head to one side, comic fashion, and stared right into her eyes. The beautiful blue of them, the violet irises, knocked him dizzier than the cognac already had. "Where have you been . . . all of my life?" the cognac made him say.

She laughed then, for the first time: a high, piping sound that emitted more from her throat than her larnyx. Rocking from her own surprised mirth, she steadied herself by a hand on his shoulder and he laughed too: long and hard at what he did not know. Or care. When they stopped laughing, both looked embarrassed; they avoided each other's eyes. As though something, somewhere in a dark, mysterious void, held secrets of two lives neither of them wanted known. Secrets that did not exist here, only elsewhere. But where?

He got up brusquely, walked over to the bar, bought a large bottle of red wine that looked good to him from the array of bottles on Carl's shelf. He walked back over to the table. Ilse watched his actions. He sat down at the table again, poured some more beer in his glass, drank some, then looked about him at the rest of the group. A waning summer was fully in the air; it provoked a lightness of spirit that enveloped the table's other couples. A bit earlier, Paul had begun to feel they were scrutinizing him too closely, and he feared they might see more of him than he wanted shown.

He didn't feel aloof now. He felt agressive. Didn't want to be alone, either. He turned to Ilse.

"Let's go somewhere," he said, simply.

She stood up and preceded him to the door. Carl put the bottle of wine in a sheet of flimsy brown paper. Paul looked back over his shoulder to the group he was leaving. Bartlett looked over at him, gave him a short, affected, vertical salute and smiled broadly, the white teeth pearling all over.

Outside, what was left of the afternoon glimmered in the oncoming dusk. The fresh air revived him from Carl's *gasthaus* mustiness. He walked alongside Ilse for a full block before he asked her where they were going.

"Over (to) the underside of the mountain," she said, with a nonchalant gesture of the hand.

Later, he looked up at the broad foothill in front of him, not more than a hundred feet high, and walked on, saying nothing. Ilse did not speak either; neither did until the *gasthaus* and Spook Village were far, far behind them. Below, on the underside, he felt tranquil walking on the summer grass.

166

"I wonder if it's alright to open this bottle?"

"*Freilich.*" Naturally.

When they reached a glade surrounded by tall, intermittent rows of swaying oats, it was too ideal to walk past. "Let's sit down," he said, gently. The long aurora of orange light set afire thick rolls of cumulous clouds.

They sat down in the shadow of tall oats, facing the last big ball of sun, their physical bodies invisible to a peopled world for miles and miles and miles around, yet less than five kilometres from Paul's camp.

They were completely alone. They were utter, utter strangers. Drinking from the same bottle of opened wine, she sipped; he took more. Ilse cried a little for whatever feminine unhappiness unknown to his masculinity and he kissed her tears, her irises and her hair. The dusk entered, spread fully into darkness, and she moved closer to him. He held her tightly, the fingers of one hand loosening buttons from in back of her dress, as she was unbuttoning his fly . . . .

The Party

First they stopped at one of the homes for the aged. It was, like the two others on their itinerant list, some 30 kilometres distant from the battalion, the "Bat"; in a hamlet hidden behind the snow-capped mountains that ringed their camp. This was the battalion's yearly goodwill tour—and definitely a new experience for Paul Merritt. The Thanksgiving party was their standard goodwill operation, originated five years previously by concerned members of the Bat and further promulgated by the sergeant-major, Sergeant Moment himself. Not necessarily an Army directive, it was binding all the same.

Money the sergeant-major had collected so unctuously over monthly pay tables, whether grudgingly given or not, was held in his keeping for this ideal. He did the purchasing: cigarettes in a great hoard, snuff, pipe tobacco, nuts, and soft candies, as well as scarves, mittens (for both young and old), even warm cotton shirts and long wool stockings mail-ordered earlier from J. C. Penney, Woolworths and Kress back home. He also bought sundry items the party committee could think of that would bring comfort to the impoverished old people and orphaned children who lived along their route.

Today, the party group consisted of fifteen men in two trucks, including Paul and Sergeant Moment. Paul helped unload a small drum of lard, a sack of pinto beans, a sack of flour and two roasted turkeys from Mess Sergeant Evans' bountiful (and ever spotless) kitchen. Sergeant Moment strolled about the spacious parlor where thirty or more of the aged indigents were clustered about. He smiled congenially and spoke flawless German, putting them at ease. He was some kind of diplomat! Paul thought, as he joined the others handing out pre-stuffed Red Cross ditty bags, one to each person. Additional gifts were held in abeyance until the men sighted a particularly needy receiver: a shawl here, some gay mittens there, a muffler, an extra pair of long cotton or wool stockings, a large box of round mints, packages of Lifesavers, miniature boxes of Whitman's chocolates and Woolworth or Kress pendants and gayly-colored head shawls.

After the gifts were passed out, it was time for entertainment. The Bat's quartet, which on other occasions sang blues, pop, and even rock, sang four ageless spirituals tonight, and for a bonus, the first verse of "Silent Night" in almost flawless (southern accents and all) German. Paul later found out they had been rehearsing it since Easter—two years previous! The look on their listeners' faces revealed surprised delight. They stomped heavy booted feet on the floor and uttered "Bravo!" They shook the black and brown hands vigorously, issuing effusive phrases such as *"die guten hertz von die schwartzen soldatten."* Sergeant Moment commented to Paul that the group wouldn't be able to sing the encore in pig Latin, much less German!

Paul discovered that many of the people living in these climes had never seen a black man in the flesh before, which amazed the absolute hell out of him. He was encouraged tonight to watch that initial fear change to enthusiastic acceptance through the common language of music. The quartet had won over some cold hearts, and now these people did not want the group to leave. When the Bat group left for the children's orphanage which was to be their next stop, every man, woman, child, dog and goat was huddled by the road to see them off. Their waves and joyous smiles as the huge trucks sped away would always remain vivid in Paul's mind.

By the time they reached the even smaller hamlet of the children's orphanage, he was feeling full of optimism. He hopped off the truck with three other Bat soldiers and entered the huge parlor that had been decorated with colored bunting for their party. He was startled to hear gasps of astonishment from child-like voices: *"Neger!"* *"Schwartz!"* He looked at the group of fifty or so children, and cringed at the fear on every face.

He was surprised to see four "brown" faces, two girls and two boys, whose "café au lait" complexions stood out among the creamy white ones. Their noses combined an inclination toward flatness with an aquiline harshness. Their hair was dark and curly, in contrast to the straight locks around them. Otherwise, they were no different then the rest of the children. They all stood no higher than Paul's shank. The boys were dressed in *lederhosen*, shirts and knobby-looking shoes; the girls in *drindls* (aproned), sweater-type blouses and patent leather shoes. These were the first brown babies he had seen in Germany. When he recognized on their faces an aloofness and diffidence, his heart went out to them. Already they knew they were different.

This did not stop them from looking aghast, like the rest of the children, at the sight of the three black soldiers. Paul thought he saw on the four brown faces a mixture of both recognition *and* apprehension.

The children all turned their heads to the wall and covered their eyes. Some began to whimper. Paul stopped in his tracks. The two young fräuleins in charge of them rushed to the ones who seemed most upset, kneeling down to their level, speaking sooth-ing Germanic words of consolment. The two brown male chil-dren recovered first. They jerked their heads around and faced the newcomers with a stare. A few at a time, the others followed suit. The fräuleins began to lead the children to the tables and chairs set middleways in the parlor. Once there, they sat in silence, facing one another, looking down at the six-part, brown plastic Army trays.

Paul suddenly realized he was the only soldier inside the building. The others must have gone back to the truck to get more foodstuffs. The children were looking at him like he was a demon from a fairy tale.

He decided he had to do something, "even if it was wrong," as soldiers were wont to say. He turned away abruptly, went outside to the truck and returned immediately with an elongated box. Its contents contained cellophane-wrapped gifts of nuts, candies, and miniature toys, tied up with bright ribbons by a cadre of volunteer soldiers the night before.

Paul faced the women and children and turned on the Merritt charm—a big, broad smile. Feigning nonchalance, he placed the box centermost on the succession of cloth-draped tables and took out each package with a studied flair, lining them all up in a neat, resplendent array of colors: green, red, yellow, blue, purple, orange, chartreuse. The two women watched him with interest; the children in wonderment. Good, he thought. Their attention was transferred to the gifts, with only a few furtive side glances at the black man lining them up. Although inwardly happy in his charade, Paul frowned, trying to appear dissatisfied. He was sure that every eye in that parlor-room was riveted on him. He worked hard to keep all emotion out of his face, pretending to be absorbed in his work.

The children's eyes were glued to the glittery packages. Paul placed the last one on the table. He allowed a satisfied look to slowly replace his serious one, then clapped his hands and yelled "Voila!"—the only French word he knew. He stepped back to admire his ebullient display and attempted a rapturous look on his face. He noticed no lapse in attentiveness among his young audience, so he decided to risk leaving the room. He picked up the empty box and started towards the door. Sergeant Moment, who had stepped in to watch his performance, gave him a bemused, "way-to-go" smile and an "I'm-with-you-kid" wink.

As if on cue, soldiers entered the parlor en masse. They carried pots of savory smelling food to the tables. Paul wondered how anyone could think of being afraid while surrounded with such wonderful smells. He re-entered the room, pleased to note that the children were running tiny tongues across their lips and fidgeting anxiously. Master Chef of Headquarters & Service Company Mess Hall, Donald P. Evans of Fortuna, Tennessee, had prepared a feast: roast turkey, mashed potatoes with giblet gravy, green peas, cranberry sauce, lettuce & tomato salad, dressing, celery, parsley snips, spinach. Three kinds of pie: cherry, potato and apple. The chef himself stood at one corner of the serving counter with arms folded, an unlit pipe at a corner of his mouth.

The serving soldiers played their roles to the hilt, acting with over-stated nonchalance and absurd, would-be officiousness as they served and distributed the food-laden trays to their waiting diners. One of the fräuleins hurried to find aprons for them, which immediately became props for budding comedians. Especially Warren Robinson from Ohio, and Josiah Harrison, from South Carolina, two of the Bat's most endearing jesters. Robinson made a big to-do about how the apron would look on him, even to the extent of putting it on "ass back'ards." The children tittered, then giggled, then laughed.

Harrison responded by putting his apron around the small of his back, then bending down to view it from between his legs. Shrieks and howls poured forth from the tables. In further imitation of circus clown antics, Robinson jerked Harrison's apron from him. Harrison bit Robinson's finger, causing Robinson to hop around the floor in pain. By now the children, the fräuleins, and the other soldiers were all squealing and shrieking with laughter. Harrison ran and hid behind Sergeant Moment, but Robinson pulled him to the center of the parlor floor and proceeded to tie the apron on correctly, but in the process began to tickle him. Robinson fell down laughing and Harrison followed him down, continuing to tickle. By the time both men crawled, tickled and giggled their way out the door, the room was in an uproar. Robinson and Harrison reappeared at the sound of the children's applause, made several exaggerated bows—aprons and all—and shuffled back out the door, showcase style, waving Army pete caps in place of top hats.

The children's fears were gone. The soldiers, including Paul, took their places as waiters. They carried Army food trays—Promethean by contrast to such tiny imbiber diners—from the children's tables to food pots and back again. All the while they cooed the little girls and got coquettish looks in return. They made the little boys giggle, and got a furtive rub on the hand or (more daringly) the face—to see if the black would come off.

There would be no more crying now, for any reason. These black soldiers had made the breakthrough and the enemy was theirs.

Well, almost. The white kids were going along with the program, as were three of the brown children. But Paul noticed one little brown girl wasn't having any of the invader's shenanigans. She wasn't even eating. From the look on her face, hell was going to freeze over on this snow-covered Thanksgiving party before she'd relent. Six years old? Who said? She had to be sixty if she was a day, Paul thought.

This little lady—Jeanette as Paul found out later—had also been noticed by Private Harrison. Even as he was doing his skit with Robinson, he saw a resemblance to his niece Lucette, who had died of a strange malady twelve years before.

Lucette was the offspring of Harrison's sister and a white man who had forced himself on her. Scorned by both blacks and whites, Lucette depended on her uncle Josiah Harrison for love and acceptance. And he had done his best to love her with a fierceness that would make up for the hate she received from everybody else. For six years he had told her she was beautiful, reassuring her that her "high yaller" color was a double "badge of beauty" the good Lord had given her. But just as her confidence was taking hold, a strange malady took hold of her frail frame, killing her in less than a week.

For Harrison, seeing Jeanette was like seeing six-year-old Lucette again, twelve years later. She had the same pensive stare, the same moodiness, the same radiant beauty and, what was worse, the same resigned (but feisty) belief that nobody gave a good goddam about her.

Harrison couldn't even speak her language, but he thought he knew how to make her laugh. First he found the smallest dish in the house. Then, taking the now famous "apron" off his waist, he fashioned it into a bib. He placed a backless children's stool beside Jeanette and lowered himself onto it. His knees jutted ridiculously into the air. Every eye in the place followed his movements, including the young girls'—though she tried to hide her interest. Paul crossed his fingers, and noticed that Sergeant Moment had done the same. Harrison held the tiny dish up in the air and pointed to its emptiness, pretending to beg for food. His pleas were ignored. Deflated, he pretended to wail loud and long, and this time was rewarded by a small giggle. He begged again, looking straight at Jeannette. Too direct. She shook her head. He wailed again, louder and more fervidly, with all the drama he could muster. A thin line of a smile commenced to begin across a young brown cheek. Assured of success, Harrison wailed even louder, adding wanting-to-eat gestures; comparing his tiny eating plate to her great big one. The crack in the girl's cheek deepened, her brown eyes danced, a grin broke. Suddenly, she gave him an Army spoon full of mashed potatoes, followed with some of her giblet gravy. The boy next to her, not to be outdone, shared his too. Harrison began to eat from his small plate. Smacking his lips at the taste, he yelled, "Ist gutes, ist gutes!" Sure enough, Jeanette picked up her fork and started eating. Soon every single black, brown, and white face in the room was bright with laughter, with gravy spillings around the edges. It was a Thanksgiving feast unequaled by any that Paul Merritt had ever experienced. It seemed that for once, in this one little corner of the world, there was someone who gave a goddam about a little girl no one else cared about.

Paul was pensive on their trip back to Bat headquarters. He couldn't get those brown babies off his mind. How many more were back there, so far behind those mountains? There had to be more: homeless, fatherless, motherless, friendless; skeptical, disbelieving, hoping, asking each soldier they saw, "bist du mein papa?" He was afraid, all of a sudden. Suppose he left a seed of his own in some woman's belly? Questions, goddammit! Too damn many questions.

Somebody else was thinking about it too. Out of the darkness, Harrison's voice reached Paul's ears. "No Negro can ever, honestly, turn away his own kin. . . . Somehow, someway, I'm going back to get that li'l girl out of there and take her back to the states with me. I don't know how the hell I'm going to do it! But I'm damn sure gonna be caught tryin'."

Nobody else spoke, but every black soldier in that truck knew exactly where Harrison's head was coming from. Bad as every one of their own childhood years had been, none of them envied those children. Unspoken but shared thoughts permeated the truck's interior. "Bist du mein papa?" was uttered aloud by an anonymous voice. The question hung in the air, then the answer, coming from fifteen, sixteen, seventeen, a whole battalion of black American soldier men: "You're goddam right I am. . . . and I gives a good goddam. . . ."

Reveille

He was running to beat the band.

Reveille was four minutes to the front of him and his legs were churning like smoothly oiled pistons down that long, narrowly winding, foreign road. He *had* to make it, what with those brand-new corporal stripes so dearly sweated for and so newly gained; and the first overnight pass he'd acquired after five months of becoming part of this proud and wonderful outfit. That and his first experience of living in a remarkably strange land.

The Quartermaster insignia on his left shoulder arm gleamed brightly as he ran. The bright haze of a breaking summer dawn in his view revealed the stark outline of one-storied, wooden billets in the swiftly approaching distance. He ran tirelessly, like the well conditioned athlete he was. He saw Francis Scott Key being run up the mast—and put on more power. Thank goodness, he thought, the flag detail always beat morning roll call. Still, though, he couldn't take any chances. He'd have to hurry. . . .

His feet were gobbling up the narrow road. The outline of a barbed wire fence encircling the camp's perimeter came clearer to his view. Even from this distance it looked like a shabby piece of goods for an American military installation. His face darkened at

176

the sight of it. It always did. It looked like the ugly, fucking shanties that he came from. His eyes swept over this old, unsightly, former DP *Lager,* with about eight huts in all, now the military haven encompassing *his* Quartermaster Company. Even the grass didn't grow anymore. Externally, their wooden surfaces had been painted so much—by dissident painters, no less—that their rotten sidings and flopping facades rebelled at each new approach of paint buckets in unskilled or uncaring hands. He grimaced at the thought but kept on running.

To top it off, as he grew closer, he saw the kraut civilian guards in their black-dyed, "fuzzy-wuzzy" uniforms and white helmets with black stripes running down the middle. Armed with carbines, no less!

Wasn't white folks crazy? What were the sons of bitches *there* for? To keep unwitting interlopers out? Or, to keep *his* Company *in*? Wasn't that a bitch!

They didn't control the main gate, though. The "brothers" had that. He was *really* glad of that. Even though he was sure to make it in there with just the barest amount of time, he would be recognized instantly as another "brother," and that would be that. When they had the krauts on at the beginning they were always checking passes. They were sticklers at it. *"Kenkarte, bitte, Kenkarte, bitte"*; goddam, he sure was glad that was out. Damn! They sure could make it tough for the po' GI. He ran on, shaking his head.

He ran slower now, observant in the day's perspective, seeing the first few fatigue-clad stragglers drag sluggish bones into the narrow asphalt street between the huts. A smile lighted up his face: no need for further haste now; all was well, and he was home.

After all, that's what this was to him now: home. (He couldn't say this out loud, of course; people would think he wasn't used to anything.) Sure, this was an all-colored outfit—but a good one, and he was proud to death of it. Lately he had been hearing more and more talk that the colored and white soldiers were going to merge together, and he wasn't sure whether he would like that or not. (What the hell: he couldn't stop it one way or the other.) Just as long as they didn't do it too soon. When a man comes from nothing, like he did, and at his present age—twenty-five, right on the button!—gets worked into something, like an ace driver-mechanic in this famous Quartermaster Company, it was something to run, jump, and shout about.

He was looking between the buildings as he ran with that graceful stride that runners make when they are far ahead of the opposition, seeing more members of his unit pouring out of the huts toward the formation point. He ran driftingly now—"cooling it," gathering together his thoughts of last night's meanderings, to be discussed over the breakfast chow table with his buddy. He wouldn't have much to say this time. After all, he hadn't "scored"—as so many of the others had. Strangely, he had wanted those corporal chevrons worse than anything. The world was full of chicks, but those stripes were hard to come by. That first three-year hitch for instance: always waiting and working up to that instant, and then missing out right at the door. Now he had walked in—and had been accepted.

Oh, he had made a pass at a cute little filly at a coffee house in the city during the early part of the evening. But that was because he felt he had to do something to keep the broad from staring so intently at his dark face. Being black was such an exasperating thing over here. They stared at you from sunup to sun-ain't, especially them country hicks from behind the mountains. They were gapers from the *be*-gin. So, while he was "cooling it" in this *real* nice coffee house, drinking Napoleon brandy by the double shot and chasing it with beer, he had "hit" on the broad just to see if she was interested in him or merely gaping at his dark face.

He didn't get anywhere and she turned her head away from him so sharply he thought she'd break her neck. After a time he forgot all about her, and drank toasts to his promotion in silence. He walked awhile, enjoying the summer night, thinking over a home he had never loved and had *always* wanted to get away from. He walked the hinterland route because it was good for night thinking, and quieter; the stars, far in their heavens, hung more peacefully. Inwardly he had felt that the man of momentum which he was striving to be had finally gained some. Now he could go along in the life he had made up his mind to live: that of a career soldier. So if he was asked how he celebrated his promotion and his overnight pass, these would quite likely be the things he would tell them—although in a different way, of course. He slowed down almost to a halt as he entered the guard gate, flanked by a white, circular edifice that divided entrance and exit. A khaki-clad Negro soldier with an MP brassard on his arm and a forty-five on his hip stepped out of the small house at the gate's center. He nodded affirmatively as he recognized the runner's face, and with his thumb beckoned him on in.

Walking now, he strutted monkeylike to the nearly formed formation. He adopted this clownish act only because a friend's face greeted him a scant few smiles away. (It's easy to be friendly with naturally effusive friends.) He felt joyful. After all, his expression seemed to say, didn't he spend the whole night away from camp and just barely make it for The Man's reveille? (Every swinging root in the *Lager* knew that that Georgia Cracker of a Company Commander was a bitch with his reveille. *Nobody, no* time, *no* time missed that diffydaffy motherfucker's reveille. Shit, not even MacArthur, hell!) Doggone right. But he couldn't tell his friend that he had bought a jug of cognac and carried it with him on his nocturnal travels—alone, got good and drunk, and a little sick, and had to spend the night in a roadside *gasthaus* till morning came. You just could not tell your best buddy these things. They sounded too incredible. People in his age group expected victories, not defeats. So he'd have to white lie a li'l bit.

"Lookit the kid!" Evident proudness, showing in his friend's voice.

"Aw, it ain't no happen's." Nonchalance showing through and through.

"Don't give me that shit. I know you done 'em up. Had yo'self a young ball!"

More nonchalance. Silent braggadocio, emphasized by shaking one stiffly outstretched hand from side to side as though the thing were of no moment. "I ain' raisin' no sand. The nest is wa'am, but the bird is gone." Contemptuously immodest, provoking laughter, completely understood, without long-winded embellishments—they will come later and the lies will flow with each encouragement—this unerudite by-play must be carried on in the brief time remaining.

"Let's have that noise! COMPANY, TEN HUT!" Repartee ends. The roaring voice of one thoroughly disciplined first sergeant brings with one command one blatant sound of eighty-six pairs of feet present for duty. In itself it is enough. The owners of those eighty-six pairs of feet present for duty out of a company of 125 total strength have heard that voice through innumerable tones, inflections, and decibels. But on this bright summer morning there is an urgency in it totally unlike all those other times before. The hush in its wake grows apprehensively maddening. The affirmation that something is wrong comes in the next, hardly ever used command.

"OPEN RANKS, MAARCH!"

Obediently the first line on the front rank takes three steps forward and halts. The third line in back takes two backward steps. The middle line stands fast. One or two overtly inquisitive heads furtively try to ask one another the inevitable questions of Why or What. They as well as all the others are petrified into immobility by an amazingly clever command:

"FREEZE!"

The now frozen human statues are stock-still. Every eye looks straight ahead, an ocean of wonderment on those immobile faces. A door from the Orderly Room just in front of them opens and the Company Commander—a white man, The Man—precedes a white Provost Marshal followed by a young golden-haired, white woman.

The look on the Company Commander's face is stern, deliberate, even angry. The Provost Marshal's face is intent, authoritative. The young girl's face is milk-white and she looks as though she is scared to death! At the formation the Captain addresses the First Sergeant, who stands stiffly implacable at attention, then does an impressive about-face, walks to the head of the first man in the column, and becomes the first man in the column, frozen as his predecessor.

Now the Captain takes the lead, starting with the First Sergeant. The girl is in the center, the Provost Marshal is behind. They walk slowly, deliberately so, past each man, all the way down the line of the first rank. The life blood of each black or colored man within these three lines is now in the hands of this undeniably beautiful, young, white woman, irrespective of their presence in another country. True, their faces do not move, nor their bodies; it is only the souls peering through those brown eyes that have a tendency to give vent to their true feelings. And those souls cannot speak now. Indeed, they do not dare!

The trio turns, looks up and down the backs and necks of each man in that column; and *that* is worse because they cannot see behind their heads! Not another word has been spoken, nor does one need to be uttered. Every man-jack in that formation knows that some overzealous paramour-to-be has attempted an assault upon this white feminine symbol of the world. They know that this type of crime—and worse—happens and has happened in other armies of the world. But never—NEVER! in the souls of black folk—does it happen exactly like this. Suddenly, the trio turns again at the first man in the second line and begins that long, slow, deliberate walk again. The drama intensifies.

Seven men down is the Runner. He recognizes the girl as the same one that he barely spoke to last night. He stiffens suddenly and the Captain sees the motion. Six men down. Five. *Shee-it! S'pose this bitch stops at me! Hell, ain't no law 'gainst hittin' on a woman. Goddam.* But if for just some feminine whim she stopped at him, then what? How could he explain where he was? He hadn't met a soul in his travels. He was in and out of joints, trying to find one that suited his mood. *Oh, God, make this bitch pass on by!* Three. *But she looked at me for such a helluva long time.* Two. Arrogance, the only course left, seeping subtly into his clouded stream of consciousness. *Bet they put the bitch up to it.* One. Anguish. Defeat. *Oh, Jesus, what am I gonna do!*

Zero.

She did not pass on. She just stood there and smiled him the warmest smile, as though he were an old friend she hadn't seen in ages!

The Captain's face held a satisfied leer. The Provost Marshal's hand went automatically to his gun holster—and stayed there. They both looked so smug, so self-contained, that in his sudden flight he pushed them aside so brusquely he had a head start before they could even recover. (They didn't know it, but the "Brothers" gave him a few precious seconds with fumbling apologies and idiotic interferences.) By that time he was a damned good distance away.

He was running to beat the band.

Only this time he was not running like at the beginning, with a purpose, trying to make it in, looking athletic, concerned, and proud, with a zest for living, hope for tomorrow, *today!* Now he was running like a fool, legs akimbo, frightened running, ever listening for the bullet that was sure to come from the Provost Marshal's gun. All his *life* he had been running, Great God Almighty! For something. To something. Last night with the promotion and the overnight pass he felt he had stopped running. Because he had finally arrived at his destination, more or less. This morning he was running back to it, hoping to go on, with less hurried strides, "cooling it," so to speak. Now he was running for all he was worth, more into oblivion than anything. Home—for what it was worth—was over three thousand miles away. But he was a good runner. He'd make it.

He had to slow down for the fence. The civilian guard said something to him. In one instant he looked at him with such venom that one would think the look alone would freeze him into immobility. He didn't answer. He didn't need to. Wasn't going to. He was part-way over the fence when the sound from the carbine stopped him short. The guard was a marksman. The lone bullet went through his throat and his body draped arc-wise across the barbed wire, dangling ridiculously for several life-beats. Then all was still.

Only not quite all. Back at the disjointed formation was the throng of people headed toward him. The Runner's friend, his rotund frame quivering from his anguish at the scene unfolded, was walking just half a step behind the girl. The Captain and the Provost Marshal were just ahead of them. The Runner's friend

182

was alternately looking at the fence in front of him and the girl to his left. Her conversation—to the void—was a tower of Babel as she walked among that varied group to where the body lay. But he heard the anguish being emitted in her mother tongue, recognized the words for their meaning. Suddenly he reached out and grabbed her hand and yelled to the two white forces of power in front of him:

"Wait, y'all, wait! Listen to her!" Pointing, holding on to her firmly. "It wasn't *him*. Ask her, ASK HER!"

They all stopped. The Captain and the Provost Marshal turned and walked back toward the woman, who was now lamenting to the heavens as the rotund body of the Runner's friend sank to the earth on his knees and alternately pointed at her and beat the ground with his fists. In all that silence his tears and sobs enveloped them in his anguish.

He lay there sobbing, beating the ground, saying those same words over and over: "Ask her, ask her, ask her," while every person there looked down sorrowfully at him.

Shade of Darkness

They were so drunk they didn't know who their adversaries were, where they had come from, or how they themselves had come to this particular pass.

Just a few minutes ago they were having a drunken ball in the place just down the street, even doing an impromptu jig or two on the dance floor to an incongruous and "square" accompaniment of zither music. It was late—darn near twelve, anyway—and icy cold outside, where the second snows had packed solid with their annual Christmas "visit." The cold itself hadn't bothered them—not with the many double shots of antifreeze they had poured into their gullets. The Three-Star Cognac they had been guzzling since sundown had provided a furnace to their glowing countenances as they stepped out the door, wishing both their much-relieved hosts and the other patrons a profusive barrage of *Frohliche Wehnachens* and Merry Christmases, respectively. (After all, soldiers were sometimes troublesome when there was so much drinking. And the *schwartzis* ... sometimes they could be difficult. ...) For one instant, Paul felt a peculiar uneasiness when the door closed behind them. Like they were utterly alone.

By all that was holy and—to military men in particular—by all that was *conceivably* tactical, they should have taken the longer way home. But such old-maidenly fears seemed so commonplace tonight—of all nights. This was the Night of Noel, the "night of our dear Saviour's birth." This was O Holy Night and they were wrapped joyously up in it as they walked stumblingly, staggering happily, singing, down the cold, quiet, cobblestoned street. They were in love with everybody! Kendall blurted out suddenly: "Peace on earth! Good will to ever' body's body!"

There were at least four of them, maybe five. Paul only vaguely saw one of the assailants sneak furtively away after one of his intended blows was warded off and one of formidable power given in return—with a crunching sound against the jawbone. The impact of the blow greatly enlarged the eyes of the sneaky assailant-to-be, and the last Paul saw of him was a hasty departure. So there were six, at first.

One thing of which the two were certain: the thugs were all white. The evil glimpsed on their faces in such close combat was magnified manyfold in their rushing charges: swinging, kicking, cursing, some of it unmistakably Southern and *all* of it unmistakably vehement. They were attempting to do with sheer force of numbers—collective feet and knees and hands—that which white men in a dogged South had over the years done with rope and faggot to other black men just like them, with the same collective hatred. Only here there was one starkly immediate difference: the manner of dress, a uniform, was the same for *every* man involved in this upheaval. Now it was as though an Army was ridding itself of an Army. Its own. That unity of the form-fitting olive-drab symbol of American defense was never to be sacrosanct again; its causes were lies, its doctrines impeachable, its tenets spurious, and after one hundred and seventy-five years and more, no American soldier ever again was to be his military brother's keeper. The dim light of a quarter moon, playing peek-a-boo with drifting, fleecy white clouds, reflected an incongruous scene of men at war—with themselves. It was unreal, unimaginable—to a passing stranger, perhaps—but to the two victims involved it was quite real, quite imaginable, only surprising that it had taken so long to reveal itself; they were the recipient pawns of one of America's smoldering hates.

They sought refuge in the wall together, almost simultaneously—Kendall leading the way, backing up to it, swinging, kicking, Paul following. They were in an area where both had walked, as it seemed to them, a thousand times: always for some normal reason, but, strangely, *always* in daylight. They knew it like the backs of their hands. A civilian cleaning and pressing shop fronted the end of this cul-de-sac. (The proprietor, a short, grubby-looking man, with a moustache like Groucho Marx, had a legion of young peasant women who scrubbed their clothes with the harsh GI soap, and water from a running stream in a small culvert to the left and rear of the building. They pressed them with hand irons that were constantly heating in a bucket of coals, just to the right of the door's entrance. The creases themselves hung alone! The owner should have made a mint, because he had trade from all the units in the area!) A shoe-repair shop with what Sergeant Moment described as having "qualitative extras" sat in the middle of the block. They bought their winter shoes there—and wore them all summer long: bought them handmade, had them repaired there, loved the rabbit fur that lined the insides. They were durable, long-lasting, had a classy look to them, and were thoroughly approved by Army protocol. Minnow's favorite commercial for them was: "Snow grip, can't slip," and he was right as rain. They purchased these shoes with money or trade: cigarettes, Nescafe, nylons from the Main PX, even with clothes from the duffel bags of their own Form Thirty-Two! There was also a restaurant that unostentatiously served a deluxe European cuisine at a surprisingly economical price; it looked, from the outside, like any simple *Weinstube* that doted on quality and comfortable sit-ins rather than on hullabaloos and grandscale advertising. (The two warriors should know: they had just left the place.) Shops adorned either side of the short street. A two-storied *Konfektionar's* store flanked the opposite side of the cleaning shop. A hewn-out break in the continuous wall, which was made of stuccoed links, was the only aperture, and it gave onto a view of an open field, now thoroughly snow-covered. White soldiers used this opening as a ladder, hoisting themselves over it to reach their unit, some four blocks behind it. It was a direct shortcut. Verboten it was—but to a soldier, a shortcut. Otherwise, to the eyes of all concerned, the continuous wall, with its curving nooks and niches, completely sewed the street off in cemented finality. It was the wall alone that kept them from being whipped to pieces.

The moonlight was inconsistent. Nearly all the street lights from the restaurant on were dark. A faint bulb from the *Konfektionar's* shop glowed dully a scant hundred feet away. Darkness encompassed the battlers. The area was quiet, save for the sounds of blows being leveled or glanced off heads and resounding torsos and/or swishing misses in the air, aimed at a groin or thigh. The two were steadfastly pummeled by the five remaining assailants and swung back desperately in return. (Instantly the thought occurred to Paul: This is how the race riot in Italy started: a couple of spooks in the wrong place at the wrong time—and alone!) Paul had never before in all his life had a fight that mattered—except that fiasco with Rose and her boyfriend back in Boston. Yet five years of soldiering had taught him how. No one needed to tell him they were being attacked on the strength of hatred alone, on the strength of their being black, or on the strength of their association with white frauleins in their midst. He knew. Reasoning did not hang in the balance here: he did; and Kendall did; and Race did. Every uniformed Negro from his battalion, and every Negro from other battalions, companies, squads, units, echelons, and every Negro that was born this morning, yesterday, last night, the day before, ever after—every Negro everywhere on the face of this earth was being viciously clobbered by this desperately vicious quintet of white men whose violent passions of hatred had at last reached their peak—on them—and whose tumultuous hatred could only be satisfied by lying in wait for two unsuspecting blacks. And *because* Paul knew that reason was, in this case, especially now, just some pompous old bitch—printed, edited, and propagandized by a score of didactic, selfish, mendacious white men in the celestial seat of social power— he lashed back at the mean, angry, hateful faces with all the energy he could muster, using every dirty trick he could pull, avoiding kicks at his groin (which was obviously what they most despised, because that was damned sure the most repeated place they struck at), and returning kicks to their groins, guts, and heads whenever he saw an opening. Just think: a few minutes ago he was drunk as a Cooty Brown, happy as a lark, in a festive mood, singing Christmas carols at the top of his voice with Kendall, alternately reciting poems by James Whitcomb Riley and Paul Laurence Dunbar. Now he was mad as a motherfucker and this madness gave him additional strength.

Once he looked over at Kendall. The bright, clear, friendly eyes that he knew so well were now fixed in a pronounced stare of masochistic and sadistic welcoming. For every blow he received he retaliated with two. Sometimes he actually appeared to smile. To Paul it seemed as if this was Kendall's last day on earth, and the determined look on his friend's face revealed that he was going to take into his record book as many sore heads and bruised behinds as he could carry. His head was bleeding, and his mouth. He clamped his teeth hard, he winced often, he breathed laboriously, and the long, sinewy, strong arms were rapierlike in their powerfully directed agility. Hardly ever did he throw one that did not connect. Then they were wrestled, their assailants trying feverishly to get them away from the wall, to get them down on the ground, to stomp them into the dust. They would not yield (indeed, they did not dare!) nor fall, although by all odds they should have. They stood, however weakly, and swung and kicked and gouged, fighting for all the world like two invincible supermen.

Suddenly a noise appeared from nowhere—an automobile, the unmistakable sound of a jeep. Now, for one instant, all combatants stopped, their actions halted in ludicrous poses at confirmation of the sound. It arrested them all with its familiarity. Then, as a body, the assailants turned and ran, grabbing pete caps and straggling comrades in their wake, racing toward the opening in the wall. Paul distinctly heard their feet scraping the stucco as they climbed gasping over the wall, heard a muffled grunt, a groan, as they landed falling, on the other side—probably on each other. Then he heard the clatter of booted feet crunching across packed snow. As he slumped to the ground he could hear their running footsteps receding in the distance.

"Git up, boon! We can't stay here! The MP's 'll write us up shore as hell and give the battalion a bad name!" The voice sounded heavily labored and strained to Paul's ears, as though the mouth was split—which it was: the tongue foggled, coherence lacking, only the intensity of the moment; a muttering but coming through to his muddled senses loud and clear—although confusing in its purport.

"But they'll help us," Paul protested, imagining them to be the Ninth Cavalry, the Posse, the main body of the Army's Expeditionary Forces coming to their aid. "We can tell 'em what happened!"

"We can't tell 'em shit!" Kendall's anger overrode his soreness. In one fleeting instant he looked at Paul as though his friend's naivete was utterly repugnant to him. Yet, solicitously, he subdued it somewhat. Right now time was of the essence. "I know them motherfuckers a heap better'n you ever will! C'mon, I know a place to hide. Cmon!"

Paul looked defeated. What were "right" and "justice" and "faith" *for,* if one didn't believe those qualities would emerge triumphant in the end? Kendall must be wrong. Still, something told him that he was not. Some intuitiveness, some hunch, something as obvious as the broken nose now splattered across his face. There was a sense of urgency, in the fullest meaning of the word. He felt he *had to* trust him, no matter what he himself believed.

He allowed himself to be dragged up, weary and sore as he was, and together they stumbled, recovered, rose at a point just barely away from the lights of the oncoming jeep, near a wire gate virtually hidden in the overhanging foliage of the pressing shop. In spite of his body's feeling so completely beaten that death alone stood as a welcoming eminence, his brain admired Kendall's methodicalness in his swift and certain acts: sweeping their pete caps from the ground, pulling him through the nearly invisible gate, closing it shut as noiselessly as possible, then spreading the evergreen foliage thickly and artistically back into place. Kendall ducked Paul's head under the foliage as the jeep neared the wall, and under cover of the jeep's noise, dragged the wavering Paul to the softest parts of the grass as soundlessly as a cat's tread, toward the rear of the store. They crawled to the culvert where the peasant women washed the soldiers' clothes at the running stream.

He made Paul lie down near him on the soft part of grass, where the recent snows had disappeared because of so much walking. Made him lie straight—as he himself, did—on his stomach, near the culvert, just this side of the building, where they could both peer out, beyond a small-holed, (thank God!) brick latticework, at the MP's jeep. The two patrolmen embarked, warily alert: one played a searchlight around the area about them, where the assault had taken place. (For some stupid reason Paul closed his eyes, and Kendall, completely in charge now, felt the gesture and nudged his friend viciously.) The two of them then watched these two authoritative peace officers of the Army move stealthily about their rounds.

Beyond a doubt they were white. Both of them knew there were no colored MP's in the provost marshal's section. That went without saying. But they scanned their height level to read something passive or impassive in the faces. They couldn't: the light was too diffuse, too undependable.

They saw more legs than anything. Controlled, directed, alert; feet ready to pivot and descend. In spite of their wounds, their pains, the men on guard were quiet as mice when the cat's about, hardly daring to breathe. After an interval of a minute or so of seeing nothing, they could hear talking in fits and starts. Kendall nudged Paul to make sure he was awake and wise to the "happenings" rather than defeated and resigned.

". . . somethin' damn sure was goin' on . . ."

". . . you ain't bull-shittin' . . . some kind of a fight, that's fer sure. Shine your light here!"

". . . those bastards from Ordnance, prob'ly . . ."

"Yeah . . . wonder who called?"

"Beats the hell out of me. . . . They sure got away in a hurry."

"You ain't a-bird-turdin' . . . musta took their wounded wid 'em." Grins nervously. Facetious.

". . . probly." Dryly. Their tension is more apparent than that of those who lie in wait.

". . . GI's a sonofabitch, ain't he? Thinkin' all the time. I *know* these wuz GI's. I kin smell 'em."

". . . Yeah . . . Somethin's wrong here . . . I kin still smell the funk, the talcum. It's too rich, too *clean.* . . . Naw, somethin' ain't right. . . . But I don't *see* a damn thing, do you?"

"Shit, naw. . . . Reckon they scaled this wall and lit out." Peeps through opening. "Je-sus, the snow looks black out there!"

"Fuck it." Disgustedly. ". . . ain' no use lookin' fer ghosts."

"You ain' bull-shittin'." Resignedly, then suddenly contemplative: "Wunder if they wuz any niggers in it?"

Almost too quickly, explaining: "Not hardly. There seems to be a gentleman's agreement with them not to be down here after dark."

Apprehensive, calculating: "See any difference in the blood spots? They tell me a nigger's blood is thicker and darker—like, maroon-colored." Looks.

". . . naw. Look's like plain ol' peckerwood's blood to me."

"Then, on the other han', could be some of them civilians. Commies or some'pin'."

"Yeah. Maybe."

"Everything's quiet, now."

"Shore is. . . . Fuck it, let's go."

"Just say we investigated a disturbance that somebody called in and let it go at that, huh?"

"Damn right. 'Les' you want to go over to Ordnance and have the O.D. and C.Q. make a midnight bed-check."

"Fuck no! They'll think it's a peter parade or some'pin' and I don' wanna go fer that shit!"

"Me neither, come on."

The warriors watched them depart, saw the legs walk past their view. Paul strained his sore head and swelling eyes to get a good glimpse of their figures and faces, so that he would remember them again. The close latticework hindered it. He watched their legs carry them to the jeep and ducked his head back with Kendall as the lights made a sweeping arc about the perimeter once more, then, slowly, made a U-turn and headed in the general direction of town. The governed jeep made a loud noise that wasn't speed at all, just an authoritative sound. But it had saved their lives. He felt they had been that close to extinction.

He was sore *all over!* Especially around his chest. Yet his mind was working forty miles to the minute, his now quieted spirit conscious of the craziest thing: the soft, sibilant sounds the perpetually running stream made—the water lapping over the banks of the dam, flowing down the culvert of the little brook. It seemed the most magnanimous sound for this silent night, holy night. It was like Thoreau's Walden Pond. Hell, it was like the little pond at Kendall's house: so peaceful, gentle, serene. The ground was cold and his fingers were feeling numb and, oddly, the rippling of the stream was balsamic.

With the jeep's sound lost in the distance, they crawled to the edge of the brook's concrete banks. They viewed the now quiet world through the latticework as they approached it.

"All is calm, all is bright." Paul mumbled softly to Kendall as the moon came out, now completely unfettered, and shone brightly in their midst.

"You're damned right it is. And you're alive, I see," his friend encouraged him.

Kendall dipped a handkerchief into the cold black water, mopped his face with it, grimacing succinctly. He dipped it again, repeating the process, blatantly cursing, issuing the sweetly familiar vulgate epithets of Negro troubles, the expressions sounding sardonically humorous and even strengthening to Paul as he listened. The battle was over and both of them—by some whim or fate or chance—were alive and could make some sport of it, no matter how painfully difficult it was to do so.

Kendall sloshed the rag about Paul's face several times. It stung and shocked and even threatened to drown him. Anything to keep him from falling asleep, Kendall thought. There was the danger. Paul protested and bitched mightily and Kendall "rolled." Even Paul laughed. He couldn't help himself. The sight of Kendall rolling on the icy cold ground, slapping it with the palm of his hand, was so awesomely comical he quickly forgot about his pains. He had to do something: this fool was going to do with a rag and some water what the white folks hadn't been able to do with *all* their savage kicks and blows!

Revived, Kendall led the way back through a seldom used trail. It led through a line of small cemeteries. Paul winced, remembering the ancient "isms" of Negroes being afraid to go through cemeteries at night. But Kendall's purposefulness in getting them out of danger and into safety *demanded* that he put such fears to flight. Why had he waited so long in life to find a Negro man with such courage, and why had all those beautiful ideals he expounded so brilliantly in the I&E classrooms deserted him so completely in the darkness of night in quiet graveyards? Why did the ancient "isms" make him think that spirits of people long gone would rise up wispily and scare the be-jabbers out of him because it was wrong to intrude upon their sacred ground— he who had virtually been born in church and who revered the gospels; he who had picked his own biblical hero, Paul, his own namesake, in making his First Communion: the thirteenth chapter of the First Corinthians? Now he realized that the man had also written "All things are lawful." Yet he was being led by a man who took the lawful and the expedient as they came and let the devil himself take the hindmost, at times dragging him through other graveyards through the moon's mist, past the suddenly arising crosses that they couldn't help but touch in their staggering walk. He knew that without weapons they couldn't stand another attack, knew that Kendall was ever so determinedly taking him to the numbered safety of house and home, where people loved them and could bathe their wounds and make them well again. And yet he was cringing in fear because they were trespassing upon the real estate of the dead.

How could he let this man down with fear of that sort? It wasn't to be done. Not now. Not ever. So he stumbled on, felt himself being dragged, jerked upright, falling with him, rising, proceeding on, on, on, to the most marvelous sight on the face of the earth: Kendall's house.

They virtually fell into the room. Erika, who was a light sleeper when Kendall was out on the town, awakened with a start, ready to light into her man with verbal tongue-lashings. But when she clicked the light on and saw not one man but two, and both of these bloody and battered, their clothes filthy, her hand went to her throat in shocked horror. Conservative as the Europeans were about fuel, she started a fire immediately. While it was kindling she came over to them to view worriedly their appearance. They looked pitiable. It seemed a toss-up to her, as she looked from one to the other, which was in worse shape. It was Paul. Kendall dragged him to the bed and propped him up there, trying to get the tie loosened from his throat. Erika meanwhile was loosening Kendall's, getting her hands in under his long, busied arms to do so, observing the swollen cheeks, the smashed nose, the split mouth, the large, swollen mouse about the right eye. "Git the cognac, honey," Kendall ordered through thick lips as he hustled Paul's Ike jacket off and started to unbutton the shirt. Erika, bringing the cognac over to Kendall, looked on in puzzled awe. As Kendall unstoppered the bottle with his teeth, grimacing as he did so (they were knocked loose), he pushed the neck of it into Paul's mouth and tilted it up, forcing him to swallow. Then Kendall pulled the bottle away while Paul gagged on the substance for which he normally had to make mental and physical preparations. Kendall took a big drink, waited an instant as it coursed down his throat, and appeared to feel instantly better. He took another. Erika frowned, but said nothing. (Another time she would have called him a pig but now, no.) He handed the bottle back to her without a word. The thing Paul observed most was this rare attitude of Erika's: whereas before she had seemed so bossy, so much the head of this house, she now seemed both astonished and infused with servile humility.

Kendall pushed Paul back on the bed. His eyes looked glassy. The cognac was eliminating some of his ashy pallor. He protested uselessly as Kendall attempted to pull his trousers off, unloosening his belt as Erika bent to pull off the half-boots. It was to no avail. Kendall was in complete charge and with Erika's help soon had Paul's trousers and O.D. shirt off. They both looked at the brown-skinned body with startled apprehension.

The body looked terrible. A rib on his lower left side threatened to protude through the skin at any instant. Welts here and there arose and throbbed, swelled to the body's surface like thick embossing on a sheet of paper. Kendall suddenly undid the shorts, pulled them down. Erika gasped, bringing her hands to her throat. One side of the scrotum had swollen to twice its normal size. The colors on Paul's skin clashed: brown, blue, mauve. Kendall stood silent for a moment, as though weighing the seriousness of it. His concerned expression revealed the seriousness of what he saw. There was nothing much they could do here. The abrasions went too deep. They couldn't fake it. Much more had to be done. X-rays, doubtless. There might be more broken ribs, more internal injuries.

"Honey, go git 'Chili.' "

"Chili" was Sergeant Moment's own personal jeep driver. Short, taciturn, almost self-effacing, one of the few "saintlied" soldiers in the battalion, he lived just three houses down from Kendall. He was a devout, God-fearing, chapel-going man, and fortune, as it reimburses its believers in life, had provided him with a raven-haired mate a scant half-inch shorter than he. (Indeed, they were so much alike in temperament and character that when she wore high heels, she made damned sure that the difference in height was upon her "Chili"—even if she had to search all over town for "short high-heels.") His real name was Lorenzo Marvin Prince, and he was a corporal. His home was Lafayette, Louisiana, and he had been nicknamed "Chili" all his days.

Erika had no trouble finding him. Not addicted to serious drinking, "Chili" was always "home" before midnight. Since Christmas was observed so differently over here than in America—the celebrations commencing one minute after six P.M. on the 25th—"Chili" had gone through the yuletide rituals with the woman he unfailingly referred to as his "wife," Hansi. The trio had come back to Kendall's house and watched him as he put cold compresses on Paul's scrotum, all of them observing the tip of the rib that threatened to poke through at any moment. Kendall ordered "Chili" to get no one but Sergeant Moment and to get him over fast! One look at the suffering I&E man on Kendall's bed was enough for "Chili" to take off without any questions. The only enlisted man in the battalion with authority to carry a jeep off post—and keep it—during after-duty hours, Corporal Lorenzo M. Prince speeded forth to Battalion Headquarters. (To all intents and purposes, Corporal Prince was a courier and a courier was on duty twenty-four hours a day. If need be, Sergeant Moment could cite military authorities. So far, there had never been any need. Sergeant Moment's word *was* authority and *that* authority was *lawful.*)

"Chili" wasn't gone thirty minutes before the assemblage at Kendall's house heard the sound of a jeep and the heavier sound of another vehicle: an ambulance. Sergeant Moment was the first in the room, followed by Corporal Leonard J. McNair, a medic from Washington, D.C., who had flunked out of Howard Medical School for "improprieties." As "Chili" entered, Hansi, a striking, petite brunette wearing a housecoat over some jeans, closed the door. McNair and Moment stepped over to Paul. After an intense yet perfunctory examination, McNair uttered without looking at anyone: "We've got to get him to the hospital right away. He's in bad shape."

"Chili" volunteered to help McNair. They wrapped Paul in a mountain of Army blankets, placed him on a stretcher, loaded him in the ambulance McNair had driven down.

Concerned, Erika reminded them of Kendall. McNair took one look at the Quasimodoish-looking face and said, "Come on, you too." Kendall's protests went unheeded as the entire entourage of that holy night headed toward the ambulance, its motor still idling, the white steam thickly rising in the frosty air. Sergeant Moment, Corporal McNair, and the two patients hastily left the section of Spook Village and headed toward the main road, while "Chili," Hansi, and Erika were left behind, wondering curiously.

Kendall explained the entire sequence of events to Sergeant Moment as the ambulance sped toward the area hospital some fifteen kilometers distant. McNair had given Paul an injection, more against a freezing body-temperature than against the pain. The patient had fallen into a fitful quiet. Sergeant Moment's face was a mask of stifled revulsion.

"Six of the bastards, huh?"

"*Was* six. Merritt broke one's jawbone and the sneaky motherfucker got his hat."

"That's good. He'll have to go to a dispensary, then to a hospital. Then we'll know who the rest of them are—or were. From Ordnance, you think?"

"Pretty sure. It wuz dark and we wuz battling so fast, but they hit that fence that's in back of Ordnance, going that way."

"It's a good thing you had the presence of mind to get him and you back to the village. If the MP's had of picked you up back there you'd have still been back there suffering. To say nothing about writing up a bunch of charge sheets."

"Well, sarge, I know how they operate. We wuz jes' lucky they didn't catch us."

Sergeant Moment scowled and said, "Bastards." His favorite cuss word. The only one anyone ever heard him use. And yet it sounded strange in the ears of the listeners, primarily because everyone in the battalion knew that Sergeant Moment was a homosexual (a white man's word; it didn't really tell a Negro anything. In the Negro vernacular, the man was a stone fag). It was the sibilant way he said "bastards" that shook people a bit. As though by his saying it heads could *really* roll, whereas one of them saying it was just another cuss word thrown on the wind, accomplishing nothing. They knew however that his revulsion was at the injustice that provoked the word. It was conceivable that some white "bastards" had attacked two members of his race and he was mad as hell about it.

"Paul," he asked, pointing, "a good fighter?" Kendall observed he said "Paul" and not "Merritt."

Kendall's smile was grotesque in the semi-darkness. "One of the best." He laughed suddenly. "He really slammed it on that guy's jaw: ViiiiVIP! He gave as much as he took. One while there I thought we wuz gonna whup 'em all!"

Sergeant Moment smiled. Kendall's one good eye saw that it was one of pride. Even McNair turned around to look at him, with the same kind of smile on his face.

"Some heads are gonna roll behind this, mark my words." The sergeant then turned to look at McNair's head. "Step on it, Mac," he said angrily.

"Right," McNair answered, speeding up, the road in front clear, cool-looking, as only a cold winter's night could look. "We'll be there in a few short ticks." The eloquently cultured voice now sounded strangely colloquial.

They were the only emergency case there—so far. The Officer of the Day, a medical doctor with the rank of captain, came to look over the two soldiers. He glanced at Kendall, attempting to examine him first—at which Kendall referred him to Paul, now prostrate on the examining table. "Get him first, Captain—if you please, suh!"

The officer looked rebukingly at Kendall, whose eyes returned him stare for stare, saw the unmovability of it, saw also the equally serious, equally authoritative expression in Sergeant Moment's face, then moved over to Paul. He pulled the blankets back and saw the jutting rib; then his eyes hastily scanned the rest of the abused body, and seeing the wounds, welts, abrasions, his face suddenly flushed with professional concern. "Medic!" he shouted to the open door. A sound of running feet was heard coming in their direction.

"Get this man ready for surgical examinations! X-rays, and I want plenty of them!"

"Yes, sir," the white medic answered.

The captain looked over at Kendall, saw the battered face, the filthy clothes. "Get your clothes off. Get on the other table."

Kendall began to undress.

"May I assist you, Captain?" McNair's voice: cultured, refined, smooth.

"He's our medic," Sergeant Moment said, as though that explained McNair's status completely.

The doctor looked at him skeptically. "Are you a pill-pusher or something of a doctor?" he asked, blandly.

198

"At present, a pill-pusher, primarily. To be sure. And yet, something of a doctor, as well."

The doctor stared at him, appraising. "All right." Resignedly. "I'm going to need some help, anyway."

Kendall smiled broadly. Sergeant Moment beamed.

Sergeant Moment helped them move the two oscillatory tables together, placing the two battlers together again, side by side. Sergeant Moment stepped back a discreet distance as the stern-seeming doctor and the washed-out medical student began to apply the medical ways of man to put new life back into damaged bodies. Fatigue suddenly overcame Kendall and a familiar noise was heard by the interested probers: Kendall was asleep and snoring loudly. The group paused to look at the disfigured nose spreading over the swollen face. Sergeant Moment frowned. McNair looked perplexed, the white medic startled. The surgeon shook his head and smiled.

"So . . . I've got two heroes tonight," he said to the sergeant-major, with light aplomb. "Or—maybe two fools."

The sergeant-major's stern countenance broke into a wide grin.

Caravansary

The hinterland O-Bus was going to Lambach.

Only a few passengers, seat-scattered here and there about its oval contour, made anything of their presence. Those in question, a boy and girl of approximately the same age and fifteen at most, sat together in stoic silence, near the front. A third, indubitably of the same party although slightly younger, and looking none the less stoic, sat behind them, two empty seats directly in front of the black soldier.

They were the shabbiest threesome the soldier had seen since his arrival almost five years to the day since World War II ended. Because they were so young, with obvious poverty hung about their slender frames in tattered garments, his now disjointed thoughts were loathe to ponder them—at first. Now he observed them in detail. Their clothing—a kind of denim-seersucker twill—light grey-blue with thin stripes running vertically about their near emaciated figures. He had seen that uniform before. Where? Oh, yes. How quickly one forgot. On the outside wall of the compound entrance, grouped with many others. And at immediate eye level. Part of many momentos and horrible photographs placed there by the Preservists of those interned;

distinguishing one helpless group or sect from another. The entire collage, if you will (the first he'd ever seen), had struck him as odd-looking, since he had always assumed *all* internees wore the same clothing—and faces on wearers of the uniform were utterly devoid of expression.

To him they had actually looked repugnant. (But wasn't that their captor's intention?) The uniforms indicated the status of the compound's inmates. They also included emblematic patches sewn on a shoulder arm: triangular, square, crescent-shaped, octagonal, others. Prisoners not necessarily of normal crimes, but prisoners of tyrants whose powers heaped diabolical and murderous mayhem, often experimental, upon bodies they deemed of no more use to their would-be world-conquering and fiendish Utopia. Remembering some particulars, the political, homosexuals, Jews, retards and nomads—as he assumes these were—rated high on a commandant's list for laboratory dissection *play* as well as gas and oven deaths (the final solution), the ultimate denouement of man's inhumanity to mankind, speaking starkly to him and to all other first-time viewers making the pilgrimage. If the three the soldier was now observing seemed non-conforming and/or migratory, it was perhaps because they were indicative of the survivors. And yet they seemed to him a different breed of dissenters. Because they were young, perhaps? Well, they *were* young.

His little tour over, the soldier was surprised that he was so soon reminded of that Place. He was returning back to his military unit after his Three-Day Pass visit "up-country." Returning initially from his dead soldier-brother's grave in Metz, Belgium, he saved the compound visit for the return trip. At his brother's grave site—amidst a sea of white crosses on a gentle, grassy plain—he had placed a wreath of mixed flowers bought from a vendor who peddled his fresh-smelling blooms not far from the gravesite. He had stood there at the foot of the vast American graveyard for long minutes, remembering his brother's two-year older age difference, his CCC Camp volunteer decision, the tears shed at that parting, his first furlough after a subsequent Army induction, and letters and photographs of him and his jocular Army buddies, whose camera-caught likenesses tried to assure the black folk back home that the enlistment was a lark. Whether any of the family believed the beaming beau gesture or not, proudness had enveloped the family. And even after word arrived that he was killed in action during the Battle of the Bulge, they would endure and persevere until his remains were shipped home. And he, having missed the action, had made a request— in person—to Graves Registration, to at last have his brother's remains shipped back to their southern stateside home. His visit to the compound had only accentuated the noble beliefs that their black family felt their firstborn son had died for, and the soldier was glad to have made both pilgrimages. It was the second one, though, he felt he would have the most trouble accounting for in his mind. It wasn't war, wasn't combat, wasn't an equal confrontation. But he felt he needed to see the results of it.

He had kept his mind open on the journey down the long road, past each point of the three barbed wire gates that once halted entrance so menacingly. Now they had been flung back (for any and all entrants) and tied with their own wire to a long accompanying fence running the road's length. Before he was past the third checkpoint he knew he was in the arena of death, and the victory was not with the Christians.

He smelled the thick, rancid odors that once burned human flesh and still, five years later, permeated the area like a lingering surrealist odor to the nostrils. In a concerned metamorphosis of his own, he felt the heat of still bristling ovens. Entering the compound proper, he toured the cemented interiors. The gas chambers, spotlessly clean, stank loudly. The Preservists had posted large readable signs in blatant lettering. "OPERATING ROOM" for the place where human guinea pigs were used for surgical dissection, for "UN-ANASTHETICAL EXPLORA-TIONS." The mute rooms cried out to his brain from their now disinfectant cleanliness.

The rooms for "GAS-ING" internees looked almost exactly like Army showers, innocent and welcoming as group therapy hygenic participants, their hidden death-dealing sprays issued to unsuspecting bathers. Their cries of death at this sudden betrayal should have awakened both the dead and the living.

The ovens resembled mass bakeries. Elongated (corpse-size) compartments, with brief iron doors whose latches sealed both the dead and nearly so, were in horizontal rows like legions of filing cabinets—only human-sized. Flat spatulas were missing to ladle them in and out after burning at maximum Fahrenheit temperatures. Iron rakes would suffice, to glean the bones from the ashes after a "considerable" time. With care, though. Inlaid gold, open-faced crown and silvered teeth were objects for commerce trade: dowries for the future; security. Not even pious words would be wasted on their previous owners.

It was only one camp, one compound, and he had to explore it thoroughly; he didn't know when he'd see another. Like all memorabilia enshrined by the Preservists, it would be a last and, most likely, the foremost eye catcher on a distant tourist's itinerary. And in this instance, they had, to the black soldier, truly reserved the most memorable emblems for last. Like going-away reminders.

"The Hanging Tree" had died. About its base, tiny as well as bigger limbs and branches lay shredding about the visitor's feet. Even "The Shooting Tree" was dying. Petals normally blooming in any summer's ambiance strained futilely to proffer open, demure-like colorful buds. Instead, surrendering like sylphs, lover-companions, or defeated soldiers, all only loved and boasted on; like summer romances, now exhibiting powdery-drooped eyelids emitted like guilty consciousness, where before volatile coquettishness and masculine triumph held sway. Those three words, looming large on placards tacked big on tree trunks, answered any and all questions. Many men had died here for no reason other than that the tree gave an immovable target for compound guards' military target practice.

A huge, iron-spiked roller, once pulled by inmates to crush rocks for paving the enemy's roads, lay as a forced symbol near a yet-remaining, (once electrically-charged) barbed wire fence. At steps farther on there was a sign:
"GRAVE OF THOUSANDS UNKNOWN"

The path past it was also smooth and tiled—now. The soldier had halted before a huge Star of David uttering an even more blatant cry:

"GRAVE OF *MANY* THOUSANDS UNKNOWN"

He believed it all, but it was the monument to the doomed that spoke the loudest.

He had never known art so instantly encroaching. Here, the sculptor and landscapist must have agreed upon the height of the male statue from the ground and the depths of it beneath the sky. It stood not too far above the eye level of a six-foot man. By design, the figure symbolized the lowest depths of depravity that beasts-who-walked like men can render upon their brothers.

The head was grotesquely bald; the face ran ovally down to skeletal proportions; the nose was huge; wrinkles, the kind that normally inundate people of great age, ran like capricious rivulets down to the nape of the neck. The rest of the body merely hung on, as though submission and death were the only choices left. (And the eyes looked as though they refused to die! Even in their weariness they alone refused to die! They stared at the last remnants of life in a vain but immutable protest.) Hands hung down an emaciated back, one grasping the other in an implacable gesture of negotiation if not dignity. Their emptiness confirmed the futility of both. Then the uniform. (An almost exact replica of the ones the bus trio wore.) Tattered, expressionless, utter. Of the two trouser legs, one draped across the great bootshoe in a startlingly laughable effort of sartorial decorum. It failed, as all other efforts failed, to gain a moment of mercy. The figure reminded its viewer of nothing and yet—glancing up and down, from head to toe and up again—it reminded him of everything that is, was and could ever be, human.

The foreign words on the pedestal beneath it suited the artist's action and the action, words:

"Ne Wieder!

Denke Daren!"

Other words from other actions spoke their protests too:

"Ne Palais!"

"Never Again!

Remember That!"

And remember he did. Long after that, the pathos and poignancy went on in his consciousness.

The distinctive uniforms fanned across his eyes. One word shipped over his brain—Gypsies. And the definition he had read somewhere: "Nomads, usually a band, traveling across wastes, plains, through villages; often stereotyped as thieves, armed with long knives; wearers of scarves, kerchiefs and large, hoop earrings (resembling gold). Shabbily dressed women, palm and card readers. An accordionist accompanying a young dancing girl and sometimes, a dancing bear." A storied fixation bedding itself into one's developing intellect? Unalterable fantasy and truth comingled? Only time—in this case, his—and experience would divine the false from the true.

He looked at the boys then at the girl, and a second long look at the girl again. A slim, frail body, a dark brown skin. (They were *colored*, too!) Hair of curly auburn locks. The eyes were brown also; he had verified this when she casually turned to speak to the disconsolate loner of their party. verifying his assumption. At his assumed age of her—fifteen—she was a beauty. She would be a knockout "Carmen" at twenty-two. A survivor now—and only the heavens knew whether she had lost her virgin purity at the point in time—she faced a world he hoped would have changed some by then; and peaceful aggrandizements would cast lures of different stripes in her direction. As for the two boy-men, they'd go wherever their grain led them. Maybe even as conquerers themselves, making a world from the one of which they had been themselves salvaged.

As the O-Bus rolled on, the soldier viewed the summer grass tall and darkly green, bright and sparkling along mostly country roads. Always, across the way, mountains and foothills of all shapes loomed and soared, packed into mapped pages of foreign geography. He saw tiny brooks disappear behind immense foliage that buffeted sky-climbing trees, caressing brief banks by hidden homes, both chalets and more modest abodes, encompassing them as a matter of course. The blatant sounds of the bus's motors roared, swelled and sometimes (but not often) purred, in the process of grinding out its run. All of a sudden he had an urge to begin learning about these nomads, to ask questions, and to start out by saying hello.

It was then the bus stopped. The first two, the boy and girl together, got up hastily and exited. The last, the younger boy in front of the soldier, jerked awake suddenly, oriented himself to his companions, and scampered to the bus's foldback door. The soldier watched him scurry across the dirt road and stagger over the gravel shoulder of a nameless point in time.

Standing to observe their sojourn below the road's shoulders, the soldier saw the billfold left by the loner of the three. Picking it up, he allowed his curiosity to urge him to look within. The trio was by then heading across a meadow, towards a foothill in the distance. The younger one was still trailing, but he was closing in. The soldier looked at the billfold. A few papers. Photos of the trio in rags. In tatters. In the prison garb. One photo of the first two together, managing wan smiles. Another of the sullen youth in a sullen pose; the eyes of the discerner and the mouth of the thinker crooked in sarcastic solemnity.

The soldier carried the billfold to the bus driver, who looked over at him, then perfunctorily, at the contents. He shocked the soldier by throwing the entire lot out his window. The driver's face revealed his own surprise: why would an Amerikan *schwartzi* concern himself with three non-entities, three "nobodies" who were merely alive to tell about their experiences. Changing gears, he went about his work, driving his bus.

The soldier returned to his seat. He looked back into the distance. The grey-blue color of the three uniforms was becoming more and more a light sheen as the brown of their faces became an indistinct blur. The meadow became an oval valley and at its crest before they disappeared completely; all he saw were three indiscriminate specks in that now lush distance between earth and sky.

Corporal Willoughby's "Waw"

Suddenly *everyone* was busy. The Ready Alert signal had sounded loud and blatant over the whole perimeter of the Bat. Every soldier and his brother knew what that meant: trouble; and to get to their own particular area for formation and instructions on the double quick. And they complied, formed into respective platoons and squads; were hurriedly briefed by their first sergeants and platoon leaders. They were marched—on the double!—to the Arms Room where they drew their own carbines and clips of ammunition. The last time they had been provided real rounds of ammunition was four months previously, on the firing range. In remembrance of a war five years past, each man was closely studying the value of every item that would encompass his person as a soldier geared for battle.

The cartridge belts they were issued held four pockets. Each ammo clip contained eight rounds. Thirty-two bullets per man. Some of the First Three Graders ("RHIP"—rank has its privileges—) got two additional cartridge belts wrapped around their chests criss-cross, like bandoliers, as if a long war was expected. Helmet liners were tucked snugly into steel helmets, feeling weighty upon their heads. (A soldier's—almost—bullet-impen-

etrable protection, though: the damn thing weighed five pounds!)
A bayonet, twelve inches of dark-blued steel, fitted into its
receptacle on the left side of the cartridge belt. Neatly compacted
packets of sulfa—for wounds—fitted into two pockets of the belt,
completing its overall usefulness. The carbine rifle was already
cleaned and oiled. (It had better be. There was an automatic three-
day Restriction for the man who didn't do his weekly cleaning.)
Battle-wise, they were as ready as they ever could be. Only the
good God knew their attitudes towards actually *killing*.

Some men were quicker than others. Orderly confusion
inundated the entire camp. The routine of instant readiness they
had gone through countless times in practice was now done with
precision-like certainty. They appeared braver, more valorous
while active; apprehensive and fitful when they had to wait. All
of which was characteristic of the Army anyway: that old "hurry
up and wait."

It had hit Paul Alexander Merritt like a ton of bricks. He
heard the Ready Alert and ignored it completely. (A discipline
offense if ever there was one, and there were plenty!) Yet he was
absorbed in his work. It was Friday, a regular class day for him.
And as usual, he was in his Information & Education office, going
through several newspapers from home, a stack of magazines,
sifting little informative "gems" from this or that source; pencil-
ing info on little three-by-five-inch cards. Kendall had come
running into his office like a savage whirlwind, a smile on the
wide mouth yea wide.

"You kin fergit about yo' lessons fer today, young soldier.
We got a 'waw' on."

"You must be kidding!" Paul looked up at him in startled
surprise. "You mean that's what the whistle-blowing was all
about?"

"None other. Them goddam Commies done finally put
some real shit in the game. They done took over Ordnance and set
up barricades all along the *Platz*."

"No shit." He said it so blandly it was almost a whisper.

"Come on, let's get to steppin'! Full field pack, carbine,
ammo, steel helmet, ever'thing. Miz Merritt's li'l boy is goin' to
waw today!"

A dazed and shocked Paul followed Kendall out of the office. For once he was speechless, especially compared to Kendall's ever present garrulousness, intensified now because, as a man of action, he was at his zenith. He made his legs move at the pace Kendall was setting towards the Arms Room. They were very nearly the last to get their "fighting" equipment. They lugged the weighty ammo clips, the cumbersome rifles with looped slings, the sulfa, bayonets, the cartridge belts. They made haste to their room, Kendall unbuttoning his fatigue jacket as soon as they entered. He flopped down on the bed and began to unlace the many eyelets of his combat boots. Paul made a feeble attempt to keep up his companion's pace, but failed miserably.

"Come on, boon, we've got to be at the formation in five minutes!"

"Okay, okay!" Incredulity still assailed him. It wasn't fear—at least, not yet. He was thinking there was so much more he wanted to do. He had eleven letters mailed out to registrars and high school principals around America, letters that accompanied results from courses his eleven students had already completed satisfactorily. Now he was deep in the process of following those up. He believed that in most cases only another elective course or two would be enough to get these men diplomas. But these goddam Communists! Shit!! Messing up his playhouse like that. Militant sons of bitches!

Morose as he felt, he had nearly caught up with Kendall in dressing. They wore Class A's—the olive drab dress uniform for downtown. This too seemed incongruous to him, like "dressing up to go to war." Fatigues would have been far more suitable. Class A's were hard enough to keep clean as it was. Besides, they only had three suits.

Kendall had his full field pack on. He came over to Paul, twirled around suddenly. "Tighten my strap up on the left side, boon. I don't want my pack saggin' 'fore we git to where we' goin'." His friend complied, harnessing the pack tightly about Kendall's broad back. Kendall then did the same for him. They checked one another hastily—but thoroughly. Everything was complete and in place. "We're okay," Kendall uttered, "Let's go." They started out the door. Paul paused, turned to look at the room. "Come on, young soldier," Kendall was smiling, as if reading his thoughts. "Just stick with me and ever'thing 'll be all right."

"All right, Sergeant York—if you say so," a grumpy Paul answered.

"Now you sound more like my boon dot." Kendall flashed him an infectious grin. Paul couldn't help but grin sheepishly back at him.

If they had been Infantry they would have been a formidable sight indeed. Weapons would have been more varied and foreboding. There would have been M-1s instead of carbines, recoilless rifles, howitzers, field artillery, bazookas, cumbersome machine guns and untold more. But they were transportation. Mobile "servants" first who, incidentally, were fighting men. Their job was to deliver the goods and the men. But today they would use everything they had on hand. Ordnance, with its varied types of equipment for waging war, was out of sight, out of mind, out of touch. The Twelfth Armored was way the hell in Passau or some damn where (they practically lived in the woods!), so it was up to the transportation men to rout the miscreants from the *Platz* barricades.

They formed ranks at one central point: the large Headquarters Parade ground, where the entire battalion often staged its military shows for visiting Army royalty or dignitaries from places as distant as the Pentagon. Indeed they looked impressive! But more impressive was the array of trucks! Their washed metal gleamed with sun-bounced sheen. Even Paul gasped as he saw them in tableau.

So many, as far as the eye could see. They were in rows, bumper to bumper columns, actually, in the *kasern's* long street headed towards the Bat's entry/exit gate. Officers and First Sergeants were inspecting men and equipment. (To Paul, this process seemed to take an interminable amount of time.) Finally, reports of readiness were relayed by every first sergeant in each of the six "line" companies, as well as headquarters' own. The report issued to and for the Bat's C.O., Colonel Rossi. "A COMPANY ALL PRESENT AND ACCOUNTED FOR, SIR!!" Each following company repeating the same redundant sound, voices

210

rising in contrapuntal nearness and farness until the tympanic sound of this military coda had played its score. The colonel returned salutes with official stiffness and all-military decorum. He gave the final order to his First Sergeant: "Have the troops mount up." The salutes again, the Sergeant's about face, his bellowing command, "MOUNT YOUR TRUCKS!!", rumbling all down the line until the last one uttered was barely audible to the place of its inception.

They boarded. Kendall and Merritt were in the fifteenth position. Not all the soldiers drove. Some, like cooks, permanent K.P.s, and permanent guard walkers, climbed in the backs of tarpaulin-covered trucks and looked out warily, holding carbines firmly. They were moving. The truckers spaced themselves at twenty-foot intervals. Sergeant Kelly brought up the rear with his wrecker. Sergeant Evans was somewhere in between with his food ration truck, puffing contentedly on his Kaywoodie pipe as though he were going out on just another practice manuever. His driver, Pfc. Reese from Indianola, Mississippi, was fastening the strap of the steel helmet under his chin.

Paul thought of Lea. He also wished he had finished writing those letters home.

The convoy entered the street outside the gate, headed towards Baden. It looked long and endless to Paul, almost exactly like the huge mural on the wall in headquarters' mess hall. They passed some of the girls—their "ol' ladies." Some looked surprised, anticipative, and waved questioningly at them. Paul saw a phalanx of black hands waving back—both in front and in back of him. He wondered what the girls were thinking, since no one had been able to get off post to tell them the news. But, from the worried looks he saw on some of their faces, he figured the Spook Village Grapevine had already informed some of them. Kendall was straining his neck for a glimpse of Erika when they came parallel of a back section where her house would be. Paul was the first one to see her running out just behind them, waving to beat the band. Erika knew Kendall's truck number. Paul hurriedly stuck his hand out and waved frantically.

"Was that Erika?" Kendall asked.

"Uh hunh."

211

"Good. *Now* I'm okay."

Paul wished he could have seen Lea's face too. He was afraid she was working downtown, just a few streets over from the *Platz*. "I hope nothing happens to her," he mumbled, barely audible.

Even on an ordinary day, the *Platz* was something to see. It only covered a distance of two blocks, ending at a cul-de-sac, with buildings joined to one another (townhouse-style) on both sides of the street. It was the widest street in town, and it had no island in the middle like so many others did. Once a week, on Saturday, it was Baden's version of a Paris Flea market. Paul figured it was called that because when the nearby peasant farmers gathered there with their wares, which ranged from roasting chestnuts to fresh-killed pheasants—they looked for all the world like a horde of fleas. Many of them wore quaint costumes of the provinces in which they lived: all garish. Girls and women in dirndls/or aprons; boys and men in lederhosen; other men in undescriptive trousers with tunics resembling the Reich uniform. It was a place for garrulity, evidenced by compatible competitions and friendly respect, plus a yen for festiveness that naturally became them. As a nation of peasants, their tableau was appropos. A spirited bond of togetherness pervaded their days, and Bat soldiers, in particular, had always felt a strong kinship with them.

Now, as the trucks pulled into the *Platz* from the two streets that led into it, the same resemblance to fleas hit Paul's eyes, with one pronounced difference: the "fleas" now had a military sense of order (rather than a tolerated *disorder*) and a *menacing* sense of purpose. The leader of this motley group towered above his crouching followers. He stood arrogantly, one leg encased in a jackboot atop a sandbag. A green Reich tunic open at the throat, with olive-green epaulets on broad shoulders, classified *any* (Hollywood) Teutonic, movie idol. A heavy shock of brown hair utterly unkempt and a wild look of defiance was etched across the handsome features. And yet there was a strange sense of the ridiculous here, particularly from the men in his ranks. Instead of looking like the formidable army of five years previously (going on six), with every conceivable heavy weapon of that enemy's army, they resembled a pageanted scene from a Gilbert & Sullivan

212

opera: one staged for laughs, rather than poignance. Paul was hard put to stifle a laugh.

These rebels were armed with outlandish weapons, from cap pistols to blunderbusses. Their leader himself had an Italian Beretta (a Brownie) rammed down in front of his belt. His "troops" displayed a various assortment of rifles, a few carbines, pistols—souvenirs from the war—pitchforks and some "Alley Oop" clubs. As the trucks converged, using a deep U-shaped wedge within the islandless *Platz*, they presented a combined might which had to have looked overpowering to the raggedy army. Even with the limited firepower of the Bat, today bolstered by its greater number of seasoned soldiers, the "war" against mostly middle-aged, summer "fleas," would be a senseless massacre. Paul was sorely piqued at the ignominy of it all. It seemed grossly unfair.

The troops dismounted hurriedly and took positions by their trucks, holding tightly to their carbines. It was difficult to find a good position from which to fire and take cover at the same time, but they did the best they could do. Even so, the truckers had the advantage of more consistent weapons—and more men.

There was a lengthy impasse. Both sides glared at each other across a no-man's-land not fifty feet wide. It was too ridiculous. For five years (going on six!) soldier and civilian had lived/or co-existed in compatible harmony. The natives knew those black faces so well they often addressed them in the diminutive. They joked with them in *gasthauses*, bought Nescafé, cigarettes and even clothes from the soldier's backs!—when the soldier wanted a drink, or a woman, bad enough! They had their own version of a Black Market. The *Schwartzis* patronized their *kinos* (movie houses), bought gifts of silverware, porcelain and leather goods from their *Platz*-mall shops. Money from the monthly Bat pay tables had given them stability in a country whose own monies were slow to rise to some comfortable level, especially behind so much of the past war's desolation. The kicker, though, had been the Negro's own inbred friendliness—a soul-imbued tenet of doing-unto-others, issued from thousands of Black Baptist churches back home—which penetrated war-torn hearts in Baden. It had become a quid pro quo between the two: *gemütlichkeit fur gemütlichkeit,* and it had worked. Now, all that was going to end by the sudden act of a rebel Communist leader whose obvious pent-up frustrations against all *amis* regardless of nationality had pressed him into this act.

Everyone tensed. The soldiers anchored their positions more firmly. Colonel Rossi had already given the order not to fire until fired upon. Kendall had taken a position on the left rear side of his truck. (He was left-handed anyway.) Paul was on the right. He looked up and down the line of trucks at the other soldiers in similar positions. At the far end Colonel Rossi and "Chili," his jeep driver, crouched behind their vehicle. Corporal McNair, wearing his red medic arm band, was lying prone behind his ambulance, his portable medical kit grasped firmly in one hand. Corporal Patrick every now and then wiped sweat beads from his forehead with the back of a hand. Staff Sergeant "Doc" Whitehead, behind the next truck over from Paul, was peering out from behind a rear left wheel. Sergeant Moment was behind the right. Private Dickenson, the Bat's heavyweight champion fighter, was stretched out full length underneath his truck. Currant, (the oddest half of this odd couple), the foppish clerk from headquarters company, was a few feet behind him, also prone.

The Communist leader surveyed the positions of the soldiers, all the while giving vehement instructions to minions on either side of him. To Paul Merritt he looked like another native whose path one might cross on any given afternoon, on a stroll or sitting in a *gasthaus* with his friends. Now the man was preparing to give the signal for his minions to fire, to start a raggedy war in which he and his "troops" were hopelessly overmatched. That *was* the bottom line.

The foolish idealist slowly raised his hand to give the command to open fire. Every soldier tensed, leveled his carbine at a human being across the way. Kendall broke the silence, grimly: "The shit's about to hit the fan."

Suddenly, before the Red Leader could bring down his hand, everyone heard a familiar and poignant human sound. A child, not more than three years old, was walking right down the middle of no-man's-land, crying forlornly. The Red Leader's hand remained poised in the air, but his head jerked in the direction of the sound—and sight. The child walked with no apparent sense of direction among the rows of would-be combatants. The pathetic baby cries, combined with the sight of the child walking betwixt two opposite rows of fire, held everyone spellbound.

Paul saw that it was a boy-child, virtually an urchin, with short *lederhosen*, a ragged sweater. As he walked, he continually balled tiny fists to wipe tears from his eyes. The Red Leader's hand slid unconsciously to his side. Some of his followers looked at him, perplexed. The soldiers looked at one another, questioningly, their faces strained with compassion, their eyes watchful of the scene. Then, the strangest and most surprising thing of all happened.

Corporal Ira Willoughby, from Bossier City, Louisiana, "C" Company, was seen walking down the no-man's-land from whence the child had come. He had laid down his carbine, taken off his cartridge belt and started walking in easy, purposeful strides towards this sudden center of attention.

Corporal Willoughby was a long, lean and lanky drink of water with a face like Andy Gump, buck teeth like Bugs Bunny and a perennially drooped bottom lip. He was the homeliest-looking soldier in the entire Bat, but also one of its staunchest adherents to a soldier's duty and obedience. He caught up with the child and faced him, bent down on his knees and began talking to him in the baby-talk language of the country; soothing him, taking a clean, white hankerchief from a pocket and gently wiping away the tears. The child cried yet a little but listened, clingingly, to the words of comfort from this solicitous brown soldier. Willoughby patted the little back lightly, talking softly to the child, walking back with him over the lengthy distance he had come. Every eye was watching, but no one said a word.

Some of the soldiers came away from their protective positions to see the spectacle up close, as if they wanted to share in it. Some of the rebels stood up also, wonderment and concern evident in their faces. Then others stood, holding their weapons askew in their hands. Two of them climbed over the sandbags, walking in the direction of Willoughby and the child. A few others from the rebel camp began to walk away from the barricades in seeming disgust. Then more. And still more, up and down the line. Then all were walking away—an odd sight. Men began slinging their guns over their shoulders, barrels down; J*aegars* (hunters) coming home from the hunt, having captured no game yet going home for a good hot meal and the quiet of a family hearth. Some of them threw down their guns and walked away angrily.

The rebel leader looked this way and that, admonishing his followers with vituperations. It was to deaf ears. In an instant there was no one on the rebel's firing line but the rebel himself. He turned to view the soldiers with mingled hate and frustration. Colonel Rossi approached him, talking. The rebel leader was declaiming bitterly. His hands flailed the air. He flung a torrent of invectives. The Colonel listened, then reached over and pulled the Beretta out of the man's waistband. He ordered his soldiers to come and pick up the discarded weapons along the now abandoned barricade.

Colonel Rossi refused to arrest the Red leader. Instead he simply turned his back and walked with "Chili," Sergeant Whitehead and Sergeant Moment back to his jeep. (Later, Paul was to learn that the Colonel's action was the equivalent of a "public spanking.") As for those supposedly holding Ordnance's skeleton personnel under siege, the Colonel, "Chili," Sergeant Moment and the thigh-wounded *Burgermeister* walked into its company office and accepted surrenders without a shot being fired. The hapless "summer soldiers" (middle-aged to a man), breathed great sighs of relief and gratefully accepted the packs of free Pall Mall (Reds) the Colonel gave them, going forthwith to their homes with his pardon. Baden's *gemütlichkeit* between the *Amis* and its natives was still par for the course. And the course was still steady.

Merritt and Kendall were assisting the other soldiers in gathering up the contraband. Kendall was angry and disgusted. Merritt was relieved.

"This will go down in history . . . Lord, today!" he uttered with pride. "I wouldn't have believed it . . . Je-sus!!"

"If this ain' a motherfucker I'll eat my peter! . . . Them

chicken-shit sons of bitches!" Kendall kicked violently at an imaginary object.

Merritt had to laugh at his friend's outburst, at his anger, his frustrations. Kendall was a fighter, valorous in a valorous situation, a heroic type who thrived on action.

"I'm beginning to believe this is one 'war' that couldn't get off the ground if it wanted to," Paul mused, still unbelieving.

"Yeah. Ain't it the motherfucking truth! . . . Who ever heard o' such shit?!! A 'waw' wid'out firin' a shot!"

"Corporal Willoughby, baby," Merritt replied, blandly, in a tone rife with meaning. "He's the Nigger with the unknown and still known equation. He's the motherfucker. Bless him. We're still living, bless him!"

Kendall looked at him in anger. Almost as though his rooming buddy was dirt under his fingernails. "What's that? Some more of that SCHOOL shit?"

"No, sir. No, my man. . . . Believe it or not, it's *little* talk. It's person-to-person SHIT! It's Providence-to-Willoughby-to-that-*kid*. As far as I'm concerned, that's the greatest human equation of them all. Fuck the books!"

Kendall was looking strangely at his friend as they walked back towards their truck carrying armfuls of rebel weapons. Paul and Kendall—a strange but compatible duo. To Kendall, Paul was too reflective—seeing lights at the end of the damndest tunnels. And to Paul, Kendall, once having tasted heroism, had not wanted it to get away from him, ever. A standoff or a stalemate simply killed him, or limited the beloved continuity on which he based his current existence. A war was still a war. The baddest motherfuckers kicked asses and took names. But no such event had taken place today.

"TRUCKERS, MOUNT YOUR TRUCKS!" Motor Sergeant Martin's booming voice broke up both reveries and frustrations of the two gallants with opposite beliefs. They boarded, climbing into their truck cab with regimented, unchallenged, servitude. Military obeisance was still first and foremost.

They eased into convoy formation, drove out of the *Platz*. Paul Alexander Merritt was pensive as they passed through the former war zone. A fidgeting Kendall gnawed on a knuckled fist with one hand, steering with the other. Paul looked over at his buddy, poked him in the side ribs with his elbow. Kendall grimaced with a feigned extreme pain, watched a familiar wide grin break out on the right side of his friend's face and busted out laughing. He shook his head and muttered, "son-of-a-bitch, son-of-a-bitch." Merritt got the message, entirely. "You fuckin' aye it is, my man, you fuckin' aye." There was no more to be said on the subject. The "waw" was over.

Heavyweight

$\mathbf{C}$orporal William—"Billy Kid"—Buchanan, A Company, had been with the 33rd Transportation Battalion (the Bat) for five years. A six-by trucker with the best of them, he was the Command's heavyweight boxing champion. Liking both the nickname and the fame, he was forever—in the jargon of his Bat's idolators—notorious for "kicking asses and taking names."

The notoriety was perfect for him. After his 1953 termination of a three-year enlistment ("This is *it*! I promise you no more!"), he would be entirely into boxing for a living. He had become enamored of main event overtures—grandiloquent, eloquently lipped from word-processed ring announcers—blatantly proclaiming his victories to boxing patrons seated about rings in Army gymnasiums. His climb to a many-victoried status had been brutally impressive—even in four-rounders—and he was basking in the glories.

Two years ago, the name "Billy Kid" had not sounded so spectacular to the U.S. Army fight world at large. But recent events concerning his fistic prowess had sent that grating oversight to flight. His now avowed Command championship had come from his recent fight at Straubing, that Army and Air Force sports-conscious city; when he had whipped the literal piss out of that hefty "peckerwood" soldier from "Sippi"; and his fame had gained gargantuan status overnight. He had become "Champion of Tomorrow!—and of the World!" Ironically, this announcement had come from a glibly enthusiastic white soldier writer in the Command's weekly *Argus*. The voluminous praise garnered him a word-of-mouth substance that was constantly ringing throughout the Bat. Ring-warring Billy-Kid Buchanan felt unshakeably deserving of every syllable—both written and uttered.

Of all the books, newspapers and magazines entering through each of the Bat's Company Day Rooms, *Ring* magazine in "A" Company *always* seemed to disappear completely. One could "bet a fat man" it was the touch of Buchanan, almost as if he had subscribed to it for it himself—which he damn well hadn't. The truth would out eventually from vagaries of the thief himself. Just ask any member who had listened to him expound on any black boxer at any morning breakfast chow. Verbal outpourings concerning the fisticuffs of Jack Johnson, Kid Chocolate (The Boston Tar Baby), Joe Louis, Max Schmeling, Randy Turpin, Sugar Ray Robinson, Kid Gavilan, Archie Moore (the Mongoose: a name Buchanan dearly loved because of the snake's stealthy cleverness), and all other boxers great and small comprised his cranium of facts. Gathered from where? Where else? The missing *Ring* magazine. Contemporary ring greats like Ezzard Charles, Jersey Joe Walcott, Billy Cohn, Willie Pep, Sandy Saddler made the fictional, white, movie-western-cowboy names most black men of the Bat rolled off their tongues, pale into insignificance. They were all "hunkies," bullshittin' dumbass niggers with jive-ass, celluloid macho. He, Billy-Kid Buchanan, lived in the world of real men.

Off duty, Buchanan had it made even more so. After his daily truck driving chores were over, having at last made corporal, he walked with a haughtier gait. The corporalcy was not for leadership smarts, or even for time-in-grade. Special Services had deemed a corporalcy a suitable rank for the Company's (and Command's) *celebrity*. He was exempt now from those degrading tasks of all day K.P.-ing and after hours walking guard duty. It lifted his soul to accepted heights. His off-duty jaunts, both off post and on, ofttimes resulted in busted noses and broken teeth to unwitting comrades whose sudden urge for fistic stardom caused their facial ruin.

A case in point occurred when Buchanan challenged eight A Company hecklers to stay one round with his murderous fists in a makeshift ring. Eight foolhardy blacks accepted the impromptu dare to their peril. And all eight fell, knocked senseless by his barrage of flailing fists. Kayos one and all. (Indeed, not only was he the "Jim Brown" on A Company's gridiron, he was a "Joe Louis" savagery, although clearly not in humility. Of that he had none.) The one-warrior massacre would be a conversation piece for days and days *and* days!

But the foolhardiness of the eight would never match the witlessness of a well-liked "second-John" (Second Lieutenant) from C Company, Howard Mendle Smarts. The Lieutenant, a Supply Officer, ("so good-natured it hurt" and eternally pipe-smoking sober), often served as intermediary bailsman for soldiers jailed overnight in downtown Baden on "trumped-up" charges. Almost always easy to reach, day or night, he would be down at the Provost Marshall's office in a twinkling. He was noted for getting his men released to him pending charges for soldier disturbances downtown by white MPs (there were no black ones). The contention of black GI's was it "took a white face *for* a white face" and some "strong white man's talk" to hasten a release. A junior member of the Bat's Adjutant General's staff, plus pursuing a career in law "from the git-go," Lieutenant Smart's arguments were almost always astutely effective. His efforts were compared to those of Sergeant Moment, who had three strikes against him from the start: he was a nigger sergeant in a nigger outfit and a fag to boot. He had to come in *very* diplomatically (although firmly); he had to beseech, cajole (literally, ass kiss); and *still* threaten intercession from the area's High Command. He mailed typewritten reports of abusiveness, brutality with discrimination, and anything else he could think of to the Adjutant General's office, which did his men little good while they were suffering blows and "black sonofabitch" insults from bestial, black-hating white MP's. It was one reason the Bat's blacks unlucky enough to become temporarily locked within the Provost Marshall's jail referred to it as a "little Georgia."

It was not so with white Second Lieutenant Howard M. Smarts. He could go *in* demanding. The horn-rim glasses-wearing exponent of justice-for-all demanded that the soldier (or soldiers) be released forthwith, using every ounce of his Adjutant General status as an opening gambit. He was far more well-versed in the dictum of the Army's (Revised) Uniform Code Of Military Justice than his confronted bestial peers, who displayed all kinds of frustrations pondering complex judicial asides—even when the black soldier was dead wrong! A live wire Perry Mason in arrest cases, Smarts nearly always took his arrested-now-released detainee with him out of Baden's dungeon (a place barely removed from the middle ages), happy as a lark to be back in his black world! The clout, the audacity, the judicial expertise of this sandy-haired southerner from Valdosta, Georgia, made his fame shine and spread all over the Bat. Even the frauleins and schatzi's, ol' ladies and 'ho's of the Bat's blacks, knew of him. Having grown accustomed to loving legends in their historical world through wars and rumors of such, their feminine bosoms cleaved to him with each black's storytelling.

That was the main reason Bat members "fell out" with Billy-Kid Buchanan, even though they would ever ponder Lieutenant Smart's senseless foolishness.

Billy Kid-Buchanan hated the white lieutenant's guts. To him, Smarts was typical of all the "hunkies" he'd known all his struggling, fist-fighting life. Whether in makeshift boxing rings in Texas, Florida, Mississippi, Georgia, or anywhere else down south, Buchanan had been sponsored by cigar-chomping, money-bets waving white promoters; ever with the blatant, vocal dictum-hype ("my-nigger-can-whup-your-nigger") placed with one white man or the other. Like fighting roosters or fighting dogs, like any "things" considered less than human. And Billy Kid-Buchanan's *look* at all that money, of which he always got so little, and the indignities it cost him personally. The hawkers' savage instructions: Buchanan and his opponent were to "beat the slop out of each other" until "blood flowed." There would be no such thing as a "draw." Blood alone was the criteria. "Nigger fighters" always fought to the death, because it was what their white patrons paid to see. And it was Billy Kid's *seeing* what those perverted white faces showed that lingered in his memory. It was only through a faked facsimile of bloodletting—from chicken wire laced about the gums—that some black fighters survived at all. Sadly, Billy Kid's hatred of whites in general, based on the gloating hate emitted from white faces around his old, remembered ringsides, would never diminish. He lived by an ancient Negro axiom: "When you ketch a fool, bump his head." It was a normalcy in Billy Kid's upbringing. And for a challenge, once accepted, one had to "bring ass to get ass." His code. And he lived by it.

The lieutenant was a white do-gooder Buchanan hated for sure. In his mind—whether he could *word* it that way or not, which he couldn't—a hunkie *always* had an ulterior motive. To Buchanan, the "el tee" was a hunkie in power, but still a hunkie; no matter how much he "pretended" to *like* black folks. If he was going to challenge Billy Kid-Buchanan, he'd have to "bring ass, too"—and plenty of it—or else get his goddam "hat." This slaughterer didn't have no love for him.

It was a no-contest from the start. Lieutenant Smart's cerebral morality play of "teaching" the militant, non obsequious Buchanan a *lesson* (in whatever "style" engendered from *his* upbringing) belonged in a Hollywood scenario where the *hero* would emerge triumphant, and *definitely not* in a downtown Baden's servicemen's club gymnasium; a gymnasium now mass-filled with black and white American soldiers, Baden's club-employed natives, and even a modicum of its Department of the Army civilians. All of C Company's first three-graders—several from Buchanan's own A Company and a score of those from Headquarters, including Sgt. Moment—had tried, vainly, to talk the would-be moralist out of a possibly shaming venture. The heroic—and soon to be proved dumb—Viking had studied "fisticuffs" as diligently as he'd studied the laws' torts and retorts; both civilian and military. Even Paul Merritt, the I&E man, had tried unsuccessfully to dissuade Smarts from this obvious *madness*. His softly uttered, but intensely released, "the reasons are *not* the *same*," followed by "he *hates white people*!" and his poignant last thought, "we—we black people—we *need* you for what you *already are!*" fell on deaf ears to an already thoroughly made up mind. Defeated, Merritt, Sergeant Moment and other caring members went back to their improvised ringside seats to await the outcome. Their combined black knowledge, known to a man, was that this light-skinned Negro was out to wreak black vengeance on whatever white man faced him in that ring today. And all of them cared, and cared deeply, more than they'd ever care to show. It showed anyway.

The lieutenant did as Billy Kid-Buchanan knew he would: everything with a dash or splash. Entering the ring, he was relieved of horn-rim glasses, pete cap, olive drab tie; removed his Ike jacket with gold bars, rolled up his khaki shirt sleeves, loosened his belt a notch, relinquishing aforesaid habiliments to an effacing, admiring private (black) in back of the ropes. Another black, Corporal William ("Bill") Kelsey, Special Services NCO, serving as referee, laced sixteen-ounce boxing gloves about the lieutenant's well-manicured hands. Kelsey led both fighters to the center of the ring and gave the usual redundant and all too familiar ritual of Marquess of Queensbury rules. Both fighters then went to their separate corners to await the bell.

In less than the time it took to pray, the bell sounded. It made the loudest noise in the world, particularly in that hushed "arena" of history-accrued, eminently divided loyalties. The lieutenant was the first to advance. Billy Kid-Buchanan looked athletically adept with his arms at posture, fists balled, balancing on balleted toes for leverage. Even wearing light grey sweat pants and shirt, he glided like an animal. The lieutenant, in army olive drab, looked foolish trying to emulate him. The officer circled, jabbing a left fist in the air about his opponent's face, missing him completely, searching for an opening. He jabbed, feinted cutely, missing the champion but looking good "on paper." For almost thirty seconds not a blow was landed and the officer provoked a clinch. Corporal Kelsey dutifully rushed in to separate them. Confidence gushed all over the officer's face. He was falling victim to the idea (based on centuries of black subservience) that the big Negro, Billy Kid-Buchanan, wouldn't dare hurt this white man. Fool. Lieutenant Smarts should have studied more closely the malicious smile that suddenly began to encompass the mouth-piece face in that one—and *only* one—white-black embrace. It was a look of hatred that shouldn't belong to any human. His well-known hatred of whiteness, even within his own cross-bred skin, had long been known to A Company's Bat members; and no equality would ever exist to change the furies. Now, at this moment, he would make damn sure this hunky motherfucker would never "hug" him again.

A vicious left hook from Billy Kid-Buchanan sent a mouth-piece flying across the ring. A smashing right to the lieutenant's face caused teeth to run in triplicate down a khaki shirt, accompanied by small spurts of blood. A right hook made the left eye dance crazily. A savage upward left punch to an unprotected stomach divested the now hapless officer of his latest meal. Then both of the gladiators' arms dropped. The white face was pummeled by fists left, right and "bolo-ed." Animal brutality took over. The sinking officer was virtually being whipped to the floor. On his knees, he hadn't yet reached the nadir of his fall, and Billy Kid-Buchanan hovering over him at range with repeated blows continued to flail away, even then, almost as though the bloodied face still had some *whiteness* showing.

It was human concern alone that saved the white man's life. Seeing Kelsey knocked away by one of Billy Kid's blows, Paul Merritt, his friend Kendall, "Chili," McNair and even Sergeant Moment all leaped into the ring and as a group held the furious-snarling Billy Kid in a no-break grip. Then McNair and A Company's medic, "Doc" Whitehead, dragged the hapless officer to a ring corner. Seconds later, two soldiers—one white, one black—were hurrying up to the ring with a stretcher. Handling him ever so gently, they muscled him through the ring's ropes and hastened him to one of the gymnasium's dressing rooms. There, the two indispensable and thoroughly well-liked Bat medics made instant ministrations. The only words spoken were by them; their prostrate victim was soundless. Only the wail of an unmistakable army ambulance nearing the service club pervaded a generally massive quiet. The officer was carefully loaded into its confines, along with both medics, as its black orderly driver revved up his motor before speeding even more blatantly away. To the watching throng outside the service club, it seemed the shortest time in history before the emergency sound vanished, and the merging macadam encompassed their flight towards the area's army general hospital.

It was ironic, Paul Merritt thought, after the gym had closed and off-duty GI's resumed their off-duty pleasures, that he and Kendall had once been swept towards the same hospital for emergency treatment. Only this situation had almost been reversed. If the fates were fickle and erratic, they were also unkind. His mind pondered two unanswered questions. First—about that beating by six white thugs the previous Christmas night— why *them*? Second—with Billy Kid doing his damndest to whip a decent white man to pieces, one who was forever going to bat for them—why *him*? Why, Lord, him? The officer was one in a million—in his book.

Almost overnight, it seemed, many soldiers of the Bat— many from A Company in particular—did not take to Billy Kid-Buchanan. Many divided emotions raged and reverberated vocally for and against a champion they had once lauded as a second "Joe Louis." The unkind words issued from painfully knowledged *survivors*, who were totally unforgiving of the way whites back home had treated them to say nothing of their friends and loved ones. The kind words echoed remembrances of once being "saved" from an upcoming, brutal attack by whites who appeared to be— or were even *known* to be—bigots. ("Klu-Kluxers," Bat soldiers called them.) One thing ultimately showed, however—sooner or later—they were *glad* to see a black man *win*. Only this victory just wasn't clean. Every black son-of-a-buck and his brother knew of Lieutenant Smarts' downtown victories on their behalf. To those more searching than others, there was more moping than gloating. In their minds, and for their futures, so long as they gave a damn for people like the lieutenant, who not only fought their battles but *won* them, there not only was hope for the race, but, also for the whole (sometimes "fucked-up") world! One had to be fair, race be damned!

Some time passed. It always did. Second Lieutenant Howard M. Smarts, with the help of the skillful medical and plastic surgeons, recovered quickly from his savage beating in the ring by Billy Kid-Buchanan. A kind of plain-Joe in looks before, the second-John was now damn near beautifully handsome. They not only "fixed" the battered eye, they *saved* it. His vision was even improved. In the future he would hardly need his horn-rims—his "cheaters." Moreover, his love for A Company men changed not one iota; and neither did his pursuits on canons of law. They seemed enhanced all the more. A Company as a whole rated him a hero, an idolatry that brought a well of tears streaming down his face at an impromptu mass gathering in its Day Room. Quiet as it was kept, it was probably the one time in the white officer's life that he wished he were black as the ace of spades, and could live with their adulation forever. Only one laconic utterance was spoken *sotto voce*, yet heard by at least one gossipy minion: "hunkie had to git his ass kicked by a nigger to see how a' ass-kicking felt . . . and in *public!*" Luckily, it failed to penetrate the officer's praise-filled ears. Directed at a known white enemy that truth would have been unanimously accepted by the black masses. But, not today, Lordy, not today.

* * * * *

The Army Integration change-over continued in high gear. Almost snowballed—viewed as a reckless pun. Even Billy Kid-Buchanan had been transferred—along with three of his own idolaters ("ass-kissers from the *jump*" and all known to A Company men) to a once all-white Company in Veen: Vienna. He didn't like it too well—didn't like it at all for a fact. The city wasn't free enough, travel-wise: being divided into four parts by the Big Four Powers. (Only in the Russian zone was an American GI cautioned *not* to enter.) Plus, the city was geographically and historically monstrous. In the International zone, however, large-printed, posted signs kept a straying GI apprised of his immediate whereabouts. This irked Billy Kid-Buchanan, who was used to roaming all over his now departed Baden in search of "new pussy," and felt limited in pursuing such conquests due to so much political protocol. No matter, he'd rove anyway.

As for duties, all the four did was either work in the Company's motor pool—washing trucks, jeeps, and weapons carriers—or serve as jeep and/or truck couriers: transporting officers or supplies to this or that unit within their specified American perimeter. To the champion, a drag, really. "Integration," the man had said—and still a drag. That arrangement might work well for Billy Kid-Buchanan's three ass-lickers, but added no adrenalin for an ambitious "killerboxer." Uppermost in his mind at the thought of his savage profession flashed the image of the then welterweight boxing champion, "Kid Gavilan" and his "bolo" strikes. He had used it on the lieutenant—for practice. And he couldn't, for the life of him, get the sports people of the *Argus*, to write more on his recent victories—his eight kayoes simultaneously *and* the Company lieutenant. That had to be world-shaking news to fight fans everywhere. Of course, he wasn't entirely stupid, he knew the MAN ever played his little "games" with contending blacks. He also felt with just a taste of chagrin that they already knew of his ring savagery—writers and boxers alike—and were *afraid* of him. Well, he'd have to find another, better way of getting media attention if he wanted fistic credits established by the end of his enlisted tenure. The first thing he'd have to do was shake off these three black leeches who followed him wherever he went. . . .

He got lucky one surprising weekend. On Saturday when the weekend duty roster was placed on his new Company's bulletin board: all three of them were listed for both K.P. and guard duty. Alone at last, he left the Vienna *kaserne* right after noon chow and began to explore the diversely gregarious city.

Strangely—perhaps because he was alone—he liked the city something fierce! He liked the townhouses, storefronts, the abounding sewers; the darkness and the light, shops, sidewalks and the sound of his own heavy, highly-polished combat boots resounding on cobblestoned streets. Walking in the middle of it when he could (like in the country) and barely escaping being run down by uncanny driving motorists, the experience was in itself a challenge. (Not like back home walking down dusty roads.) The city, sophisticated or not, still supported people carrying rope-sacks of food and cycling *fahrrads* (bicycles) like they did in Baden. His American uniform and light-skinned (high-yaller) face was stared at, as in Baden, but not with the "fear and trembling" such stares evoked there; because race-mingling and power-mingling held a great surge here. Truly, in the City of Dreams, intelligence in the main held sway over politics. An attitude of "show me" and "let's talk" seemed to out-vote blatant, unsubstantiated racial statements—especially in a city that had housed—in siege and out—a multiplicity of races.

He stopped in several taverns: drinking a tankard of beer here, an octel of wine there, a viertel of *steinheger*; at an even cozier *wein stuberl* he asked for a *Karlovitzer*, that red, deliciously sweet wine that always gave him a mean buzz. After a while, realizing his boxer's proclivities for keeping a clean body, this alcohol business would have to cease. More food and less spirits ought to do it. At least for today.

Right now he was hungry as a dog. Darkness was falling and he was pondering a place to eat. (Actually, there was no end to them.) Why not the West Bahnhof? The train station? One could always count on their food. Whether first or third class. (Where the hell was second class?) The third for him. He'd dine with the peasants—more in keeping—besides, didn't it all come from the same kitchen? Damn right it did. Hungarian ghoulash . . . that was good eating. The thought sped him to the *bahnhof* quicker than he thought.

He picked a table among several empties.

The table in front of him presented a young, pretty, black-haired fraulein. And two young men. Idly, he wondered if they were together. The instant his eye caught her he knew she was what he wanted. He was lucky in other ways, too: her tablecloth only went so far over its edge and he saw with mounting lust those beautifully crossed big legs. A curvaceous ass simply had to go with them. The legs made a movement as she caught his stare—and confirmed his hopes. No doubt about it: this mother was foxy. Just what he needed: bedwise. Even an athlete needed pussy. And weren't those big, brown eyes a knockout? In the path of lust a passing waiter in semi-tuxedo attire was beckoned and he ordered a small *Karlovitzer*. With spirit heightened toward a possible sexual conquest, he felt his libido stirring. One guaranteed hard-on coming up!

The *bahnhof's* loudspeaker boomed, announcing arrivals and departures of trains going to long distance places across the continent. The two men at her table rose at once, gathering tattered suitcases at their feet and rope sacks of veggies: potatoes, spinach, cabbage, radishes, white onions. They bid her fervently emotional *Auf Wiedersehen's* and hurried out. The girl remained. His long sigh of relief was almost visibly breathed.

He eyed the good-looking woman for long minutes on end. A lucky rascal (she had eyes for him, too!) her gaze never left his face. He was hesitant towards suddenly moving from his table over to hers; but he sure as hell wanted her and he needed to do something! Goddam! He hadn't had a woman in weeks!

From across the table he thundered, *"Bist du aleines?"* (Are you alone?)

A startled look from her but to his joy a positive, *"Ja."* Yes.

"Gut. Ich acht." Me, too. His pidgin street German was limited, but no more so than that of other Bat members who had amassed over five years of European occupancy. With confidence, a man could even make the devil work for him.

"Wollst sie ein bier?" Care for a beer?

"Nein, danke." No, thank you. Perhaps she didn't drink spirits.

"Ein Cola, ca?" A soda pop, perhaps?

"Nein. Ich willst nicht. Danke." No. Nothing at all, thank you. She didn't want anything. Damn! An ass pocketful of money, he wanted to offer her the world. But, at least they were *talking*. Suddenly he wasn't hungry either.

"Wo gehen sie? " Where are you going? *"Dortmund."* *"Heute nacht?"* Tonight? *". . . Villacht."* Perhaps. *"Ich weiss nicht."* I'm not sure, yet. Maybe yes, maybe no. She sounded promising.

He detected encouragement in her declarations. *"Ich bist aleines, acht."* I'm alone, too. He had to pursue this . . . he was gaining . . . making points. *"Willst sie mit mia gehen?"* Can't we go someplace together? *"Wo?"* Where? *"Spazierngang."* Just walking. *"Machts nix."* It makes no difference . . .

She rose first and headed for the door. After waiting the entire length of two frustrating seconds, he hurriedly dropped an over-amount of money on the table and followed hastily behind her, and out the station's departure doors. He caught up with her on the outside platform. They walked along together, but in silence. His head was a little woozy from so much drinking.

"*Mein nome ist 'Billy-Kid.'*" He tossed aside the Buchanan.

"*Icht bist Ilse.*"

"*A gutes nome.* " A good name, he thought, and meant every word.

They walked off the platform, their feet crunching the cinders paralleling railroad tracks. He figured that he had her, but the spirits were telling him to rush it. He edged closer beside her, smelling her talcum, inhaling her freshness, her femininity. She looked up at him, at his height, gave him the widest smile. He had it "dicked" now.

They walked past a coal shed. Railroad tracks were broadening out. He was feeling exhilarated—and reckless. Once or twice he stumbled. He recovered, grinning sheepishly." *Langsom, bitte,*" she cautioned, concerned. Be careful. He saw a sign on a building in the far distance, signifying a *pension*: a *gasthaus* with rooms, a shack job. It was across the tracks, however: a wide expanse of tracks.

"*Es gehen,*" he said, pointing. Let's go there.

"*Nein. Das nichts durchfahren. Die andere weg ist besser.*" It's forbidden, too dangerous that way. Better to go around.

He thought she was stalling—if not *teasing*. He could feel his anger rising, an ancient anger of rejection by white folks; of promising but not delivering. "Come on!" He snatched violently at her arm.

"*Nein! Nicht Durchfahren! Ist Verboten!*" It's foolish . . . The trains! Her face revealed absolute terror of crossing those tracks in that immense darkness. And it *was* pitch black.

"Come on—damnit!" He reached out violently for her again but she broke away, backing away from the now gone gentler side he had appeared to present before. Now, fear encompassed her face.

He advanced on her, she retreated, seeing an evil in his face that might have been imbedded in it for years, just waiting to surface and surfacing *now*. He lunged for her, she broke and ran fleeing for her life.

In his lunge he had fallen, and now steadied himself on knees and hands, feeling the rock-sharp cinders prod his senses to pained wakefulness. But the drunk was too strong, and with no food to thwart an equivalence, his body was captured by it. His eyes wouldn't focus properly. The sweet finesse of balance that had carried him over, around and through so many fistic boxing matches in the past was limp as a faggot's wrist, and twice as weightless. Up ahead she was a long distance blur in the night's blackness. But he had to have her, and at all costs. Like everything else in his life, he had put far too much of himself into the doing. And the doing was him, Billy Kid-Buchanan, bone and sinew. Now *he* was running, panting heavily, not at all like the well-conditioned athlete that had made him the superb fighter that he was. But too much alcohol and no food at all since noon-day chow had "messed" with his muscular coordination, and his "target" was somewhere, up there, in the distance. There she was. Just up there.

And she was coming to a dead end on the path. A small train shed, flanked by a curved, double iron buffer, ended her path. And gave her choices. She could either turn completely around and run *back* towards him or seek other refuge by running across the wide expanse of train tracks in the inky black distance. Moreover, not only was the shed no help, it was also thickly padlocked. Each thought terrified her all the more. In her lifetime, stories—and two *knowing sights*—of people killed on railroad tracks had haunted her dreams for longer than she cared to remember. Now *she* was being forced into this tragedy by the inexplicable pursuer . . . and he was *gaining* on her.

Fear of the known in front of her and the unknown in back of her hastened her sudden decision: she chose the known. Running across railroad tracks to the far side of their expanse, using diminishing light paths as her guide, she planned to leap the breast-high fence to the safety of the *pension*. It wasn't her best choice, it was her *only* choice.

Billy Kid-Buchanan followed, gropingly, legs akimbo, stumblingly. Ilse made it across one, two, three sets of them. A hasty look back, she saw him at four sets behind her—but relentlessly groping forward. After nearly tripping over the last set of tracks, she recovered her balance, commanded strength for both arms and legs and, grasping the wooden fence top with a firm grip, arched her entire body over it in a soaring, no-hands free fall. She barely stopped to savor the shock of her fall on the sidewalk; instead she felt compelled to look back in the direction where her pursuer might be. And he wasn't there. Innate female curiosity, mingled with compassionate concern, made her stare longer through that mordant darkness for a visible show of his being. The other fear—that of the known—returned; she found herself brushing away imagined dust and lint parcels, as she made her way to the ever so near, *gasthaus pensione* . . .

Billy Kid-Buchanan hadn't seen the long tongue switch handle, standing vertically up to a night sky. Running into it, he was sent sprawling. In the fall, his head banged against a track rail. He struggled to get up. As he did so, he heard an all-too-familiar sound. Far away. *Or was it?* He fell back down again, and vibrations within the timbre of the track's rails where his head lay rattled his memories of impressions acquired as a youth long ago. He remembered old movies of Indians putting their ears to the railroad tracks to hear trains that were far away but *coming!* He was having trouble getting up. What was wrong with him?

He *had* to get up! The vibrations were getting stronger, the sounds were getting nearer. In the batting eyes of a liquored head now excruciatingly painful from its assault on immutable steel, he could see white beam lights, plus some red ones, winking and blinking in a distance perilously near. A blatant and shrill all-knowing whistle inundated his consciousness, while the first flood of fear riveted his face amidst thick beads of sweat. He was even beginning to smell the oils and fuel of an approaching engine. Damnit, it was getting closer!! Panic seized him even more as he made one last, desperate, all-out effort to rise.

He thought he heard a screech of brakes. Git up, git up! his own voice thundered at him. Git up, damnit!! And the body hadn't answered, hadn't responded to the agile, boxer's mind that had controlled it so many countless times before. The only reply was a night piercing scream coming from the depths of the body that was once Billy Kid-Buchanan, mingled with even more mingled sounds of train brakes that autopsied a once fine human body into globs of parts. The savage fighter that might have been a "coming" rival against those in his cherished heavyweight division had lost to a foe outside a ring: himself. Like much of the roving, displacement, battle for survival his life had been, he had even lost it, in a country that was not his own.

Jean

The one I met, walking,
Without rouge, lipstick, hair un"pressed"
(just good-groomed)
Dark-skinned, black (like me), tall,
Swivel-hipped, clean-looking, pretty,
High-breasted, big-behinded,
Large, expressive eyes, long,
Big shapely legs, feminine gait,
Feminine woman, my kind:
Thirty-four, twenty-six, thirty-eight,
(Hips, by God!)

I, late for work—but getting there—
Anxious like a dog.
Anxious, earning this day, needing it
(more than ever, now)
Having the knowledge that
This poor, unhandsome slob
Loved her—loved her to the teeth.
Right now!

Maybe her bus will stop—
Stop by the barbershop—
At the end of the evening
Discharging passengers,
And she will alight
Fresh as a daisy, ending the day.
Maybe I'll be there,
Bump into—"excuse me"—
Tell her "I'm sorry,"
Contend with a frown,
Get a smile in return.

Walk to the corner
Slowly behind her,
Look like a fool,
Wait for the whispers
To tell me I'm wrong.
Then, free myself from
Such didactic cowardice
And think of some minister
In a Baptist church.

Blues for Black

I . . . don't have to remind myself . . .
That black is beautiful . . .
I know it is.
I have lived within its varied,
Broad and sometimes
Abysmal deeps for years.
I have swam in its black, murky waters
The entire length of the Nile and
In the inky, fathomless depths
Of the Euphrates
I swam and swam and swam and swam
And . . . God knows I can't swim a lick!
Rhetorically, I've seen black kings sell
Black princes to white slave traders.
In the bottom-less holds of white slave ships
Bound for an alien shore
I have plotted right along
With other angry discontents . . . like me . . .
A mutiny so fierce
That an entire white ship's crew
Jumped overboard.

I know this blackness well:
It is an indelible part of me,
And has been for a long time.
Will ever be for an even longer time,
So long as black breathes breath;
Implacable and ever sustaining itself
Within the blackness of infinities of Infinities.

My soul has become inured to this blackness
And there is no substitute
For it.

I am Gideon, Solomon, Simon;
I am the arch-angel Gabriel:
I awake the dead *and* the living . . . I
Am the man who cried I AM !!!

I am a black voice
Crying out from the deeps:
From murky Mississippi waters;
I am the recurrent echo from a Georgia,
Alabama and a Texas cotton field.
I am the roaring sound of perpetual,
Dusty mills;
My skin is dusty with the cover of finely
Ground wheat,
My lungs bursting with the cry for anti-
Bodies
To sustain my existence on this earth
Woe, this is woe, o hideous woe!
"My lamentations are weightier than my
Groanings."

I, also, am a little black boy lost
On his first day in an all-white school;
A black cry from the wilderness
From a swollen valley of despair.
I am a black poet heard from the tombs
A singer crooning softly yet succinctly:
Steal Away! Steal Away! Steal Away!
I am an escapee, hiding in the woods,
Behind Harriet Tubman's skirts or
Masked as a sailor with Frederick Douglass;
Riding shotgun, perhaps, with Nat Turner
And John Brown, dying heroically.
I am Countee Cullen, Phyllis Wheatley,
Booker T., Will Edward Jackson . . . my father
. . . I am Jean Toomer, Richard Wright,
I am Daddy-O, nigger, Negro, black

I am ethnic and James Thomas Jackson.
I am America: the land of the 'Free & the Brave'
I am Africa: Ethiopia, Haiti, Sans Souci,
Toussaint, Henri Christophe, Dessalines;
I am Hannibal, crossing the Alps on elephants;
Unlike Alexander the Great I cry
Because there are no worlds for me to conquer
At all . . . in the world I live in.
There is nothing here for me but lies and yet
I know that I am a black Phoenix
Mindful of all the years of my black
Suppressions,
Rising from depths of my own black ashes.
I am a Black Prometheus unbound!
In my hands is the white lightening
Imprisoned by me!!!
For once, to furl at *my* bidding

O woe, o woe, o senseless woe
I have news for you, now listen: there'll be

> New lamps for old,
> New lamps for old,
> New lamps
> for old . . .

Poem From the Temple of My Mind

I

Where home once stood . . . (even then) . . .
Its chances of becoming extinct by racist
Hordes
Were great. Home is the birthplace where
One grows and thrives and nurtures,
Sprouts, runs, observes . . .
For life is early, sudden, warm, jubilant,
Violent:
Exhibiting happy, ignorant, youthful idiots
Romping
Ecstatically through vales, over plains
Across the dunes, through cotton wood forests
Or, through canyons of concreted steel and
Cement.

Poets write about us, eulogizing us,
Knowing all the while that many of us
Are un-acknowledgeable bastards, a free
World's Untouchables,
Yet needing us for our kindred spirits;
Often, perceptive dolts, that rise up out of
The blue,
Out of the infinite: eyes staring, dull,
Glossy-glowing;
Heavy with repressed inhibitions *and* released
Inhibitions;
Minds, youthfully aware of ghettoes: Watts,
Little Rocks,
Selmas, Newarks, Sharpvilles, Bi-Afras . . .
Yes, even Warsaws, Houston, first loves,
and second loves: A war, a black soldier
Falling in love with a pleasantly peasant
Italian girl

Strolling amidst the ruins of Pompei.
A flowing, black-haired wench named
Francesca;
Or, a sweet, dark-skinned beauty named Fancy,
From Greensboro, North Carolina, love,
Dammit!
A sunset splashing through a Georgia wood,
Forbidden to enter by blacks from white
Georgian laws
(The woods, to them, were for lynching, not
For loving!);
I, me . . . man . . . caressing a black soldier,
On an Italian battle field, giving words of
Comfort
To his dying, each of us equally afraid yet
I,
Knowing, one must love one another or die
Completely. In a war neither of us cared for
Or invented.
And I am the recipient of *all* laws: black &
White . . .

II

A legend named Santa Claus: red suit, white
Beard and all,
A stone peckerwood, entering and emerging
From sooty chimneys, his costume completely
Devoid of soot
And me, youthful idiot that I am believing
That all this profound bullshit was true.
Moreover, this old dude, riding away on
Eight reindeer
To the next house, and the next house, and
The next . . .
The Hi Ho Silver, Away bit and the poetic
"On Donder, On Blitzen, On Cupid, On Comet"

. . . Yes, Sir . . .
It was all so beautiful . . . to my and our
Young minds . . .
So beautiful . . . for that time . . . should
I ever be that
Naive again? Hardly. It would very nearly
Be a pity if . . . such bullshit . . . had
Not been
So detrimental . . . in the youthful valley
Of our young minds.
And, to be on the safe side I have
Just today, plugged up all the chimneys!

III

Now there's the rhetoric and the historied
Accumulations
Of lies penned on paper. With hopes, I suppose
For their implanting in books.
Another side to this value-less coin. Harder
To un-do,
This;
Harder to convince the older masses or, even
Impress
The youth of today with ingrained impressions
That once held forth so hopefully
In the ever young temple of my mind . . .
And theirs . . .

Truth must be served, and I must serve truth
If only . . . if only . . . for the tabooed
Love of that
Lissome wench
In Pompei, Italy: Oh my! What a love!!
Or that dark-skinned beauty in North Carolina
And those other dark-skinned beauties in
Between.

And other dark-skinned beauties round about
Me.
In the pronounced ghettoes of the Watts I
Favor
To improve.
I have at last reached the peak, the summit,
The mountain top.

These are the poems, some of the poems
From the temple of my mind
These are the poems, some of the poems
From the temple of my soul.

Coda . . . #1

Go! Tell it on the mountain!
The icy creeds that have no roots, just fears
. . . Wind songs played on Jewish harps
To closed hearts, cancerous minds, over-
Sexed bodies . . .
The night has a time for weeping, are you not
Weary?
Have you enough luminal to last
Until the dawn? The stores are closed
And the minds closed with them. Make Haste!
Tomorrow is coming and going all at the same
Time.

Yes. There is the sound of a distant drum,
There is a cadence of un-rhythmed feet
Heading for the dunes . . . the perennial
Hour-glass of time
Spills more sand about this barren land . . .
No birds fly to give directions,
No wind songs sung: indeed, there is no wind;
Except the muted wind of fear, the fear of
Death . . . and the horrid thought of one
Becoming suddenly
Extinct . . .

Voices I hear: (Do you hear them, too?)
Voices form the mountain top
Listen: shhh . . . is that a bugler blowing
Reveille? Or taps? Yes. Taps.
He blows for death.
Unlike Pan, he is not frivolous in his nature
He is the idyll of some un-enchanted forest
He is the coda of lamentations
He is the town crier of assassinations.
The world is a dearth of death to him:

Useless death, senseless deaths, deathly,
Deathly deaths.
Deaths from Meridian, Mobile, Trenton, Watts . . .
Death in embryo, infamy in deaths unclaimed . . .
Grave where is thy victory?
Death where is thy sting?
Here. Here. Here in this place called Liberty.
Here in this rancid place called AMERICA—
Better . . . we all moved to the mountain top
And stayed there—.
All is not peaceful down here.

Coda . . . #2

The wind fans the bulrushes along the Nile
It is a gentle breeze, wisping across its
Shore.
Cicadas and jackdaws make merry noises
Like gay fools, hell-bent for fool's survival.
Victoria's Falls vie with tymphany and
Euphoniums,
Clashing cymbals accentuate her glorious
Might.
Huge, fierce cats stalk the darkened jungle
In quiet yet beautiful, sinister mystery.
Beware, beware,
But why beware? Has not the jungle its own
Laws too?
The laws of animals . . . And are they greater
Than the laws of man?

Man has an intellect. He need not destroy.
But is he more beautiful than the Nile?
And can he duplicate the Falls?
Make them impervious to destructibility?
He doesn't seem to . . . yet he likes to plunder
. . . to hate, deprive, murder, kill the dream,
The dreamer, burn the page, burn the book,
Kill Jews, Kill Niggers; lie, deceive, concoct
Kill himself . . .
The stupid bastard. Or is there beauty
In this stupidity?

Daybreak

1

The night has cried enough!

The stars have impelled our destinies,
The sands of time have accentuated our presence
The bugler blows a new dawn
And we are awakened today
Into the light of day

Yes, this is Reveille . . .
Our wearied bodies move like rusted hinges
On creaky doors.
The mornings' glow infuses our awakened spirits
With new hope in a new land
In an old land and the voice of the turtle
Is heard once again
In our land . . . and in our time.

Hear: the blatant tramp of our marching feet
See the foul decadence recede into oblivion
Know that we will never be
As so many of us once were
Nor would ever hope to be gain.

Yes, . . . Time marches on . . .
Can't you see that grizzled old man
With his punctured hour glass
And his reaping scythe
Mowing down the adversaries
Of our former plight . . .
Dragging the debris of it
In his wake?

O Time O Time O Father Time!
Invincible father, lead your black sons

Along with you, we've got to MOVE!
We've tarried too long in this one place
And we are sick to death!

2

I'm tired.
That weary old song . . .
"We shall overcome . . ."
Has no fascination for me,
Hell no, I didn't like the damn thing
In the first place
I'm writing some brand new
Lyrics for it as of right now
So you can remember and
The words are:
"Hold on, I'm coming, hold on, I'm coming . . ."
And I am, too!

3

Daylight has assailed me rapturously.
My vision is clear
My strides are purposeful
Listen to me, nation:
James has got himself a new religion . . .
Or an old religion in a new body
My soul is buoyant with the ecstacy
Of freedom
Now, can I get a witness!

4

Black man, black man
Use the strong potent soap of Soul Words,
Un-wash your brains . . . you can do it!
Remove those idiot fallacies from your psyche
Make a new Jerusalem all your own . . .
You can do it.

The power lies within you
As it always has only you let
The powers-that-be suppress you
With too many lies, deceits, untruths
So MANY that you have become
Implacable pawns
In the Mans' white hands
On his all too controlled checkered board.

Black woman, cleave to me:
Your black lover who has loved you
Over eons of time in my/and our
Submerged Black Histories
Without your ever knowing
That you were beautiful, to us,
And that we loved you
And that we love you still.

Yes, hasn't the night cried enough?
Great Day in the morning!
Let this be a great day in the morning.

I am all for it
I have grown so weary
Of shit!

Poem for Medgar Evers

This the cry of the centuries!

A nation within a nation cries.
Some Rip Van Winkle suddenly awakes
To view the change of centuries past
And flips!

Yes! Medgar Evers of Mississippi
Lies slain on the cold earth of his home
His grieving wife runs toward the line of fire
To her murdered spouse while her children
Hover in dark corners of their room.
While a wildly stupid de Beckwith
Stupidly leaves the weapon at the scene
And flees. (He knew his deed was wrong.)
Fused with hate and frightened of blackness,
He flees to the sanctuary of other
de Beckwiths-to-be . . .
Just like him . . . although cowered by
Inactions,
Yet bolstered by the magnanimity of
Mississippi anti-black, pro-white votes.
No, Medgar Evers, your glorious death
Does not go unheralded, unknown, unsung;
No, not unaware, un-trumpeted even though
This murderous bastard
Yet runs for Congress . . . in Mississippi . .
For you are our cry too.
Yes, we other black, supposedly non-entities
Rebuke your damned Congress-es.
Your damned vindictiveness, your
Vitriolic hatreds, your caucausian fears, all
You conglomerate, mustard-tongued bastards
I reap reams of obscenities upon your families.
Upon your mothers, fathers and call them dirty,

Obscene names . . .
I curse them all for all your conglomerate
Guilts.
The incinerators of Dachau, Auswitz and
Buchenwald
Cremated all the wrong people!
Or that our so-called America was lucky and
All the time I thought
We were so blest . . . My God . . .
Is Jesus asleep?

Who will you kill tomorrow
Mr. de Beckwith?
(He'll have to be black, of course.)
Another black dreamer, of freedom and justice?
For freedom is a sometime thing
It is the only absolute on this earth
That . . . while living . . . really matters.
Intelligence, from a black man, goes for no-
Thing;
Impassiveness is folly;
Live and let live is use-less, un-workable
Useless-ness: Hot air, turds, farts;
It is the fighting and the dying
And the raping
Of other blacks that is galling . . .
Re-incarnating
More freedoms, for more black people
That suck the sweet breezes that blow
From magnolias or the wispy aura of air
From stately cottonwoods
That finds minute freedom
Under their sheltering arms . . .
Yeah, Rip, you grizzled old buzzard . . .
Be careful how you tread.
Africa has at last come to L.A.
And Houston, and Selma, and Shaker Heights;

And Watts, Pomona, Encino, and Morehouse, Brown
And Spelman;
And has existed in Mississippi all the while
You were snoring.
Perhaps you had best return to your slumbers
Sleep the deep sleep of the ages, if you will.
There is a black Rip now, a Black Prometheus.
He stirs, he marches;
We are seated in a black, celestial Omnibus
We shall touch hands with our black, African
Brothers.
We shall make great love to our black, African
Women again.
Never more will we be distant . . . one from
The other as it has seemed . . .
We will be Africa, America-Africa
And we shall not be ashamed of her, our
Mother country
Or she of us, her kindred.
And vindictive assassinations such as yours,
Mr. de Beckwith
Will not go unsung, not now, not ever
Because we will love our black being
And our black beings.
And we will band together
To fight our enemies
Wherever they might be.

The Breadwinner

Here
In concrete
In wind
In sculptured main masts
In swinging vaults
In flying buttresses
In joist-joints and sixteen-penny nails
Nailed hard, solid and true
By black carpenter helpers
With salty sweat flowing down black faces:
Across, over, around and thru
Sad, brown eyes that know the difference,
Past black lips that seethe with yearnings
Yearning lips that kiss black women
On their sensual lips
Late at night (and) when the kids are asleep
Or, early in the morning
When slumber's not deep and there's no reason
For two to not want too. . . . .

The daddy ain't rich
But his woman's good-looking
And both are enmeshed
In the making of love
And the river, the rivers: the Nile/or Euphrates
An all-cleansing Jordan
     Runs
Somewhere in their being
Somewhere . . . beside them . . . somewhere
Between them the river
Runs
     Somewhere, through their minds
     Through their separate goals
     Through their heat-meshed hearts
     Through everything they own

Twelve leagues from today
Twelve leagues from now . . .
   And for all other leagues
   Following thereafter. . . .

Michael Powe: Epitaph To A Beautiful Person
(Dedicated to the son I would have . . . if I had a son.)

> *"Hurry down, Sundown*
> *See what tomorrow brings . . ."*

The tumult of life's most raging years
Fills in some the rage to change
What is unchangeable but which must change.
A meadow lark pipes shrilly across a lonely
Waste
The hum of human voices bus vibrations
On busied telephone lines. The road is long
And covers many years . . . for a youth . . .
Eighteen, nineteen, twenty . . .
The family families: now here, now there,
Now here,
Yes; the young, strong loins of youth, the
Bright ideals
Surge to the front and feast with reason!
Change, change. A new Jerusalem, a new Jeru
Suddenly exists. For where love dwells so
Dwells Jerusalem.
Armies come and victors and victims and
Dreams
Are stymied for moments; an hour perhaps,
A day
Yet not for long. The whistling of a
Meadow lark
Is penned on parchment from a mother's vision.

> *"Sent for you yesterday*
> *And here you come today!"*

Her child walks in her footsteps . . . indeed
He is the ma-child,

The boy-child, the man, the victor-to-be, the
Soldier
Even;
He, too, remembers the golden sonnet, the
Minute poem,
The symphony of words that accentuate wisdoms
Penned by the matriarch who spawned his being
And of which he follows in immeasurable pride.

> *"Tomorrow may bring sunshine,*
> *And tomorrow may bring rain."*

Pasa por aqui: he passed this way, he passed
This way, He passed *this* way, he passed *this*
Way, And on he passes.

Sundown, be not so expedient in your endless
Travels
Why hasten to fold your cloak of light:
Ever moving westward to endless horizons
Leaving behind our endless night
Can you not travel alone? You are so
Invincible.
Why seek *this* companion for your infinite
Destiny?
We need the dear ones . . . already they are
Too few.
Why make our lives an eternal dirge of
Saddened litanies:
Too many Good Morning, sadness-ses, Bon Voyages;
Too few abiding here until the end of time . . .
Yes . . . Good Morning, Sadness, Bon Voyage
There is much sadness in our valley today . . .
I shall miss you, Michael Alan Powe . . . . .

Watts . . . '68

Now, hear *my* song from *this* distant singer.
Once there was a dream here, now it's deferred,
Gone to those more capable, perhaps, more
Beautiful, even . . .
I do not know the criteria, nor do I care to.
Catch *my* soul, you ignorant bastard, catch my
Soul.

Perhaps this dream belonged
To a two-year-old-black child on a battered
Tricycle
Or to an eccentric Mexican whose hands
Formulated massive, glass-tiled towers creating
A dimension soaring over our ghettoes' blight;
Too stark for viewers at the very first glance.
Perhaps it belonged to un-pregnated mothers
With Promethean bellies
Bellies obese from mustard greens, collard and
Hog maws
Or, from black barber shops where black
Comaraderie flows
With the click of scissors on kinky heads
Or, from that foxy, youthful, mother-to-be
That just got pregnated last month
Or does it belong to the mongrel dogs
That infest our neighborhoods . . . creeping
Scavengers . . . Mongrels that do not attack
Negroes, yet growl
Savagely at whites, after 10:30 p.m.
(They've got no business being here, they
Should be snug in their Beverly Hills
Palaces, prone, in antique four-poster beds
Aloof,
Utterly aloof to the goings-on of our tiny
Ghetto.)

Yes. We desire change too, but Change is
In no hurry
To desire us or we to change . . . how can we
Believe you?
You never gave a damn about us before so why
Should we be so happy to believe you now?
After all,
You've lied to us for years; what the Hell's
A few more months or years?

And does this dream also belong to MISS WATTS
'68
Looking beautiful, sexy, fine . . . "Man,
Look at them thighs!"
Hair: Natural, clothed in an African robe
Retailed at Gee-Gee's for . . . "What was
The figure?"
$19.95? Ooo whee!!!

No. No. this dream belongs
To the lengthy railroad track
That passes 103rd Street, past the Watts
Writers' Workshop
Heading for downtown L.A. and points beyond
Past aged and junked Cadillacs, Chevvies and
Fords
Past W in-O Junction and mild tasting sherry
Past consumptive bodies racked with cigarette
Cancers
In infected lungs.
Past Hamburger Havens and Hot Dog Dells
(I'm glad I'm not an Oscar Meyer Wiener)
But I can't do any better for the money.
I am a cheese-burger man: Tomatoes, hot sauce,
Ketchup,
The whole business, pal: pickles, the dream

Of tiny things that don't shake the earth in
Issues . . .
I go vagabondish . . . past fleeting telephone
Poles
That stand as gaunt sentinels in the night.
Down, down, down, first one jungled tract
Then another. Until . . .
I am lost or swallowed into another oblivion
And I am glad because
The Watts that I am leaving is the Phoenix
To which I am returning
And the blackness I leave behind in Watts
Rises to meet me again in Houston
And there I'll lie
Until death claims me or, some other wasteland
Embraces me . . . for fickle moments as if I
Were . . .
No more than just some other mongrel dog. . . .

PART III

Excerpts from a play

Bye, Bye Black Sheep

Act 1, Scene 1—Morning, early. The deep, thick grays of dawn already descended upon the city of Gotham, a metropolis of over eight million people. A foreground of miniature sky scrapers, rooming houses; a few street lights, faintly burning. The street itself, empty; shrouded with the last dark of night, before dawn. A sudden quiet, too sudden. And then a woman's piercing scream rents the air.

A drunk suddenly appears as if from nowhere, stumbling along, a contented, happy smile on his face, bellowing thickly some discordant notes from a song. For an instant his voice is darn near melodious—as though freed from inhibitions—even cultured; were it not for his inebriated condition. He even manages to sing the first few parts of this well known bar of music. He is dressed well enough: suit, tie, hat and shoes. The tie is askew, the collar unbuttoned. The suit a conservative single breasted, with all three buttons of the coat opened. He could be forty-five or forty, with normal features, no midriff bulges, almost athletic, with a glow from his countenance undoubtedly caused by his drunken state. His baritone, stunted as it is, bellows forth with "Oh, Promise me . . ."

The voice breaks off after the sound of the first screams reaches his ears and just before the beginning of the second. Since he is innocent of any wrongdoing, his first realization is that of concern. But the SECOND, more piercing scream, coming more hollowly now from the bottomless depths of mortal fear, changes his countenance completely. At this instant a figure flees past him in urgent haste, brushing him aside. Even as the light of morning whispers in the day's first glow he observes that the man is of a different race than he is, and observes, too, a buttoned/or zippered jacket with a streak across the left arm as the figure runs past him.

Forgetting the man, he instinctively runs towards the direction from which he came. Sobriety returns quickly as everything quietens. Curiosity now impels him to go forth—and look.

He moves slowly at first, then trots, runs to the adjacent alley dividing other tenanted houses from the mellifluous neon glows of the city about them. At the alley he halts cautiously, peers through the dimness, sees a shape, a huddled figure, crumpled. He hesitates, then strides forward, uncertainly, towards the form.

A figure, that of a woman, lies still, unmoving in the narrow passageway. He bends over cautiously, reaches a hand out, touches something: cloth; the lapel of her coat. A cloud wisps by from a yet visible piece of moon, lights this darkened alley, revealing the face of a woman, tresses of hair and the look of death on her face. Streaks of blood yet run down her face and the man's hand feels wet with the touch of blood from the tunic by her left breast.

He jerks his hand away savagely, and eyes the wetness in the light of the moon. His expression changes from curiosity to fear, yet he remains concerned. And then to his surprise, another noise, like a foot tripping over something: a stone, some object; a muffled but distinct curse which naturally causes him to look in the direction of the voice. He sees a figure dart out in a direction opposite from where he stands. He can only glimpse the figure— so swiftly does it move—although he sees too by some basically inherent recognition that it is different from the startled and fleeing one that brushed his shoulder before. Quite likely it is one of his own people.

But logic is lost in the now twice frightened man and in his fear of this inebriate night. Two ghouls, two phantoms *and* a dead woman on this macabre scene are two too many, particularly with the blood of a victim from his solicitous touch still on his hands. His countenance deepens almost to hysteria. In fact, hysteria encompasses him. Then he flees crazily, from the alley to the street, now flaming with the brightest light from day yelling, yelling to the top of his lungs:

"POLEECE!! POLEECE!! POLEECE!!!!"

The dawn breaks fully and light as the now hoarse sounds of the man's voice lower to a decrescendo of that mighty, powerful and all-encompassing word.

Lights from many divergent rooms, heads and torsos from many directions thrust themselves into this brand new maze of thunder within this city of all cities. Gotham City becomes fully awake . . . .

* * * * *

Act Two, Scene Two—Scene: A neighborhood. The house is a white cottage-type, a white picket fence stands just high enough to give a heightened effect to the house it surrounds. A shingle, a foot in diameter either way with the words, "Davis Gift Shop," is brightly lettered on it. Ceramic pottery, figurines of a Victorian era, bric-a-brac of several kinds dot the window sills at the two large front windows.

Detective Mark Jenner walks through the swinging gate, up to the brief porch, uses the brass hand knocker on the door.

Sound: (a pleasant voice from within) Come in. The door is open.

Mark enters. The two wide rooms are lavish with bric-a-brac of all sorts: from figurines to grandfather and cuckoo clocks; from quill pens to finely-embossed stationery. There are many types of gifts here and the rooms are in perfect order. Things glitter and shine and attract the eye. Yet there is enough room for movement. An elderly colored man wearing a spotless white smock, tie askew, looks up from polishing a tiny brass stagecoach to nod to the visitor. He is short in stature and has a pleasant, round face, dark brown skin, with hair tending to bald. Fringes of gray on both sides of his ears. He speaks:

Man: Good Morning. How are you?

Mark: Good morning. Quite a place you have here. (admiring, looking at this and that)

Man: (solicitously) Is there something you want in particular?

Mark: Not really. I'm Mark Jenner, Detective from Homicide. You might say I'm here on behalf of a friend of yours, Dusty Gonzales. At least he says that's his name. Who might you be?

Man: Davis. Maurice Elmer Davis. Originally I come from the South. They just love to give you three names down there. They really have a system. Ha ha.

Mark: Then you're the man I want to talk to. About Dusty, I mean.

Davis: You say that name like it galls you. To me Dusty is Dusty. And always will be Dusty. He's more than just a person. He's an institution. He's tasted the very wine of life. He's gone out there in that many-varied void and embraced it, said to it: here I am, you son of a buck, do what you will, 'cause I'm damn sure gonna learn you. And he's true. Nothing phony about him. (Davis gives a final swipe with his towel on the stagecoach, observes it critically, then sets it carefully down on the table amidst an array of other miniature objects.)

Mark: Evidently you're fond of him.

Davis: Yeah. It's been twenty years since I met a man like Dusty. He has the gumption to do what many men wish they would do. But society and our societies' codes prevent them from it. Of course we have to have law and order. We can't let our civilization go to pot. We can't have men running around loose, dropping the seeds for a lot of illegitimate bastards all over the place. There's got to be law with the order. Or too many of us would perish. Slaughter of the Innocents and all that, you know. (He reaches for a gold looking candlestick, holds it aloft and eyes it critically, his face frowning. He applies some liquid wax on a cloth and polishes the object. He looks over at Mark.) Get a chair over there and sit down. Make yourself comfortable.

Mark: (straight forward) Do you personally believe he killed that woman?

Davis: (bitterly and with just enough emphasis) Hell, no.

Mark: (laughs suddenly) You two are alike. You come right to the point.

Davis: Got to. Too many Negroes have been executed falsely because some darky stumbled and fumbled around for answers. True, Dusty's human like any other man and could fall by that wayside like any other man. But you will never make me believe he killed her.

Mark: (Probing) What I want to know is, what gives you such implicit faith in him?

Davis: (reflecting) Danged if I know. For one thing, he's so sensitive and so utterly awake. He's come from so far, so long. He values human life too well. When you knock him down he'll come right back at you from another direction. And yet when the guy so much as nods his head to ponder a thought, every son of a buck and his brother swears he is asleep.

You may not know this but he's in love with my daughter. And he won't admit it because he and I have had so many startling conversations, I'm afraid he thinks I know too much about his attitudes.

(jocularly) The last time he was here, I watched him talking to her. Now get this: Jean has had many suitors. She's heard the lines. Dusty attacked obliquely. Know what he talked about? The Universe. About the Southern Cross. About the dippers reversing themselves like empty soup spoons in the morning. About shooting stars and making a quick wish. About a walking Bear making big strides across the heavens. About a man and his dog with a gun. And—lemme see (scratches his head)—he talked about Galileo, Copernicus and Omar Khayam. He never once approached her on the subject of love directly. Never committed himself outright about it. And yet—all the time he was making love to her. Ha ha, he he. And you wonder why I like him. He's such a happy rogue. (Laughs until tears come to his eyes.)

Mark: (smiling with him) Yes. At times he impresses me that way, too.

Davis: (his face serious, questioning) I bet you haven't got a confession out of him.

Mark: (in all honesty) No, we haven't. He's not cooperative. He's either shielding something, someone, or just has a plain mean streak in him that prevents us from learning his side of the picture. It's baffling.

Davis: (Placing the candlestick down on the table, walking towards Mark, his face one of intense concern) No it's not. It's race pride. The law is the last people on earth Dusty would trust. Not that Dusty doesn't know law or even have a profound respect for it. He knows it all too well. Not all of it, maybe, but he knows the law's perspectives, its inherent intentions. Also its aggrandizements. He knows that nobody listens to niggers where a white woman is concerned, because people have such built-in prejudices—black and white. He knows that you're only going to look at the thing from a purely physical side: that of lust, rape and carnal intent. A colored man in his right senses don't go shouting to the world that he is friendly with this or that white person; because the white persons are going to look on him as being naive, and his own people are going to look on him as a fool.

I believe to my soul that the bulk of us are satisfied with our own race. We dearly love procreating our own bastards—legal and otherwise. To us you are the invaders, you are the ones who arouse our furies, you are the ones who compound our rages. God damn! You've invaded the wombs of every nationality on earth! You're the ones who've mongrelized the races of the world. But if one Negro so much as stops on a corner and gives a white woman—any white woman: old, young, a child, even—

directions to the Post Office, a white crowd gathers. And a few black ones. People are just that conditioned. You're the damnest propagandists the free world has ever known. And yet you wonder why this man don't come out readily and confess that he killed this woman because he wanted her body. God, but you're humbugs! (There is a silence. Davis stands where he has advanced. Mark sits still in his chair, eyeing Davis candidly.)

Mark: You're another Dusty, you know that. You must sleep with your fists balled up.

Davis: (with clarity) If I did that my wife would take all the cover. Sure, I'm sensitive. Good friends are hard to come by. And a good, learned friend is harder still. So many of us Negroes are afraid to learn things for perfectly obvious reasons. We have to have jobs that pay money to make it from one Christmas to the next. When we start being too eloquent and didactic with our pay masters, our continued economic outlook is placed in jeopardy.

So we wear false faces. We comment infrequently or timidly. We look impassive on major issues as if they don't concern us. We let you take the initiatives. We let you bullshit us with your "technologies" and your "findings," your "discoveries" and your "conclusions." It's no sweat off our balls in particular. We'll let you slide. We're not necessarily given to violence at the ready—to white folks, that is—we are too few. We also feel that we're chosen whether we are or not. There's a better day a 'comin' by and by. And all that. You're so many. We have to whip you by the barest caprice of Providence. By the sudden rising of a Jackie Robinson, a Countee Cullen, a Thurgood Marshall, Martin Luther King, Chester Himes, James Baldwin, Peter Abrahams. By people black like me who come from the voids, from sudden rising clouds; even by men like Dusty Gonzales.

These people remind us of what we have, of what we should do. They renew our poise and make us distinctive. They tell it on the mountain. And you can't mess with a mountain too much. Especially if it is a big mountain, 'cause it will fight you back. Boulders from its blasted debris will fall on you and kill you. And our joint prayers will bury you deep. (Now the silence is unearthly. The two men face each other, like two combatants. Davis looks frail against Mark, but the essence of battle is in his stance.)

Mark: (wearily) I should have known I was entering the inferno when I came here. But I had to know. I sure didn't think a simple murder case would turn out so complicated.

Davis: (relaxes yet slightly vehement) That's the trouble with being a Negro in this country. People forget that the Emancipation Proclamation was signed. That we are entitled to all the rights and privileges of any American. (wearily walks back toward table, picks up candlestick again, seeming to be looking off into space) White people still want to use us, not as equals but as slaves and servants and court jesters. And we don't like it worth a good goddam. You provoke a Negro to anger when you try it. Even that eff-ing word "Negro" arouses my furies. It sounds like something unanimously contrived. Something we know in our hearts does not exist. We hate you to call us "boy" because you mean it. You had better not call us "nigger" because we'll murder you—some way or the other. We despise that word, "Negro." If that's the best Noah Webster could do he could have simply left it completely out of his synonymous Ark and simply called us "blacks." Because black is our mother country. And it is so old. Older than you.

Mark: (grasping) Do you think the races will ever reconcile themselves to one another? Do you think that—the colored man—will, some time or the other be accepted, quite naturally, as almost any white race, anywhere, especially in America? I'd like to know your opinion.

Davis: Who knows? Dusty has a more balanced outlook on that answer than I have. I get mad too easily. Especially if phonies are in the midst.

Dusty gets mad too, but not so mad that he can't put a joker in his proper place. I don't know where he learned debating, or from what fountain spring his rhetoric flows. I don't even know what impels his incentives. But that's the man to ask that question.

Mark: Is your family here? I'd like to meet them.

Davis: No, they went shopping or walking, some place. I don't know when they'll be back.

Mark: That's too bad. I just wanted to meet 'em. So many things surround Dusty in this case, so many human elements. I just thought I'd try and examine them all.

Davis: You said that like you were a psychologist or something. Are you?

Mark: (Writhing a little) Not exactly. Although I have had psychiatric training.

Davis: A sociologist?

(Mark nods his head)

Davis: It follows. A sociologist or a psychiatrist. This may offend you a little but the white man is always trying to figure out the Negro, some way. And I do mean FIGURE OUT. Out of the picture (gestures) that is. So often it seems that way. (Davis attacks the candlestick again, polishing it, rubbing it fiercely, his face frowningly concentrated. Mark watches him intently then asks)

Mark: Do you do pretty good in this shop? (he gestures with an open hand)

Davis: (a bit sullen) Now you want to know my bizness. (He looks out at Mark skeptically then resumes his brisk rubbing. There is a silence for a long minute, then Davis slowly places the object down on the table, raises his head just as slowly, his face revealing some new thought that has just occurred to him.) Tell me something. How did you happen to come to my place? Did Dusty tell you about it? (He waits, challengingly, for an answer)

Mark: No. It was Dusty's landlady.

Davis: (incredulity lighting up his face) Mrs. Green?

Mark: (blandly) Yes.

Davis: (half smiling, as though he should have known this) Oh hell, yes. She's the old biddy that kicked the thing off in the first place. Uh hunh! (he muses, knowingly) I gather (slightly sarcastic) that you have already interviewed her. Or interrogated. Or whatever it is you do.

Mark: (ignoring it) Yes. We've talked to her. It was through her that we arrested Dusty.

Davis: (impishly frowning) Please sir, spare me the miserable details. I read the account of it in the papers. "Sensational murder. Landlady discovers tell-tale spots of blood-soaked clothing in assailant's room." Big Deal. I suppose by now she's writing out her memoirs. I can just see it now: the public will eat it up. (now intensely cynical) "I HAD A MURDERER FOR A TENANT." Paragraph: "It all started when I went to clean Dusty's room as I used to do once a week. A mysterious lodger at best, he was acting even more strange and mysterious this morning. And blah, blah, blah, ad infinitum." (He throws a hand at the air disgustedly)

Mark: (Mark tries to suppress a smile at Davis' mocking mimicry but fails in his attempt. He squirms in his chair. Half explaining) Well you know how women are, easily excitable. And prone to make a big thing out of something. Don't forget, she did what was her duty to do. You just said yourself we have to have law and order. We can't let the guilty go unpunished. I'm sure you are a reasonable man, Mr. Davis.

Davis: (agreeably) Oh yes, Lieutenant, yes indeed. I'm as reasonable as they come. It's just that I've met that old biddy. I have quite a few associates but few friends. Dusty's my friend. Sometimes we shared a bottle. Boy, can that guy drink! Ooo Whee! He can go!!! I could escape from the drab routines of domesticity in this house to the learned halls of Dusty's room. There, where wisdom, reflections and knowledge reign supreme. There, where two men could orate, discuss, delve deep into the foibles of man's world without the nagging disinterestedness of womenfolk. Know what Dusty told me once? He told me he used to sit up all night long in an Army Mess Hall just talking and drinking buttermilk. And I believe him! You ever read "The Devil and Daniel Webster"?

(Mark nods his head, unspeaking, the glimmer of a smile
on his face)

Davis: I hadn't. Until Dusty turned me on to it. I thought it was
magnificent. Ben Johnson was one hell of a writer. He
made Daniel Webster an impish bastard. Approach a
problem from any angle. Obliquely, full face, from behind, even. Dusty's like that. He's various, yet insistent.
He gets that ball and runs like hell with it. For an unsung,
unheralded man, he's got bundles of rhetoric in that brain
of his. What's more, he believes in himself. And he believes in people. That they are still the hope of the world.
Now Mrs. Green is from another planet. Pluto, probably.
(Mark smiles, then instantly turns serious) She's one of
the confirmed, lonely spinsters of this world. Everything
in her house reeks of antebellum, post-Victorian America.
If she had any business sense she'd get her a hundred
pounds of lemons, a sack of sugar and a barrel of flour.
Make tea cakes, serve lemonade and show that mauso-
leum of a living room off every day from ten to five at six
bits a head. Man, she'd make a killing! Because—thank
the good Lord—that South ain't never coming back! Or
Mrs. Green, either, for that matter! As it is, she is drenched
in thirty years of a loneliness she doesn't even deserve;
and a ritual of a decayed, Southern social aristocracy that
she didn't even invent. In a world she never made. She is
just that far removed (holds finger and thumb two inches)
from utter insanity. I've been there maybe five times in all,
since I met Dusty. There isn't one African piece of art in
the joint. I know. That's my business. There is nothing
there to associate her with our rightful heritage. So it's no
mystery to me that she didn't dig Dusty. The Dustys of
this world are few and far between in my life, in Mrs.
Green's life. And in yours, too. I'll say this for her. She's
got notoriety now. She might even make a few friends.
Oh, she turned up her nose at my little "ye old gift shop"
here. Probably swear and be damned I ain't making no
money at it. But like the Indian says: heap see, few know.
(Mark has sat and listened intently. Observing Davis's

movements, hands going from object to object, polishing this, arranging that. There is a quiet. As though Davis has talked out.)

Mark: Mr. Davis. (Davis turns to look at him) When we interrogated Dusty one thing he said baffled me—more than any. Baffled us all. He even shouted it at one point. You know what that was?

Davis: (wondering) No. I have no idea.

Mark: He said; "I have no peers!"

Davis: Dusty said that?

Mark: Uh hunh. It's a strange thing to say, isn't it?

Davis: (musing, face frowning) No. Not to me. There's an old Southern expression: "Every tub stands on its own bottom." And although Dusty believes in unity, he also believes that in times of duress a man stands pretty much alone. A David fighting the Philistines. All of them. All by his lonesome. Only the Maker, who saw fit for him to be here in the first place, is his Absolute Superior. So, whatever defenses he relies on in time of trouble, has to come from that one great, invincible, invisible force, of which he and he alone is the helmsman. As for Dusty himself, he has made and established his own identity in spite of the conventional society that hates him for his convictions. No one can take that away. In the middle ages they would have burned him at the stake. In this society they simply kill him with ostracism. And even that don't work. Not with Dusty. And no one can match him—not readily. He's a little unique. And he knows it. (He pauses, then continues) Remember what I told you about Daniel Webster— and Dusty? Remember what I told you about him using the oblique approach to Jean, using the moon and stars as a gambit? That's novel. The way he did it. Putting her there, as a figure, celestial, yet doing a duty as stars do, in the Universe's grand scheme of things.

Mark: (smiling, shaking his head) You two guys should be in a University.

Davis: (pleased, smiling) Thank you. But we belong as we are.

No big fuss. We're liberty ships, not yachts. We're useful pawns, not staid bishops; roving ambassadors, not Secretaries of State. We can't be weighted down by so much grand pomposity. We oscillate between the precipitous summit and the prisoner's base. We've got a lot of love for so many of the natural things of this goofy world.

Mark: How I envy you . . . your spirit.

Davis: (tartly) Now don't try to take that away from me!

Mark: (guffaws) I'm glad my partner isn't with me. This case has already befuddled him enough.

Davis: (with equal rapport) News for you. I'm glad my *wife* isn't here!

(they both laugh)

Davis: (blandly) Being born black does that to us sometimes. We've got to fight so much, and we've got to think so much; and we've got to give so much more than other people. And we have such precious little to give.

Mark: (musing, quoting) "Our lives, our fortunes, our sacred honor."

Davis: (helpfully) That too, at times.

Mark: (rising) Well, I've got to go.

Davis: (placing object down on table, walking over to Mark) It's been nice meeting you. I've contacted a lawyer friend of mine to handle Dusty's case. Although I doubt very seriously if Dusty will trust him "with his life" —as he puts it.

Mark: (agreeing, half smiling) I doubt it too.

Davis: I'll do my damndest to get him out of there. Character reference and all that.

Mark: Mr. Davis, you're hard to beat. I can arrange for you to see him if you want.

Davis: This may surprise you. But I think the one person that could do him the most good now is the sight of my daughter's face. I talked with Dusty on the phone. He told me not to come. He insisted on it.

Mark: Well, I can arrange for your daughter to see him too.

Davis: That's damned nice of you. But that will have to be up to my daughter. Like most women, my daughter has a will of her own. I won't coerce her to go. But I will try to suggest.

Mark: That's all you can do. (extends his hand) Davis looks at it for an instant then, grasps it firmly)

Mark: Thanks very much for letting me talk with you.

Davis: (smiling) Well, you didn't get to say very much.

Mark: (seriously) But I learned a great deal more.

Davis: (intently serious) Just as long as it will help Dusty.

Mark: It could. It well could.

(Mark goes out the door. Davis stands there watching him, then picks up an African statue and begins to polish it. With a new cloth he begins to rub vigorously as his voice unconsciously soars over the quiet, passively)

Davis: I hope so, Mr. Lieutenant. I sure do hope so.

The curtain falls.

Acknowledgements

"Waiting in Line at the Drugstore" first appeared in the *Los Angeles Times* on 4 April 1975.

"Of Roses and a Black Family's Unusual Visitor" first appeared in the *Los Angeles Times*, date unknown.

"Awakening to a Common Suffering—and Pride" first appeared in the *Los Angeles Times*, February 1977.

"Stars in a Black Night—Beacon for a Black Dawn" first appeared in the *Los Angles Times* on 12 September 1976.

"Juneteenth Was Freedom Day—a Long Time Ago" first appeared in the *Los Angeles Times* on 9 June 1978.

"Not a Bad Dude" first appeared in *An Honorable Profession: A Tribute to Robert F. Kennedy*, edited by Pierre Salinger, et al. Doubleday, 1968.

"Welfare and the Single Man" first appeared in the *Los Angeles Times* in February 1971.

"Black History: Notes on a Lingering Melody" first appeared in the *Los Angeles Herald Examiner* on 9 February 1983.

"My Africa—It Is All This, and More" first appeared in the *Los Angeles Times* on 12 February 1976.

"Watts Workshop: From the Ashes" first appeared in the *Los Angeles Times* 21 December 1980.

"Black Friday: The Day Kennedy Was Shot" first appeared in the *Southwest Review*, Autumn 1976.

"Black Memories" first appeared in *The Antioch Review*, Fall 1967.

"Michael Powe: Epitaph to a Beautiful Person," "A New Blues," "Coda . . . #1," "Watts . . . '68," "Poem for Medgar Evers," "Blues for Black," "Poem from the Temple of My Mind," "Coda . . . #2," "Daybreak," are from *Soul Going Home*, edited by Tobie Hopkins, Watts Publishing, n.d.

"Reveille," "Shade of Darkness," "Jean," "Some Notes on the Frederick Douglass Writers' House," are in *From the Ashes: Voices of Watts*, edited by Budd Schulberg, New American Library, 1967.